THE ESSENCE OF SOUND

THE ESSENCE OF SOUND

Full Spectrum Vibrational Healing for the Meridians, Chakras, Auric Field, and Figure Eight Energies

BY EVELYN MULDERS

Medical Disclaimer

This book and the products recommended are not intended as a substitute for medical recommendations from physicians or other health-care providers. Rather it is intended to offer information to assist the reader to participate and co-operate with physicians and health professionals in a mutual quest for optimum well-being.

The Essence of Sound - Full Spectrum Vibrational Healing for the Meridians, Chakras, Auric Field, & Figure Eight Energies
by Evelyn Mulders

Cover Design/Book Design/Illustration
by Verena Velton

Artwork
by Avery DeRousie, Shari Sali, Julia Lum, Ruby McPhate

Copyright© 2020, Satiama Publishing, a service mark of Satiama, LLC
Published by Satiama Publishing
PO Box 1397
Palmer Lake, CO 80133
http://www.satiamapublishing.com

All rights and international rights reserved. No part of this product, including but not limited to cards and guidebook or any portion thereof may be reproduced, distributed, or transmitted in any form or by any means, including photocopying, recording, or other electronic or mechanical methods, nor may it be stored in a retrieval system, transmitted or otherwise copied for public or private use, without the prior written permission of the publisher, except in the case of "fair use" of brief quotations embodied in critical reviews and certain other noncommercial uses permitted by copyright law. For permission requests, write to the publisher, addressed "Attention: Permissions Coordinator," at the address above.

The intent of the authors is only to offer information of a general nature to help you in your quest for overall well-being. In the event you use any of the information in this book for yourself, which is your constitutional right, the authors and the publisher assume no responsibility for your actions.

First Printing, 2010; Second Edition Printing 2020
ISBN 978-0-9972825-6-6

BISAC CODES:
OCC042000   BODY, MIND & SPIRIT / Alchemy
OCC011000   BODY, MIND & SPIRIT / Healing / General
OCC043000   BODY, MIND & SPIRIT / Nature Therapy

PRINTED IN CHINA
10 9 8 7 6   5 4 3 2 1

Table of Contents

Acknowledgements 7

Forward by Dr. Bruce Dewe 9

Forward by Sabina Pettitt 10

Introduction 11

Chapter 1 The Discovery of Sound Essence 13

PART 1: SOUND ESSENCE AND THE SECRETS OF VIBRATIONAL HEALING

Chapter 2 The Power of Sound 21

Chapter 3 The Magic of Water 27

Chapter 4 Nature's Rhythm and Hierarchy 31

Chapter 5 Energy Anatomy 37

Chapter 6 Sound Essences 41
    Meridian Sound Essences 47
    How to Use Meridian Sound Essences 51
    Chakra Sound Essences 52
    Aura-Joy Sound Essence 59
    Infinity Sound Essence 61
    How to Use Chakra, Aura-Joy, and Infinity Sound Essences ... 64
    Sound Essence Protocol 65

PART 2: SOUND ESSENCE AND THE ENERGY SYSTEMS OF THE BODY

Chapter 7 Meridians & Five Elements 71
    Yin/Yang Couple 77
    Sovereign Fire Couple 83
    Ministerial Fire Couple 89
    Earth Couple 95
    Metal Couple 103
    Water Couple 109
    Wood Couple 117

Chapter 8 Chakras 125
    Root Chakra 129
    Sacral Chakra 145
    Solar Plexus Chakra 169
    Heart Chakra 191
    Throat Chakra 209
    Brow Chakra 231
    Crown Chakra 255

Chapter 9 Auric Field 269
    Etheric Body 271
    Emotional Body 273
    Mental Body 275
    Astral Body 277
    Etheric Template Body 279
    Celestial Body 281
    Ketheric Body 283

Chapter 10 Figure Eight Pattern 285
Chapter 11 Kinesiology 287

Conclusion 289

Appendices
    A. Testimonials for Sound Essences 293
    B. Sound Essence Questionnaire 299
    C. Chakra Identifying Statements 307
    D. Flower and Sea Essence Descriptions 313
    E. Aromatherapy Descriptions 321
    F. Kinesiology Monitoring
        Self Monitoring 331
        Partner Monitoring 334
        Setting Up Indicator Muscle 336
    G. Contacts for Kinesiology 337

Bibliography 339

Acknowledgments

I would like to thank all my teachers; the ones who I physically studied with, the ones who came to me through books and the ones who were brought to me by living life and listening to nature.

I would like to thank all my students for their role in my growth and evolution. The teaching students gave to me is the very reason I have written this book.

I would like to thank my parents for their optimism, encouragement, patience and support. I would like to thank my son, who is by far my greatest teacher and support.

I would like to thank my friends and colleagues as many have contributed to the work of this manual.

A special thanks to Dr. Bruce Dewe for the endorsement of this manual for the purpose of teaching this material through the International College of Kinesiology Practice.

Thanks to Yarrow Alpine for introducing me to the universal vibrations such as herbs and sound.

Thanks to Phillip Rafferty for his contribution on the research and writing of the Auric field bands.

Thanks to Donna Eden for her book Energy Medicine and Dr. Richard Gerber for his book, Vibrational Medicine that helped me to discover the importance of vibrational remedies.

Thanks to Peri Best for her research and writing on the effect various notes have on the human body.

Thanks to Sabina Pettitt for her research and making of the sea and flower remedies of Pacific Essences.

Foreword by Sabina Pettitt

Evelyn Mulders is a woman ahead of her times. She created the Sound Essences in 1999 and has worked diligently over the past 10 years to understand their meanings and uses. Her use of the template of traditional Chinese medicine is possibly the most credible bridge available on the planet today for linking allopathic medicine and vibrational medicine. What I know to be true is that Evelyn's research standards are high and her commitment to vibrational medicine is unquestionable?

When I met Evelyn at our Energy Medicine training in 2002 , she was already using the Sound Essences in her professional Kinesiology practice and just as I have used Pacific Essences in conjunction with my acupuncture practice to sustain the harmony and balance achieved in an acupuncture session, Evelyn was using the Sound Essences to create the same result after a professional Kinesiology balance session.

Evelyn is an astute Kinesiology practitioner and gifted teacher and quick to make connections and be able to interpret the underling causative imbalance of physical, emotional or mental dis-ease.

One of the major universal constructs that Evelyn and I share, and ardently believe, is that the whole universe is energy vibrating and that when there is conflict, disharmony, stress, chaos, dis-ease results. In fact the energy body is the first place that a health professional can diagnose potential illness and ipso facto it is necessary to balance the energetic template in order to achieve healing. Moreover physical health is a direct result of harmony and balance in the energy body.

This book will speak to the health professional or the novice. It provides a clear understanding of the energetic pathways of the meridians and chakras and how each of these energetic templates impacts on the well being of the whole person. It will also assist the layperson to self select essences which they understand may help them to accomplish some shift in their behaviour or emotional or mental patterns.

One of the other blessings of essences which Evelyn has identified – that human beings have choice and once we can identify something that we desire to shift or change we can be greatly assisted by using a vibrational remedy.

Imagine that you can hear the sound of gentle waves caressing a sandy beach. And now imagine the sound of rush hour traffic. Notice your whole body response to these two experiences. My guess is that you will feel calmer, more peaceful and nourished by the sound of the waves. And that's exactly how you can feel when you use essences to assist you in personal transformation and greater health and well being.

Sabina Pettitt, M.Ed., Dr.TCM
Co-founder Pacific Essences®

Foreword by Bruce Dewe

Evelyn Mulders has an innovative approach to sound therapy. Her book, *The Essence of Sound*, is very easy to read, and simple to understand, yet packed full of information. Evelyn explains her hypothesis in a manner that makes sense and produces 'sound therapy' products that enable busy practitioners to use her method without any fuss.

I would never have thought of capturing a sound as an essence, nor would I have thought of using the Tibetan bowls or tuning forks in the manner she has. I was fascinated the moment I saw the beautiful display, intrigued by her presentation, yet sceptical enough to need to be convinced that her sound essences could (and did) work. I volunteered as a demonstration model so I could experience the process firsthand.

The misters that Evelyn uses surround one with sound in complete silence. Yes, one experiences the "sound of silence". Sceptics, prepare to be surprised, the process works. One can contemplate the emotion, the issue or situation at hand as part of a meditation or kinesiology balance; experiencing the benefits of the meridian, chakra, or auric field sound without the infringement of a practitioner physically making it in some form or other. It is unique, it works, it is pleasurable and it is fun.

The essences are great and so is the book. If you were just looking for an easy introduction to the chakras, meridians, and auric fields, and not really interested in sound, you would still find this a great guide to use for self healing and for working with clients.

I am so delighted with Evelyn's work that I have certified the workshop as an **ICPKP Approved Workshop**.

Bruce A J Dewe , MD NZRK, Co-Founder ICPKP

Introduction

The purpose of this book is to bring awareness to the value of universal energies and to introduce new vibrational remedies, Sound Essence, that can potentially enhance health and personal growth. We live in times where we have surrendered our innate universal understanding of health to those that have studied the healing world through textbooks. Our health care providers need to be complimented with people re-empowering themselves with the wisdom of what nature has provided for our wellness.

Nature is our provider and the farther we remove ourselves from it, the farther we get away from health and vitality. Typically we only look at one third of our being when addressing and diagnosing the signs and symptoms of imbalance in the body. Considering that two thirds of the body is being ignored correlates with the success rate of cure. There is a much greater potential for optimum health if our three-dimensional body were to be supported.

This book was written to help take the mystery out of the three-dimensional aspects of the body and to bring awareness to the healing potential of vibrational remedies. We are physical, emotional and spiritual beings and all three of these dimensions intertwine and represent our state of health. If at any time one of these bodies is out of balance it will eventually pull another one of the dimensions out of balance creating sickness. Each dimension has its role in stabilizing our health and requires support.

Our physical bodies can be supported with air, water, food and herbs. The emotional and spiritual body needs support from other elements of the universe, which include sound, light, colour, crystals, gems and flowers. Other aspects of supporting our whole body come from positive words and loving touch. There are many diverse ways in which we receive healing vibrations from the universe. It is important to be open to the experience. Remember how you felt when you saw that incredible sunset with its magnificent colour, or the sound of waves lapping up on the shore. These are all considered healing vibrations for your spiritual body. Being with nature helps us regain our sense of grounding which allows us to connect with nature and once again connect to ourselves. By connecting with ourselves we are more apt to listen to what our body is telling us. Be still and have the confidence to listen to your instincts.

This manual describes the anatomy of the Energy Field and breaks it down into Meridian, Chakra, Auric Field and Figure Eight energies, all the while exploring vibrational healing possibilities for our energy system. Describing the energy anatomy while discovering the vibrational ingredients of each Sound Essence takes the reader into an in depth discovery of why and how the essences work. While enticing the reader to participate in his or her own personal healing journey, this manual could be considered a manual for personal introspection, it offers a clinician information to support clients on their own journey. By exploring and integrating into our lives the healing attributes of the various vibrational remedies we support the health of our whole being, physically, emotionally and spiritually.

It was through the discovery of Sound Essence that I was given the understanding of the importance of universal vibration and its impact on our energy system. Every time I had a question about vibration and our energy fields, I was given a greater understanding and may have unintentionally unveiled forgotten information as in the case of the semitones completing the Chakra Sound Essence system.

Creating the "sound" vibration of Sound Essence and continually experimenting and blending it with other vibrations has been a kaleidoscope of marvelous experiences. Because the energetic body is presently starved for nourishment, consciously replenishing it with vibrational remedies may be the missing link to vibrant health.

We need to become deliberate users of healing vibrations.

May I now invite you to join me on this journey of self-discovery using Sound Essences as the navigator?

Chapter 1

The Discovery of Sound Essence

CHAKRA BALANCERS

The story of how I created the Sound Essences begins in 1998 at a reunion of graduate herbalists. Our teacher, Yarrow Alpine had brought our attention to universal brations and organized a special experience for us one evening. A crystal bowl player came to play her bowls in a log house set amongst the acres of trees and herbs in which we had spent the day exploring and studying.

That evening, I experienced what sound could do for the body. I can't say that the earth shook or that I had some rare disease cured but I knew from that moment on, I would be different. It was the resonance of the crystal bowls that really moved me. It may have been a spiritual connection because I felt more complete than I had ever felt. This experience left me wondering why everyone didn't get the chance to have this inner sense of completion since isn't this what we are looking for every day of our lives? The crystal bowl experience led me into a whirlwind of questions that I saved for the morning gathering. My first question was; can sound be infused into matter? I had the gut instinct that it could be, but really wanted to fast track a way of doing this so I could get everyone else to feel the way I did without having to travel into the Canadian woods and organize a crystal bowl player. I wanted to capture this vibration to share with others. Yarrow replied, "Evelyn, I do not know, I suppose this is for you to discover".

The question about infusing sound into matter left me wondering and pondering for over a year. I was an engineer technologist at the time, so I was busy working in my logical brain wondering if I had to hire fancy electronic equipment to organize this experiment. Time went on until one day, I was traveling by a small lake in British Columbia, Canada, which had a rock shop along its shore. Just moments after passing the rock shop, I got the idea to use the crystal bowls to vibrate the water. I giggled for an hour as I was driving; I really had come full circle. Of course the vibration from playing the bowls would imprint the water in the bowl. As water will take the imprint of any vibration you give it, it would easily take the imprint of sound.

I immediately hired a crystal bowl keeper and told her she would be doing some odd things for that day. She giggled, excited about the project. I brought a male mentor with me for representation of the male energy of the universe. I had the crystal bowl keeper put spring water in the bowls and she played each whole note as we meditated. The water started to bubble and it boiled without heat in the bowls, giving us confirmation that the sound was being imprinted into the water. As I was transferring the 'C' note water from the root chakra bowl into a traveling vessel, the water appeared red as it was being poured. I rubbed my eyes and looked again and the water was actually clear. I realized in that moment that I was given the information that while infusing water with sound, I was also infusing it with colour. I went home with my sounded water and this was the beginning of SOUND ESSENCE.

I used the Sound Essences in my clinic and married them with flower and gem essences for my clients with great success. What I realized was that the Sound Essence really potentized the other essences. At first I was using Sound Essence like a Bach Flower remedy, drops under the tongue. This had value, but I had a sense that there was more to explore.

One day I had a small headache and I used the Sound Essence drops under the tongue as a remedy for the headache. Much to my dismay, my headache was not relieved. In my disappointment, I had the idea to put drops of the essence on my fingers and hold my fingers away from the physical body and in the region of the headache. In seconds, the headache was gone.

This small awareness made me realize that the Sound Essence works in the etheric field and should be applied in this field for best results. I then began to produce these essences in mister bottles. This worked very well. I am noticing now that more and more essence practitioners are using misters rather than drops under the tongue. The resonance of all the essences including Sound Essences seems to be picked up directly in the etheric field.

While working with Sound Essence, I realized that there were seven whole notes, seven days in the week, seven colours of the rainbow and seven charkas in the etheric field. I surmised that possibly the whole notes resonated with the seven energy centres, known as the chakras. The Sound Essence remedies totally evolved at this point. I created a mister for each chakra that had variable sources of vibration. I intuited the gemstones that I would put with each chakra and the aroma that would suite each mister. The sounded water was the macerate for the chakra specific gemstone and the sacred geometry. The colour was inherently infused. On the mister bottles the labels displayed the symbols and positive words, which would be subliminally received every time the mister bottle was used.

Summing up, each Chakra Sound Essence mister has the vibration of thought (positive words), colour, sound, sacred geometry, ancient symbology, crystals and gems, and aromatherapy. Unbeknownst to me at the time, this apparently is the perfect vibrational formula for each chakra. Dr. Richard Gerber, in his book Vibrational Medicine, mentions that each chakra resonates to the vibration of each of the seven senses. So, if you were wondering why a Sound Essence mister works differently than just hearing a note of the crystal bowl, you will remember that each Sound Essence mister carries the vibration of more than just sound; it carries the vibration of colour, ancient symbology, sacred geometry, positive affirmations, crystals and aroma. It is full spectrum nourishment for our energy body that feeds our senses. It is like having a balanced meal for each of our energy centers. We need to feed our etheric body healthy vibrations in the same way that we need to feed our physical body healthy food.

While using the Sound Essences in my practice, I noticed that the heart chakra carried a lot more energy than any of the others. During the imprinting of the note F, we collectively said a small prayer for the men of the world. It is my sense that being a man in this time of planetary evolution is somewhat complicated. The old ways taught to them by their fathers are outdated and less than effective. Women are transforming and require more connection with their men. I believe that men at this time in this society are in an evolutionary phase. The heart chakra Sound Essence is designed to support the men through this transitional phase, enabling them to open their hearts. At trade shows when men come towards the Sound Essence booth, I notice that a high percentage of them are drawn to the heart chakra Sound Essence and of course this makes my heart sing.

THE CHAKRA SEMI-TONES

One day, as I was looking at the harmonic scale and realized that there were not just seven notes, but twelve, another question arose; how do the semi-tones fit into the chakra system?

I researched for over a year and finally went to a channeled source for the information. We discovered that the semi-tones were bridges for the chakras and affect the back of the body. Each semi-tone is located at a transitional spot on the spine. For example the C♯ is located where the sacral meets the lumbar. The E♭ is located where the lumbar meets the thoracic. F♯ is located where the thoracic meets the cervical. The G♯ is located where the cervical meets the skull. The B♭ is located where the physical meets the etheric.

These semi-tones also support those going through the transitional phases of life, C♯ is related to birthing, E♭ is related to the individuation stage, like a teenager finding his own way, F♯ is the phase of finding your own calling in life, G♯ is where you are, walking your talk and B♭ is the ending phase. What I have noticed is that those who have been working with the seven whole notes in the chakra system and then have the opportunity to experience the semi-tones get a boost in their transformation. It seems that the semi-tones may offer a yin/yang element to the chakra system.

Aura-Joy

Many users of the Sound Essence product enjoy the effect of these vibrational misters and want to share them with others. I had many requests for an all-in-one mister. I created a remedy which included the vibration of all twelve notes, the chosen seventeen gemstones including silver, and the five sacred geometry shapes, a fabulous healing aroma blend and called it *Aura-Joy*. People love this blend of vibration. It works like a rescue remedy and lifts your spirits. It quickly balances the entire chakra system and makes one feel wholesome. *Aura-Joy* is also used to keep the energy in the therapy room coherent.

One day at a Body, Mind, Spirit Expo, I had a vendor come by and thank me for my work. I giggled and replied; "you are welcome" with a curious grin. I asked her what she had noticed in her use of the Sound Essence. She said that the Sound Essence misters offered our universe the experience of the fourth and fifth dimension. She implied that the Flower Essences supported humans on the third dimension and the Light Essences from Australia supported the sixth dimension. Now everything was complete with the Sound Essences supporting the fourth and fifth dimension.

Meridian Vitalizers

Another terrific experience at a trade show was from a vendor who was intrigued by the Sound Essences and offered a trade. Always ready for an adventure, I agreed without knowing what I was trading. She chose her Sound Essence product and it was my turn for the exchange. When I went to her booth, I discovered she was a tarot card reader. She read my cards and this is some of what she said: There is more to this Sound Essence than what you brought here. You have a habit of doing first things last and last things first. This rang true for me. She went on to say that I had another product that started with an "M", I jumped in and confirmed that she was referring to the Meridian Sound Essences. This was a project that I had started several years ago but got stuck on some details. She insisted that I continue with the project and so I complied.

I had the water for the Meridian Sound Essences imprinted with tuning fork vibration. Knowing that meridians interface the physical with the etheric, I wanted to marry sound with an herbal imprint. I was given another clue from a colleague who had called to say he had a message to tell me "2c". This could only mean one thing- homeopathy was the medium in which to collect the vibrational imprint of the herb. With this information, I immediately instructed my receptionist that we were to order homeopathic herbs related to each meridian. She laughed and insisted that I was to make these remedies myself. I complained that this would take weeks and probably months before we would have a finished product. She shrugged her shoulders and repeated her inner knowing and we proceeded to collect the herbs needed to make tincture for fourteen meridians. I had already grown most of the ingredients and they were easily accessible. I had waited for over four years to get to this point with the Meridian Sound Essences and now within two short hours I had fourteen tinctures macerating. The surprise to this equation was that the tinctures were outside just four hours before the time of the lunar eclipse of 2004. A lunar eclipse is the very breath of the yin and yang energy. I had been divinely guided towards this very moment in time to infuse the nature spirits into the tinctures. Combining nature spirits with herbal remedies is known as alchemy. Once the homeopathy was prepared at 2c, the blending of sound completed the compilation of the Meridian Sound Essence. The meridian formulas complete with sound, homeopathy and alchemy were blended in couples. Yin and Yang meridians were blended to represent the five elements, Fire, Earth, Metal, Water and Wood. The Fire element consists of four meridians. These were also coupled representing, Ministerial Fire and Sovereign Fire. The Central and Governing Meridian Essences were also coupled, to complete the set of seven Meridian Sound Essences.

Meridians are the interface of the physical and energy body. Sounds supports the meridians in the energy level and herbal homeopathic imprint supports the meridians on the physical level. The homeopathic imprint is read by the organs and glands related to the meridians.

Infinity

The Infinity remedy was created on a "dare" as it were. I was at a conference where distributors of the Amethyst biomat had kits stacked up on display. I asked what the kits were for and the reply was "to remove negative energy out of the room so the amethyst mat would provide the ultimate healing experience."

I scoffed at the notion of removing negative energy and replied; "why wouldn't you use something to raise the vibration in the room instead?"

In that quick moment I could hear someone daringly say, "well then, why don't you make us some of that?"

And now that you've come to know me along this journey, I am sure you can pretty much guess what happened next. Yes, I graciously accepted the challenge.

I completed the formula, or so I thought, and tried it out. But to the disgrace of my integrity, I got the sensation of getting "high", which is something that I am less than comfortable with. I felt a "lifting off" sensation and then a "stuck" sensation. I tried again over the next several days each time a little more warily until weeks later I found myself driving two hours into the mountains, a place without commodities such as power and sewer, where I had hoped to consult with my mentor, Peri Best. Upon arrival, I immediately took violently sick and could barely get out why I had journeyed to her home. I finally got out the three notes I was using in the remedy and she played them on the piano and they gave me that same "high" feeling. I was pondering how the three notes made me feel totally out of sorts when she exclaimed, "you are using three notes from a four noted chord, and if you were to add the fourth note to this sequence, you would go to infinity!" I could hardly believe my ears, there was no way she could have known this to be the title of the new remedy.

Once the fourth note was included, I tried the remedy again and felt that "lifting off" sensation along with a "grounding sensation" and I felt as though I was expanding in size. I sensed the weaving of my physical body with my energy body and knew at once this was the remedy to support all those wanting this figure eight type of connection.

SUMMATION

The meridians have vibrational support with the blending of sound and homeopathy of the **Meridian Sound Essences**.

The chakras have vibrational support with the blend of sound, colour, thought, crystals gems, sacred geometry, ancient symbology and aroma of the **Chakra Sound Essences**.

The auric field has vibrational support of all twelve notes, the chosen seventeen gemstones including silver, and the five sacred geometry shapes and a fabulous healing aroma blend of the **Aura-Joy Sound Essence.**

The Figure Eight pattern is supported by **Infinity Sound Essence**. Infinity carries and exceptional vibration by blending a four-noted chord with flower and gem essences that help to expand consciousness.

These remedies each support an energy system and collectively support the entire anatomy of the energy systems. Sound Essence is truly Full Spectrum Vibrations Healing for the entire energy network.

PART 1

Sound Essence and the Secrets of Vibrational Healing

Chapter 2

The Power of Sound

Sound affects us in many different ways as we experience this daily. Listening to a live musical event can positively move us on an emotional level. Other sounds like traffic and sirens degrade our energy. Sound is interesting because we not only experience the sounds that we hear but we experience the vibration of inaudible sounds, these would be the vibrations that our energy body picks up such as radio waves, microwaves, and electromagnetic frequencies. Experiencing the frequency shift in my body from the singing crystal bowls gave me the understanding of the powerful impact sound has on our bodies and in our lives.

Imprinting the vibration of sound into water and using the tools of alchemy for the creation of Sound Essence gave me the opportunity to share the experience of frequency shifting with others. Sound Essence holds the vibration of sound but is inaudible to most, however clairaudients can easily mimic the sound of these essences. The Sound Essences have supported people in their healing and spiritual growth since 1998. While many still wonder how the essences work, others just know and trust. My hope is that when you experience the vibration of the Sound Essences you will need no explanation on how they work, you'll just know that they are working to support you in any way needed.

HISTORY OF SOUND

Sound Vibrations are considered to be associated with creation of both the world and our individual life patterns. Sound has been with us since the beginning of time. Sound is related to the oldest methods of healing. Sound and chanting were the two common healing modalities of ancient rituals.

Laurel Elizabeth Keyer researched the threads of sound in ancient cultures. "I found that Chinese healers had used singing stones in their rituals. These were then, flat plates of jade which, when struck, gave off musical tones. They had designated the Grand Tone of Nature, Kung, which seemed to correspond to our musical note of F. The Sufis considered Hu to be creative sound. The Tibetans considered the notes A, F sharp and G to be powerful sacred sounds. We are familiar with the importance given to the words Aum and Amen. Amen was more than a period when it was uttered. It was derived from the older "AUM" which represented all of the sounds, which the human voice was capable of expressing and therefore associated with the creative principle designating God."

The mystery schools following these teachings associated rhythm with the body, melody with the emotions and harmony with lifted consciousness to spiritual awareness.

What is Sound

Sound is the vibrational energy moving through matter. Vibrations vary through a wide range of frequencies. The lowest sound can only be felt in our bodies, the higher sounds can be heard by our ears and the highest frequencies can no longer be heard or felt but are still detected by our energy body. We are aware of most of these frequencies but the effects of these vibrations of sound travel well beyond what we can detect with our ears.

There are two common terms that we use in reference to sound. These terms are harmony and resonance.

Harmony is when two or more frequencies blend together creating a pleasant or healing sound. This harmonic sound is represented through mathematical relationships tying sound into the realms of sacred geometry, proving that all the vibrations of the universe have a connection. It is like when we play the crystal singing bowls individually; they would sing a certain tone. But if we wanted to play them together in a concert, we would tune them to play in harmony.

Resonance refers to what happens when a sound interacts with matter that vibrates at a frequency that is in harmony with the sound. It is like having two tuning forks with the same frequency in one room and when one is played from across the room, the second tuning fork would reverberate and ring as well. Or if you sing into a crystal bowl with a matched pitch, the bowl begins to sing.

Sound and Sine Waves

Sound and sine waves are synonymous. Sine waves correspond to light and the electromagnetic spectrum and the vibration of sound. Everything, meaning our universe and reality, is based on sine waves, which means it's based on sound. What makes one object different from another is the pattern and wavelength of the sine wave. Everything in our world is a waveform, or could be seen as sound. Everything, the planet, our bodies, plants and rocks vibrate. Absolutely everything is a waveform. The proof that sound affects matter can be simply shown by putting sand on the face of a drum and by sounding the drum, the granules of sand will take on various geometric patterns. Sound moves matter and the sound vibration causes change in molecular structure. Sound has the potential to change our bodies, thus offering healing.

Sound as a Vibrational Remedy

Health can be defined as being of sound body, mind and spirit. This means that the body, mind and spirit are resonating harmoniously to their highest potential. By being healthy we maintain a resonant frequency. When sick or suffering from imbalance we are in discord to this resonant frequency therefore the process of healing is simply restoring this optimum resonance to the body, mind and spirit. The basic principle of sound healing and vibrational medicine is that every organ, bone, cell or system has a specific frequency and the concept of disease suggests that a counter frequency has encoded itself over the healthy frequency causing some part of the body to vibrate out of tune. By using the vibration of sound, it is possible to shift the frequency of the imbalanced part, enabling it to entrain to its normal frequency, resonating at its highest potential, seeking the state of optimum health.

There are two ways in which vibrational remedies such as Sound Essences support our health. The first is that they can provide the sine wave or frequency that is missing. Secondly, they introduce a pattern of harmony where there is discord.

Everything in the universe vibrates and has a sine wave. Vibrational remedies that support the body's vibration include thought, light, colour and sound. Other vibrational remedies come from plants and minerals. The healing frequencies from the plant kingdom are homeopathy, flower essences, aromatherapy, herbs and food. The healing frequencies from the mineral kingdom are crystals, gems, ores, metals, and essences made from these vibrations.

If our energy is blocked in some way and we do not have the full spectrum of frequency in our energy field, offering the body various vibrations allows the body to pick up the vibration it needs to support the overall resonance of the body. The body's innate intelligence knows what it needs and integrates the missing frequency into the energy field. This is the beauty of using vibrational remedies; as the body only chooses what it needs.

The second principle for understanding the importance of vibrational remedies is that we are three-dimensional beings. We consist of physical, emotional and spiritual bodies. These three bodies need to be coherent, in a pattern of harmony for us to experience optimum health. Most imbalances in the body are due to stuck or blocked energy. Energy becomes blocked because some part of the body, mind and spirit is vibrating out of tune with its natural healthy resonance. The spiritual body aspires towards a connection with the universe and a sense of finding itself at home. The emotional body aspires to resilience so it can monitor and assess feelings without getting pulled into the drama. The physical body aspires to good muscle tone, effective breathing and adequate digestion and elimination.

If our spirit is suppressed because of feelings such as despair, loss of self, isolation and loneliness and if our emotions are stressed because we get caught up in the drama of a situation for too long, or if we are physically stressed because of lack of sleep, or eating incorrectly or not staying fit, we create incoherent vibration of our three-dimensional body. By exposing the body to sound and other healing vibrations, the energy often releases naturally and the flow of energy returns, creating balance in the body.

The part which is out of sync, will be drawn to the healthy frequency and begins to vibrate in harmony with the rest of the body. It is like an orchestra warming up. Each instrument has its own sound but when the orchestra has all the instruments tuned to the perfect frequency and are playing in concert, magical music abounds because all the instruments resonate harmoniously.

Each of us resonates to our own vibrational frequency. By using vibrational remedies we keep ourselves in alignment with our innate frequency. If we get overstressed, overly emotional, or out of sync we can turn to sound vibration to shift us back into our innate frequency. We can keep ourselves stable with the use of Sound Essence and restore our own harmonious frequency.

Spiritual Growth and Sound

Using vibrational remedies is often a journey of self-discovery and self-healing. Another purpose for wanting to shift frequencies is for personal growth or for expanding consciousness. Shifting our frequency for personal growth can affect our body, mind and spirit. If our body is not in tune with our spiritual growth, our overall resonances will be less than coherent. Working with vibrational remedies such as Sound Essence keeps the energy flowing freely for spiritual shifts to take place. Primarily we can use vibrational remedies to become more awake, more conscious, and more divine. The purpose of using vibrational remedies is not simply to heal an imbalanced condition but to shift us consciously allowing us to realize that in divinity, all is whole.

An important aspect in shifting frequency is to bring awareness and consciousness to our world. We change our frequency to regain that sense of connectedness with others and to nature, knowing that we are all one.

Aware or unaware, visible or invisible, these vibrational remedies impact us powerfully. Every individual who works to raise his or her vibrational level to enter into clear and balanced frequency is contributing to the alignment and enrichment of this world. The time has come when these adjustments into attunement are imminent for more and more people.

Sound in a Bottle

Sound is one of the most powerful healers for the human energy field. By imprinting water with sound, the vibration is captured in the water molecule. By misting the human energy field with this vibration, our field resonates with the healing vibration and shifts the energy pattern. The waves of vibration affect the vibration of our figure eight pattern, auric field, chakras and meridians to create a consonance that helps our body into alignment.

Our bodies vibrate. We all have our own vibration and depending on our attitude, how we think, and how we react changes how we vibrate. It's our reaction to the outside world that creates resonance. If we use vibratory tools such as sound we can create harmony in our energy field. This vibratory energy of sound is picked up by our energy body and creates a resonance that harmonizes incoherent vibration.

Imbalances of the physical body can be detected through the energy field whether it is in the figure eight pattern, the auric field, charkas, meridians or acupuncture points. Sound vibration shifts frequencies in the energy field and ultimately alters the frequency or vibration of the physical body. By using biofeedback such as Kinesiology, we detect imbalanced or blocked frequencies in the energy field before it manifests as sickness or disease in the physical body. Kinesiology is also used to determine the source of optimum vibration which when applied creates resonance, hence balancing the whole body. Simply stated, with the use of Kinesiology we can access and find the resonant vibrational match from the body's energy field (meridians, chakras, auric field, and figure eight pattern) with vibrational remedies such as Sound Essence and expect the whole body to benefit.

Like our vision, humans can only see a small fraction of the visual spectrum. There are infrared microwaves that we feel the effect of and can't see. Unheard sound affects us. We can't hear it with our ears but our energy body picks up on this sine wave and uses it to bring this resonance into the electrical or energy field. This unheard sound reverberates just like the sound we hear.

Like ringing a tuning fork, at first you can hear the sound and then after awhile you can't hear it anymore because our ears don't pick up the sound but the tuning fork is still vibrating and the sound waves are still carried through the air. This silent sound is the vibration contained in the bottle. The sine waves are there, you just can't hear them. If you were clairaudient you could then hear the sound.

We are in a state of constant change. We change our pattern automatically in attempts to achieve higher aspirations or spiritual connection, we then need to get our body in harmony with the pattern of the new field. There are levels of experience that relate to and are activated by different tones and sound in all living beings. Generally speaking, low tones activate deep, often painful emotions, middle tones tend to comfort, and high tones activate ideas and thoughts. On a scale of eight tones the lowest tone and the highest tone come together in the octave. To understand the octave pattern, visualize the central and governing meridians as on continuous figure eight. The central and governing meridians together unify and stabilize all the other intervening tones and their corresponding meridians. This holds the divine life essence dimension of all living beings. Vibrational remedies support this change. The body is able to receive the new vibration and if there is resonance, it will shift the energy field to a newer state, hence shifting the vibration of the physical body, every organ, bone, cell or system. The body gets a tune up and the spirit gets to wake up and we come into resonance with our new desired frequency.

Because everyone vibrates at a different frequency, what is a good vibration for one person may not be the best for another. We are all moving through changes in health and attitude at different times and in different ways, so we all have an individual need for certain frequencies.

There are even discrepancies amongst the experts about which notes represent each chakra or meridian. By offering the body a full spectrum of vibration and allowing the body to choose the frequency needed to support optimum function, a truly wholistic approach to wellness is achieved. Using a biofeed back system such as Kinesiology can offer great support in finding the optimum choice for our well-being.

Chapter 3

The Magic of Water

Water is truly a magical and sacred substance. By exploring these properties we come to better understand how signaturing water with various vibrations helps us nourish and maintain the integrity of our energy body. Our energy body is the template for our physical body and any imbalance in the energy body will eventually manifest itself in the physical body. To keep the energy body healthy with various spectrums of healthy vibrations we need water as the encapsulating medium.

The ancients worshipped water and used it for ceremonial rituals. Water is truly the life-blood of our universe as much as it is the very essence of our own blood and the essence of our being.

In the universe we are solely connected with water, as we need water not only for survival but also for emotional and spiritual health. Water is the primary component of all body fluids such as lymph, digestive juices, urine, bile, mucous, sweat and tears. The mineral salts and electrolytes that help carry electrical currents in the body and to the brain are carried in water. Everyone feels better walking along the seashore, paddling in the river or just sitting by a creek or a fountain.

Water is the magical substance that gives us life. Keeping our water sacred and treating it with respect, will ensure health and vitality for our planet and us all.

Researchers have proven that sacred water is qualitatively and quantitatively different than other water. Sacred water has the capacity to encapsulate and transmit energy. Water takes in energy and emits energy and this is why it is important to hold it sacred. It has been proven by various scientists that by projecting loving thoughts to the water, the water changes its structure towards a more cohesive and positive manner. Dr. Masaru Emoto has given us the visual proof of these scientific findings. Dr. Emoto has frozen various water molecules and photographed them. Regular water has a random crystal appearance, but sacred water, water that has been blessed or water that has been charged with sound, forms very symmetrical crystalline formations. This research demonstrates that water can be transformed and potentized by charging it with healing vibration such as sound, colour, ancient symbols and loving positive thoughts.

Water molecules have an innate tendency to create three-dimensional forms. The fact that the hydrogen atoms need to attach to the oxygen atoms at exactly 104.5 degrees gives this molecule its peculiarity. By being three-dimensional, water molecules have the ability to encapsulate and absorb other molecules. Water basically encapsulates and dissolves everything it meets, making it the universal solvent.

Water responds to every change in its surroundings by expanding, evaporating, contracting, melting or creating rhythmical waves. As water keeps changing, it moves naturally. While water is moving, it is considered living as it is constantly collecting and depositing new information. It does this naturally, chemically absorbing molecules, but also by absorbing subtle information. As water travels not only does it pick up physical information, but it also has the capacity to store and transmit more subtle information like vibrational information. Water as a universal solvent will take any kind of information you present it with. These vibrational imprints can be healthy and vitalize our environment or harmful and pollute our environment. We need to become conscious on how we effect water and how it effects us. Water, if used correctly, is the most powerful channel for conducting resonance and communicating life supporting vibrational energies to every living thing.

The difference between a live body and a dead body is the life force. This life force comes from our vibration. The principle of resonance gives us the understanding that all living matter and beings communicate via vibration. Everything in the universe vibrates and has a vibratory rate. This is how information is transferred from one being to another and how animals are tuned into one another. This explains how schools of fish and flocks of birds move congregationally in unison.

It is believed that every molecule of every structure of our body is composed of individual sound patterns and emits a vibration that is unique to its structure. In a healthy body with healthy organs and glands, the molecules work together in harmonious relationship with each other. Our whole body resonates at a particular frequency and any disruption to this frequency causes pain, discomfort and disease. Our bodies are made mostly of water and the water in our body is what holds our resonance. When the water in our bodies holds a structured pattern, the cells are able to communicate efficiently between each other through patterned frequencies keeping our body at optimal frequency. The more structured the water in our body, the greater is its ability to hold vibrant energy in the body.

Scientists have proven that when water is exposed to moonlight, crystal energy or to pyramid shapes, the actual configuration of the water changes. An important conclusion from this type of experimenting is that structured water supports the healthy function of all systems. Some research has shown that structured water in the body promotes enzyme function. Proper enzyme function allows the body to assimilate minerals and vitamins from our food appropriately which supports overall health.

It is therefore important to keep our vibration or resonant frequency as close to our true pattern as possible. Because water is such an important channel for resonance it will take on any information, good or bad, it is important to expose ourselves to as much positive vibration as possible.

We can gather positive vibration from the plant kingdom through food, herbs, homeopathy and flower essences. We can gather positive vibration from the mineral kingdom through rocks, crystals and gems. We can gather positive vibration from the cosmos through light, colour, sound, geometric shapes, and symbols. We can gather positive energy from each other by way of positive touch, positive word and positive thought vibration.

Healers throughout history have potentized water with various vibrations.

- The Egyptians potentized water with crystals, gemstones, and sacred geometry, knowing that keeping an urn of water in a pyramid holds healing energetic patterns.
- Shamans have potentized water by intent and prayer.
- Samuel Hahnemann potentized water with the biochemical signature of herbs and called it homeopathy.
- Dr. Bach used water to infuse the vibration of the flower's emotional message for the human's soul and called it flower essence therapy.
- Evelyn Mulders potentizes water, with the vibration of sound for the vitality of the meridians, chakras, auric field, and figure eight energies and calls it Sound Essence.

The imprinted water is often referred to as a vibrational remedy. The vibrations stored in these remedies are picked up by the body's energetic network of meridians, chakras, auric field, and figure eight pattern. In Chinese medicine, it is recognized that subtle energy or vibrations flow from the environment to the nerves, blood vessels and deeper into the organs along special channels called meridians. East Indian medicine recognizes that the auric field and the chakras pick up the information from the subtle energies. The chakras act as transformers to translate subtle energies and relay them as hormonal, nervous or cellular messages in the body. It is through these subtle energy receptors known as meridians, chakras and auras that vibrational remedies prove their potential. The body resonates to vibration and is constantly scanning for a vibration that will optimize health. It will adopt a healing vibration from one of these remedies if it is a match to a missing vibration that is causing imbalance.

As these vibrations are exposed to the body's energetic network, the body chooses and infiltrates the energetic messages from these vibrational remedies. Life depends on these vibrations. The body has an innate wisdom for health and vitality and by offering the body vibrational remedies we can support its magical wisdom.

Chapter 4

Nature's Rhythm and Hierarchy
How Nature's Vibration Affects Human Energy Systems

Light – Purest Energy Vibration

There was a time when we were in tune with nature and innately knew what we needed from the earth and our universe to provide optimum vitality. The universe supplies us with all that we need. We can shift our frequencies towards health by embracing the various vibrations mother nature has supplied us with.

As we move through the realms of matter we must first admit that everything in the universe is in a state of vibration. We first had darkness until God said, "let there be light" and there was light. All life on earth depends on light from the sun, which is the ultimate source of life and energy. Light is the paintbrush of the creator. Pure white light was immersed in the darkness and when the two came together; colour emerged. Total light would blind us and total dark would render us unconscious, hence colour is the healing force. The vibration of colour is the bridge between light and dark. The pure white light has bountiful healing powers, as we can feel from the power of the sun. Colour comes to us at a lower vibration than light. Some might ask that for healing purposes why wouldn't we just immerse ourselves into the pure light since it holds all the colour spectrums. It is like sitting in a garden of medicinal herbs; all the herbs have healing properties but there are specific ones that will help heal the imbalanced organs or systems. There are times when a single colour like a single herb has a more potent effect on our body than a myriad or mixture will have. The right colour is the right food at the right place at the right time.

Colour – Sound Made Visible

In 1665, Isaac Newton beamed sunlight through a prism and found the presence of seven basic colours. The human body is like a prism that reflects light and colours. Colour therapy is the science of the use of different colours to change or maintain the vibrations of the body to that frequency which signifies good health and harmony and general well-being. Healing through colour was one of the first therapies.

Our bodies are an intricate mix of physical, emotional and spiritual components. The bridge between the solid physical component and the light spiritual component is the colour in the aura. Colour is the bridge between the inner and outer being. Colour is as necessary to the spiritual being as food is to the physical body.

Our emotions and actions affect the electromagnetic field, which surrounds us and is reflected in our aura. Colour has the capacity to restore the balance when a blockage or imbalance of this energy has resulted in disease. Using colour can help restore vitality to the aura through the projection of specific colour rays, which are absorbed by the chakra centers. Colour therapy exposes the life value that light gives our body.

Life is colour. All minerals, plants and animals have colour. Each organ has a specific colour. Each colour has intelligence, frequency and polarity, knows its functional role and works selectively. Colour is a vibratory energy that can activate a particular organ, gland and system in the body. The application of the correct frequency of the electromagnetic force field will change the altered function of the body and help return it to its original healthy patterns. It is this vibrational energy, which is the result of applying colour that is important in the healing process.

Each of the colours has a different effect on the body even though they are all interrelated. All the colours work together to relieve, cleanse, build, heal, and balance. The body's ultimate goal is to seek balance and the use of colour therapy has no dangerous side effects. Colour is known as a key component for the meridians in the Chinese Five Element Theory and colour vibrations influence us in a very special manner through the Ayurvedic seven chakras and the auric field. Essentially each of the seven colours of the spectrum is assigned to each energy center, chakra, and to each band of the aura. As colour works through the aura, chakras and meridians, changes in the energy field are made, the energy body will only accept the amount needed, as a pail of water will only accept the full amount needed and the rest spills over. The vibrations of colour are energy of the life-force itself and are here to aid us in our spiritual growth and progress toward the oneness which is our ultimate purpose.

SOUND – COLOUR MADE AUDIBLE

The next lower vibration from colour is that of sound. "In the beginning was the word." The word implies the primal sound vibration. Sound is audible information whereas colour is visual information. If our hearing was to possess all ranges of frequencies, we would be able to hear the music of flowers and grass, mountains and valleys, the singing of the sky and stars and the symphony of our own body. Stephen Halpern provides a fabulous image of the relationship of colour and sound. Light and colour are expressed as vibrations. He uses the example of a piano keyboard with its seven octaves of the musical scale imaginably extended to the full range of 40 - 50 octaves and suggests that in this range, the keyboard would produce colours rather than sounds when played.

There is an incredible correlation of sound and colour and there is fabulous synchronicity when the two are used together for healing purposes. Using sound in healing is relatively new in comparison to the use of colour and aroma and mineral therapy so there is still much discussion on the attributes of each note. Every note has a certain colour associated with it. Sound and colour may be used to affect the same imbalance in the body, however it is believed that each affects a different level of the body. When we describe the physical, emotional, and spiritual attributes of colour, we inherently describe the attributes of the notes associated with the colour. Some believe that sound does not heal independently of colour. Sound and colour are said to be one. When sound is colour it is the most visual and when colour is sound it is the most audible.

Tuning fork sound vibration was used in the making of the Meridian Sound Essences. The crystal bowls were used in the making of the Chakra Sound Essences. As the bowls were played the author witnessed colour dancing in the bowl and recognized that if the vibration of sound has signatured matter, so too inherently has colour added its signature to the matter.

Colour	Key Note	Scale	Chakra	Mantra	Vowels
Red	C	Do	Root	Lam	"u"
Orange	D	Re	Sacral	Vam	"o"
Yellow	E	Me	Solar Plexus	Ram	"O"
Green	F	Fa	Heart	Yam	"ah"
Blue	G	So	Throat	Ham	"eh"
Indigo	A	La	Brow	Ksham	"e"
Violet	B	Ti	Crown	Om	"m"

Form – Created By Sound

As we move through the realms of matter and admit that everything in the universe is in a state of vibration we then move from light, to colour, to sound, to form. If we were to place sand in the crystal bowl and play the bowl, the sand would vibrate and create form. Plants, animals, and minerals are form. These vibrate at a lower rate than sound. The vibrations from plants and minerals have an enormous healing affect on the human body. Foods and herbs affect the body mostly on a chemical level. Plants offer healing vibrations through aromatherapy, homeopathy, flower essences and through their spiritual messages to our soul self. Healing with crystals, stones, aromatherapy and vibrational remedies (flower, shell, sea and sound essences) along with colour belong to the category of information therapies. There is no chemical substance that affects the body, rather it is the information emitted by these therapies that affects the body.

Plant Form
HERBS – HOMEOPATHY – AROMATHERAPY – FLOWER ESSENCES

Plants offer healing vibrations for us in many different ways. We use plants and herbs for food and medicine to support our body biochemically, to restore meridian balance and to alleviate signs and symptoms of distress. Plants also support our bodies emotionally and spiritually through homeopathy, aromatherapy and flower essence therapy.

Homeopathy is a bridge between traditional medicine and vibrational medicine. Homeopathy has no biochemical trace in its remedy thus working on the energy imprint of the herb to heal the body. Homeopathy is paired with sound for the healing effect of the Meridian Sound Essences.

Aromatherapy healing comes to us by way of scent and affects our emotional realm. The plants' most potential is in the flower. In aromatherapy, it takes hundreds of flowers to create an essential oil. This process condenses the healing properties into the oil that creates this incredible aroma of nature that we use to soothe our minds and emotions and balance our bodies.

Aromatherapy is a simple and natural method of utilizing the vibration of concentrated energies from the plant kingdom to unlock our minds, bodies and spirit. It changes our thought forms and beliefs by altering moods and emotions, which create conscious shifts.

Emotions are stored in the body, in every organ, gland, muscle, meridian and system. Feelings are first taken into the body through the chakras and then fed into the meridian system, which affects every organ and gland. The aromas of the Chakra Sound Essences correlate specifically with the seven chakras of the body and hence the meridian system to heighten their frequency.

Since each organ and gland has a vibrational frequency, as do emotions, the emotions will settle in the organ or gland with the corresponding frequency. Dr. Robert O. Becker states that the human body has an electrical frequency and that much about a person's health can be determined by its frequency. We all have different frequencies as every disease has a frequency. Disease occurs when the body's vibrational frequency drops and matches the vibration of disease. Essential oils can raise the body's frequency because the flower's power vibrates at a higher frequency than us and transfers this higher frequency to us; enabling health.

Flower Essence Therapy captures the imprint of the plant's signature in water. The plant's expression of itself is in its flower. The entire purpose of a plant is to produce the flower, which holds the highest vibration and potency of the plant. The flower carries stored information from the plant kingdom and offers this healing information to us.

Mineral Form
CRYSTALS AND GEMSTONES

Minerals are in no way less colourful and spectacular than flowers, and the same holds true for their therapeutic values. As aromatherapy from flowers affects us on one dimension, the healing power of the stones affects us on another. Again it is the information inherent in the flowers and the stones that offers healing to the body. Gemstones have been appreciated for their healing and harmonizing powers since the beginning of civilization. Gemstones have grown in the depths of the earth and bear light and colour in its purest form. Gemstones offer this information to the aura and the chakras to harmonize our soul and body. If a need is fulfilled, healing will take place. If we offer our bodies a variety of information therapy, it will absorb the vibration it needs to create balance.

Crystals and gemstones heal physically, mentally, emotionally and spiritually, rebalancing and realigning energy. Crystals and minerals are other forms of information therapies.

Each gemstone and crystal stores its own information and has its own influence on the aura, chakras and meridians. These stones imprint the essence with particular energy and healing qualities of their unique crystalline structures and colour vibrations.

Chapter 5

Energy Anatomy

Overview of Meridians, Chakras, Auric Field and Figure Eight Energies

The three oldest recorded healing systems both viewed the human body from a holistic and energetic approach, recognizing that the body includes the physical, mental, emotional and spiritual components. The figure eight pattern comes from Tibetan healing practices, the auric field and chakra system comes from the Ayurvedic tradition and the meridian and five element theory comes from Traditional Chinese Medicine. These systems map energy pathways in the human body and use this knowledge to assist the body in healing through the holistic approach of addressing the physical, mental, emotional and spiritual components of the body. This human energy system has an anatomy to it. It can be simply organized as such:
  ORGANS and GLANDS
  MERIDIANS and FIVE ELEMENTS
  CHAKRAS
  AURIC FIELD and GRID
  FIGURE EIGHT PATTERN

The Figure Eight Pattern

The Figure Eight Pattern is universal energy seen both in and out of our body.

Inside the body it is found in tissues, muscles, organs and on a cellular level in the pattern of the DNA molecule. Outside the body it can be found in the meridian system, as the central and governing meridian intertwine, in the chakra system weaving the front and back of the charkas, and in the auric field connecting the physical body with the energy body.

The Figure Eight Pattern not only integrates each individual energy system but integrates all energy systems for a harmonious network of information. The figure eight energy system weaves all our force fields into resonance. It holds our energetic patterns and structures together. The figure eight weaves the dense body with the light body, it intertwines the flow of energy between your ego self and your "I AM" presence.

THE AURA

The aura, which is Greek for breeze, surrounds every creature and everything in nature. Auras surround stones, animals, humans, plant life and even trees. Auras surround anything that has a vibration.

The aura is a multi-layered energetic sphere that encapsulates the entire physical body. Our body is multidimensional consisting of the physical, emotional and spiritual dimensions. The aura which is our energy body representing our emotional dimension is the bridge between our physical body and our spiritual body. Colour is the bridge between pure white light and darkness. Our physical body hypothetically represents darkness and the spiritual body represents pure white light, the colour bridge is then the aura and our emotional body. The colour spectrum is represented by the band of seven colours and so too is the auric field associated with these seven colours.

The aura is the protective atmosphere that surrounds and embraces us, filtering environmental information. The aura is said to have seven bands each vibrating at a different frequency and each corresponding in energy with one of the seven chakras. It is believed that each auric band is associated with the body through the chakra that corresponds with it: the etheric body is related to the root chakra, the emotional body is related to the sacral chakra, the mental body is related to the solar plexus chakra, the astral body is related to the heart chakra, the spiritual etheric body is related to the throat chakra and the celestial body is related to the brow chakra and the ketheric body is related to the crown chakra.

The aura is our first energy interface and delivers information to the chakras, which in turn forwards the information to the meridian system, which transports it to our nervous system and further to the organs and glands.

CHAKRAS

The word chakra means a spinning wheel or vortex or disk of colour and light. A chakra is an energy center of the body that receives, assimilates and expresses life force energy. When we define "life force" we know "life" to be the blood and circulation system of the body; "force" is then the energy that manipulates the physical body. This force comes to us first by way of these spinning vortices called chakras, the chakras then distribute this energy through to the meridians and the meridians connect with the body's nervous system affecting the spine and brain. Each of the seven major chakras is positioned from the base of the spine to the top of the head. The chakras are named after the part of the body in which they spin and the organs in this area are directly affected by the corresponding chakra. Starting at the bottom there is the root chakra, sacral chakra, solar plexus chakra, heart chakra, throat chakra, brow chakra, and crown chakra. These chakras are on the outside of the body and when they receive information, this information is passed on to the meridian system.

Each chakra has a key issue and once they are balanced the body's energy system often feels better and this may also enhance life force (root chakra), sexuality (sacral chakra), personal power (solar plexus chakra), love and compassion (heart chakra), self-expression (throat chakra), insight (third eye chakra), the universal connection (crown chakra). Each chakra influences the organs, muscles, ligaments, veins and glands in its energy system.

Chakras have a very strong association with the body's glandular system and therefore have a tremendous impact on our emotional environment. We record every thought and feeling into one of our seven chakras. As the chakras govern the endocrine system, bringing the chakras into balance helps bring the hormones and therefore emotions into balance. Our emotions and our viewpoint have a direct impact on the state of our health. Most physical imbalances are manifested by an attitude. A gland of the endocrine system governs each chakra. Bringing the chakras into balance helps bring the hormones and therefore emotions and attitudes into balance.

Physically, each chakra is connected to a nerve center, one of the seven senses and one of the endocrine glands. The seven colours and seven musical notes and the seven symbols also vibrate with the chakras. The entire magic of balancing the chakras is in affecting the seven senses related to the seven chakras.

Root Chakra	Smell	Aromatherapy
Sacral Chakra	Taste	Food, Herbs, Homeopathy, Flower, Shell, Gem and Sound Essences
Solar Plexus Chakra	Sight	Symbology and Sacred Geometry
Heart Chakra	Feel	Healing Touch and Crystals and Gems
Throat Chakra	Sound	Music and Yantras
Brow Chakra	Light and Colour	Colour Therapy
Crown Chakra	Thought	Prayer, Mantras and Positive Word Affirmations

The healing modality that resonates with each chakra imparts special information to help balance this chakra. It is the information that is held in the vibration or wave-form of the aroma, herb, symbol, colour, sound or word that resonates with our energy system and helps to raise our vibrations.

In addition to each chakra relating to one of the senses, every chakra has its favorite smell, taste, sight, touch, sound, colour and thought. These are the components that we will be exploring in this manual.

Our chakras are a reflection of our consciousness. Chakra work leaves people feeling more centred, grounded and in harmony with their surroundings. Balancing a chakra, especially if it is the weakest link in the chain, can cause remarkable effects allowing the entire chakra system to strengthen.

Meridians

The information gathered from the chakras on the outside of the body is distributed by the meridians to the inside of the body and is picked up by the body's nervous system, the spine and brain and related to the major organs of the body.

The meridians are considered an energy network connecting the interior physiological system with the exterior energy system, the internal organs with the surface of the body and the flesh with the spirit. The function of the meridians is to provide the circulation of our life force throughout our body, thus nourishing the tissues and linking up the whole body with the energy body, keeping our internal organs, limbs, muscles and tendons and bones intact and to allow the body organic integrity and vitality. Meridians have an affinity for vibrational support especially from herbs and sound.

There are fourteen major meridians and twelve are named after the organ system they serve; stomach meridian, spleen meridian, lung meridian, large intestine meridian, kidney meridian, bladder meridian, liver meridian, gall bladder meridian, heart meridian, triple warmer meridian, small intestine meridian, and the circulation/sex meridian. The other two meridians run along the centreline of the front and back of the body. These two channels, the central and governing meridians, act as reservoirs for the life force energy. They help sustain and support the energy for the other twelve channels. The central and governing meridians also play a fundamental role in linking up the seven chakras.

One way to overview the meridians is to sort them into Chinese five elements: Fire, Earth, Metal, Water, and Wood. Each element has a yin and a yang meridian with the exception of Fire; it has two yin meridians and two yang meridians.

Chapter 6

Sound Essence

Overview

The action of all essences can be compared to the effects of having a very moving experience like the effects felt hearing a particularly pleasing piece of music or admiring an inspirational work of art. The light or sound waves that reach the senses may evoke profound feelings in the soul, which affect the body by altering breathing, pulse rate and other biorhythms. The essences awaken an experience within the soul similar to the soul experience of the creator of any art. This is called resonance. This is the phenomenon that occurs while using flower, sea, gem or sound essences. The life force or the sin wave conveyed by each essence awakens the particular qualities within our soul.

Sound Essences are subtle energy remedies created from the healing vibration of sound. They affect the human energy field physically, emotionally and spiritually by nourishing the energy field with their healing vibration. They promote health and harmony.

All physical matter has a vibration as well as its physical form. Humans manifest a lower vibration in stress than they do in a healthy relaxed state. If through stress or unhealthy lifestyle choices, the body's vibration is lowered to match a certain sickness or disease, the body will in fact take on that sickness. It is important to nourish the energy field with favourable vibrations to maintain health and vitality.

By keeping the body's energies flowing and raising its vibration, disease and sickness simply do not have the right environmental conditions in which to thrive. Whenever the human body is bombarded by too much stress, the entire system is thrown off of balance and loses its functional harmony.

It's known what to feed the body in times of sickness and what herbs help certain imbalances but most people have yet to come to recognize the importance of also feeding the energy bodies which include the Figure Eight Pattern, the seven bands of the **Aura**, the seven main **Chakras** and the fourteen main **Meridians**. These energy bodies serve as netting that encapsulates the body like the membrane of an eggshell and acts as a vitality filter. If there is an imbalance in this netting because of an emotional or spiritual imbalance the shield will deteriorate and mirror this imbalance onto the physical body and develop what is known as disease or sickness. The imbalance first occurs in the energy body and if this imbalance is not corrected, it will manifest itself into the physical body and is described as heart disease, diabetes, cancer, etc. Understanding that imbalance occurs first in the energy body and if unaddressed creates physical imbalance, it only makes sense that the focus of healing would be to balance the energy field, which includes the figure eight pattern, the aura, charkas and meridians. It is therefore important that this shield is vibrationally nourished so it can support the physical body. Just as a balanced diet nourishes the physical body, colour, sound aroma, crystal, gems, ancient symbology, positive thought, homeopathy, and aromatherapy nourish the energy systems.

The Sound Essences are a composition of these various information therapies. Each Sound Essence holds vibrational information that supports the vitality of the human energy system. These information therapies all resonate at various frequencies and interface with any field that is lacking vibration. Vibrational information is as vital to our energy system as air and water are to our physical system.

Sound Essence is a four part system that supports the anatomy of the energy field which includes the Meridians, Chakras, and Auric field, and Figure Eight Pattern.

First the Meridian Sound Essences are used to support the meridian system. Then one or more Chakra Sound Essences are chosen to support the chakra system, and *Aura-Joy* Sound Essence is used to support the auric field in raising and holding the energy of a higher magnitude. Finally *Infinity* Sound Essence is used to re-inforce the Figure Eight Pattern.

The meridian system is the interface of the physical body and the energy body. The Meridian Sound Essences support this interface as they blend homeopathy and sound. The homeopathy resonates with the biochemistry of our body. The cells pick up the plant signature and use this information to support the organs and glands related to the healing properties of the herb. The sound married with the homeopathy resonates specifically for the meridian for which it is intended.

The chakra system then interfaces the meridian system to the auric field. The Chakra Sound Essences support this interface by carrying the vibration of the information therapies held by the earth such as crystals and gems, sacred geometry and aromatherapy and those information therapies held by the cosmos such as sound, colour and thought.

The auric field is a blend of energy bands that gather information on a continual basis. It is this netting that energizes the template for optimum health. It is of the highest degree of importance that this energy field holds its integrity. It needs to completely surround the body as if it were encapsulated in an egg. The *Aura-Joy* Sound Essence supports this energy system by offering the vibrations of twelve notes, the seven whole notes that correspond to the seven main chakras and the five semitones that serve as vibrational bridges for the whole notes. *Aura-Joy* is a vibrational medicine that restores balance to the auric field as it embraces the full spectrum of healing vibration found in sound, colour, aroma, crystals and gems, ancient symbology, sacred geometry, and positive word affirmations.

The Figure Eight Pattern has vibrational support with Infinity. This remedy is most incredible, working with a four-noted chord that totally grounds one and then soars them off into a lighter space, maybe close to a meditative state. It has flower essences in it that helps to expand the cerebral spinal fluid for consciousness expansion and other flower remedies for improving intent, going with the flow, adjusting subtle body frequencies to a new energetic state, contacting spirit, drawing wisdom from life's experiences, inner tranquility, attuning to the gentleness of nature. But all in all it really has mobility to it that one experiences; similar to figure eight energy.

When to Choose to use Essences

Nourishing the energetic bodies is as important as feeding the physical body. Eating three meals a day plus supplementing the diet with herbs and vitamins feeds the physical body. Being exposed several times a day to vibrational therapy nourishes the energy body. Exposure to vibrational therapy four times a day is like having a meal three times a day that provides strength and stamina to the whole body.

Assist the body in healing and maintaining health using vibrational therapy in the following ways:

A. When not feeling well; this can be low energy, stress or feeling irritable. The fact that there is stress indicates that the electrical circuitry has been overloaded. Sound Essences help to reconnect and stabilize the weakened electrical area while the body goes through the necessary healing process. The essences support the body's innate intelligence in repairing itself.

B. When injured or hurt as with bruises, sprains and swelling. An injury is an assault on every level of the being and overloads the electrical circuits. The essences promote the recovery and recuperation process.

C. When suffering from a headache or heavy feeling in the head. A headache is an indication and a message from the body that something is not balanced. The essences bring energy back into the system allowing the body to regenerate balance.

D. When there is a life change, such as a job change, a new home, or a change in relationships. Changes like a newborn coming home or a teenager leaving home. Good changes or bad changes can charge the emotional field and overload the circuits emotionally. The Sound Essences help stabilize the circuitry and hence stabilize emotions through times of transition.

E. When faced with challenges such as a job interview, court case, important meeting, big exam or presentation, a contest or sporting competition. Vibrational Therapy such as the Sound Essences will support and stabilize the body physically, emotionally, mentally, and spiritually.

F. When going through therapeutic sessions for self help and healing for the purpose of making positive change, gaining understanding or improving life on some level. Therapeutic sessions, by design stir the body physically and emotionally to effect change. Vibrational Therapy supports the body through change and helps to integrate the change into the lifestyle. Sound

Essences continue to support the process after the therapy session when used as home care. Use of vibrational therapy as home care benefits both the practitioner and the client. The client can continue to affect the benefits of the balance at home through the support of the Sound Essences so the following therapeutic sessions will become progressive.

How to Choose and Use an Essence

Choosing the essences is very simple, and selecting those key essences can itself be a process of inner awareness. Through quiet reflection, meditation, self-observation and conversation with others, it is possible to become aware of key issues and challenges. For the best results, choose an essence around a single behaviour or issue to be changed. Some people prefer to use more intuitive methods of selecting essences, such as the use of a pendulum, muscle testing or direct sensing through the hands or fingertips.

Essences are rather different than other remedies in the fact that more is not always better. Taking small doses regularly throughout the day is the most effective. Recommended dosage for essences is four times a day and this keeps the vibration constantly available for absorption in the energy field.

It is important to shake any of the essence bottles to energize it before use. This activates the life force of the essence and attunes the vibration of the essence to the user.

What to expect from using Essences

Generally, something is noticed or felt within two to six weeks. Some people will notice the effects almost immediately. All essences work subtly. It is rare that someone would experience an immediate catharsis or a total transformation. The essences work to transform life on a deep level and because they are so subtle, sometimes this transformation may not be directly noticed. Others may be the first to call attention to these changes in attitudes or behaviours. Some people may begin to find their old behaviours and attitudes uncomfortable, and adopt new ones without resistance. This increased consciousness then becomes the tool for change. Essences are not a "quick fix." They are strengtheners of the soul forces that enable growth and wisdom from life's challenges. They invoke a healing journey, and are the allies and guides along the way. The essences are not intended to painlessly wipe away problems or provide instant fixes. They are support for shifting frequencies.

ESSENCES AND OTHER THERAPIES
All Sound Essence can be used in conjunction with these healing techniques:

Spinal Reflex Points
Rubbing on specific vertebrae in relation to the muscle/meridian being corrected. Rub up and down the spinous process one or two vertebrae above and below vertebrae indicated for balance.

Neuro-Emotional Points
These are emotional release points that are mapped on the body giving the body energy and balance. These are to be gently massaged.

Neuro-Vascular Points
Gentle and light holding points mostly mapped on the head. These reflexes are said to unlock the vascular energy flow in the muscles that affect organ balance.

Neuro-Lymphatic Rubbing Points
Rubbing points that are mapped as specific reflex points that are responsible for increasing lymphatic drainage in organs thus causing organ balance.

Acupressure Holding Points
Paired holding points that support Traditional Chinese Medicine theory and affect muscle and organ balance.

Meridian Tracing
These are energy pathways associated with organs. Meridians are a direct link between the inside and outside energies of the body. Tracing the meridian will positively affect its affiliated organ system.

Zone Therapy
Zone therapy is an extremely simple technique. Anyone can do it. The body is divided by vertical lines into five zones on the left side and five zones on the right side. These zones relate all parts of the body within each zone. The fingers and toes affect corresponding parts of the body and are the primary areas of treatment. Zone therapy works more directly on the nerve endings that are connected with organs along the zones. This therapy is a very effective pain remover.

Hand and Foot Reflexology
Reflexology like acupressure holds that the reflexes link each organ of the body to a certain area of the hands and feet, with the nervous system serving as the connection. Whenever an organ is not functioning correctly, the reflex will be tender and even painful upon applying pressure. Stimulation helps to break up the lactic acid, which forms as small crystals. This short circuiting of the nervous system results in a surge of energy flow to the directed area.

Ear Acupressure
A therapy that charts the body in the ear in just the same way as reflexology charts the hands and feet.

Temporal Tapping
Temporal tapping in kinesiology enables the practitioner to input sensory information, usually affirmations, but in this case the sensory input is the information from the vibration of the Sound Essences.

Figure Eight Energy
Energy pattern that corrects electrical circuitry. Trace the figure eights with the sound remedy on the fingers.

Aromatherapy
Aromatherapy is the healing art of using the essential oils directly on the skin.

All the Sound Essences can be used in conjunction with other healing modalities such as:
- Reiki
- Healing Hands
- Healing Touch
- Therapeutic Touch
- Touch for Health
- Professional Kinesiology
- Applied Kinesiology
- Polarity
- Acupressure
- Shiatsu
- Reflexology
- Yoga
- Chakra balancing

Meridian Sound Essences

Meridian Sound Essences are yin/yang meridian coupled essences relating to the Five Element Theory: Fire, Earth, Metal, Water, and Wood for making seven essences of the fourteen meridians. The Fire Element consists of four meridians, two sub elements of Sovereign Fire relating to the Heart and Small Intestine meridians, and Ministerial Fire relating to the Circulation/Sex and Triple Warmer meridians. Earth relates to Spleen and Stomach meridians, Metal relates to Lung and Large Intestine meridians, Water relates to Kidney and Bladder meridians, and Wood relates to Liver and Gall Bladder meridians. Central and Governing meridians combined for the yin/yang couple complete the set of seven.

Meridians are the energy system that interfaces the outside to the inside of the body, relaying information like a network of transformers. Meridians affect every organ and physiological system including the immune, nervous, endocrine, circulatory, respiratory, digestive, skeletal, muscular and lymphatic system. Each system is fed by at least one meridian. The flow of the meridian is as critical as the flow of blood; your life and health depend on it. Pairing the meridians into Elemental theory takes the healing deeper into the body.

Meridian Sound Essences help the body to keep the interface of communication balanced and healthy. These essences embrace the understanding of homeopathy and the vibration of sound.

Meridian integrity can be enhanced through the use of herbs. Homeopathy carries the signature of an herb, which the body's meridian system can recognize and use to keep the chi flowing through the meridian channels.

The effect of sound balancing meridians has been proven by Energy Kinesiologists using tuning forks as a meridian correction.

The Meridian Sound Essences combine the messages from the herbs with the vibration of sound to offer meridians a healing vibration that they can tune into. It is believed that these essences affect the meridian intelligence under the skin and on the outside of the skin and into the third and fourth level of the etheric field.

Yin / Yang Couple – Manifesting Abundance

Central – Primary Purpose
The Central Meridian governs all the other meridians. It represents our connection with our source. The Central Meridian Sound Essence can be used to revitalize sexuality, the procreation capacity and the divine joy as in knowing one's place and having all you need to manifest abundance.

Governing – Soothing
The Governing Meridian's key focus is choice. Free will is the first and greatest gift of our creator. The enhancement or the balance of this meridian using the Governing Meridian Sound Essence allows for the capability of a decision without doubt or self-recrimination. It supports the feeling of knowing that you know. It is the essence of the warrior.

Fire Element - Joy/Love
Sovereign Fire Couple – Prioritizing

Heart – Transmission of Knowledge
The Heart Meridian has to do with the electrical functioning of your heart. The electrical fibrillations are easily disrupted so the Heart Meridian Sound Essence serves to regulate and reinforce the tissues and the electrical conductivity.

Small Intestine – Adaptability
Small Intestine Meridian has to do with assimilation on all levels. It has the ability to take in and utilize information effectively on all levels physically, emotionally, mentally and spiritually. The Small Intestine Meridian Sound Essence will create an interface that allows only the information that is beneficial to be assimilated, it acts like a filter or a grid that is intelligently discerning, one that is constantly opening and closing to ideas, emotions or food.

Ministerial Fire Couple – Maintaining Balance in Life

Circulation/ Sex – Trust in Own Instincts
The Circulation/Sex Meridian supports us in transformation. Life is a process of accumulation; accumulation of experience and reaction, which builds up in responsive ability and leaves a residue. The Circulation/Sex Meridian Sound Essence has the capacity for cleaning and clearing this residue through the pro-creative and circulatory systems.

Triple Warmer – Encouragement
The Triple Warmer is the meridian that facilitates the coordinated action of all 520 hormones in the body. The hormonal system is constantly adjusting to accommodate shifts in the internal and external environment. Without coordination, these hormones send out mismatched messages or signals to various organs and systems. The Triple Warmer Meridian Sound Essence provides a constant ray of light bringing the hormones into alignment so that they can function in a co-ordinated manner maintaining balance.

EARTH ELEMENT COUPLE - SYMPATHY/EMPATHY – Making Choices for Highest Good

Spleen – Integrity
The Spleen Meridian regulates body chemistry. The Spleen Meridian Sound Essence offers the capacity for enthusiasm and discernment. The Spleen Meridian Sound Essence helps the meridian to be consistently fueled to maintain consistent speed to maintain optimum energy levels for all the body's regulatory mechanisms, including blood sugar levels.

Stomach – Discernment
The Stomach Meridian facilitates reception on all levels. It transports safe substance or thought through the system but if the substance or thought is harmful, the Stomach Meridian escorts it harmlessly out of the system. The Stomach Meridian Sound Essence facilitates the wisdom to discern and decide how to best handle the substance or thought.

METAL ELEMENT COUPLE - GRIEF/GUILT/RELEASE – Living in the Moment

Lung – Enthusiasm
The Lung Meridian Sound Essence is essential for enthusiasm, the capacity to embrace each moment. It is vital for us to actively reach out for the future, yet have the capacity to let go of the past. Let, bygones be bygones. The Lung Meridian Sound Essence is invaluable in bringing one into the present moment.

Large Intestine – Adaptability
The Large Intestine meridian has to do with receiving and letting go on a more fundamental level. The large intestine is a key to the integration of hydration or moisture in the body. Whereas the lungs take in the air, the large intestine removes moisture. That matter that enters into the large

intestine is dehydrated. The Large Intestine Meridian Sound Essence facilitates ease of transition on all levels; physical, emotional mental and spiritual.

WATER ELEMENT COUPLE - FEAR/ANXIETY – Opening Space for Enlightenment

Kidney – Patience and Trust

The Kidney Meridian facilitates the process of transforming reflexive instinct into conscious thought where choice becomes a possibility. The Kidney Meridian Sound Essence is a filter and purifier for our emotions and this facilitates clarification on all levels. It supports us in being consciously in choice.

Bladder – Circumspect

The Bladder Meridian has to do with the issues of control and release. Control and release of emotions in the Kidney and the Bladder Meridians are similar in that they are products of civilization. Working with releasing emotions in these two meridians can be very helpful when working with animals or severely handicapped people. The Bladder Meridian Sound Essence will not bring consciousness or awareness, but will facilitate release of negative emotions, which opens space for consciousness or enlightenment.

WOOD ELEMENT COUPLE - ANGER/RAGE – Managing Stress

Liver – Graciousness

The Liver Meridian manages stress of all kinds. Toxins of all sorts, chemical, emotional or spiritual, are integrated into the liver. Change on any level including shifting our consciousness can cause stress in the body. The Liver Meridian Sound Essence protects the liver by acting as a cushion in defense of any internal or external changes.

Gall Bladder – Communication

The Gall Bladder Meridian has to do with support; the ability to provide what is appropriate when necessary. An imbalance in the Gall Bladder Meridian is a sense of being out of step or out of time. No other systems can function optimally without the appropriate support of the gall bladder. It has the ability to provide what is necessary when needed. The Gall Bladder Sound Essence is the support for the entire system.

How to Use Meridian Sound Essence

- Mist on the hand and rub your hands together
- Mist on the hands and trace the meridian
- Mist on the fingers to assist pain relief using figure eight energy techniques
- Mist on fingers holding ESR points
- Mist on fingers holding beginning or end of meridians
- Mist on the fingers and rub the spinal reflex points
- Mist on the fingers holding acupressure holding points
- Mist on the fingers holding neuro-vascular holding points
- Mist on the fingers rubbing neuro-emotional points
- Mist on the fingers rubbing neuro-lymphatic points
- Mist on the fingers and apply to associated points
- Mist on the fingers and apply to reflex points
- Mist on the fingers and use in association with temporal tapping
- Mist on the fingers and use in association with ear acupressure
- Mist on the fingers and use in association with hand and foot reflexology

For external use only.

Chakra Sound Essences

Chakra Sound Essences are subtle energy remedies created from the healing vibration of sound from the crystal bowls. The Chakra Sound Essences hold the imprint of the vibration of each whole note and semitone of the harmonic scale. As the vibration of colour and sound co-exist, it has been noted that once the vibration of sound has charged the essence, so too has the vibration of colour inherently charged the essence. These essences are jointly charged with the information imprint of chosen crystals and gemstones. This is the stock elixir often used by practitioners. The stock elixir holds the imprint of sound, colour, crystals, gems, sacred geometry, ancient symbology, and positive word vibrations. Adding aroma completes the formulation of the Chakra Sound Essence misters.

The whole notes C, D, E, F, G, A, and B resonate with the seven main chakras. The five semitones C♯, E♭, F♯, G♯, and B♭ are bridges for the seven chakras located on the back of the body supporting the transitional aspects of the spine. For example, the C♯ is located where the sacral meets the lumbar, the E♭ is located where the lumbar meets the thoracic, F♯ is located where the thoracic meets the cervical and the G♯ is located where the cervical meets the skull and the B♭ is located where the physical meets the etheric.

These steps (semitones) between the tones (whole notes) are crucial points of injected energy. The seven whole notes resonate specifically with the seven main chakras and the five semitones support the five middle chakras. The Sacral Chakra then has notes C♯ and D supporting it as the Solar Plexus Chakra has E♭ and E supporting it. There is no bridge between E and F as this is already a half note separation. The Heart Chakra is supported by F and F♯ and the Throat Chakra is supported by G and G♯ and finally the Brow Chakra is supported by A and B♭.

ROOT CHAKRA – note C - base of the spine

The characteristic of a balanced Root Chakra is a strong and determined feeling that life is good. There is a belief that dreams will easily manifest and there is worthiness of abundance and security; there is prosperity in all areas of life. There is a connectiveness to the physical which builds the foundation for all higher chakras as the Root Chakra is the source of life-force.

A balanced Root Chakra is essential for grounding and focus. It anchors us in the flow of life and is the foundation for everything we do in our life. A strong Root Chakra gives us a positive approach and outlook on life and helps us to stay connected to the "we are one" attitude that we need to employ to keep our universe healthy.

Note C physically supports the spinal column, bones, teeth, nails, anus, rectum, prostate, and blood cells.

I CAN DO IT

SACRAL CHAKRA – note C# - transitional point between the sacrum and lumbar spine

C# supports the Sacral Chakra. This vibration bridges the characteristics and attributes of the Root Chakra, note C# which is related to foundation and family and the Sacral Chakra, note D which relates to movement and a relationship with one another. This bridge moves us out of the family tribe and into a dance with a partner in life.

Characteristics of someone with a balanced C# vibration would walk through life embracing their sexuality and sense of self and could express their emotions without reservation. Note C# physically supports the lower back, ovaries, prostate, uterus, testicles, bladder, and kidney.

IT'S TIME TO SHOW OFF THE BEST IN ME

SACRAL CHAKRA – note D – in hip region

The characteristics of a strong Sacral Chakra are the connectedness to self, other humans, animals, nature and the spiritual world. A balanced Sacral Chakra connects us to our pure creative energies that truly nourish our being; it houses our creative juices. There is a sense of awe with every sight, sound and experience as if life were new and original. The essence of the Sacral Chakra

I ENJOY THE SIMPLE PLEASURES IN LIFE

is to allow the soul to embrace the body. A balanced Sacral Chakra is being comfortable in the physical body, with sexuality and with the expression of sensual emotions. Someone with a balanced Sacral Chakra would exude sensuality, peacefulness, and joy. They would be nurturing, focused, capable, spiritually aware and emotionally responsive with a healthy appetite for life.

Note D physically supports the pelvic area, reproductive organs, kidneys, and bladder. It supports all liquid functions in the body such as blood, lymph, gastric juices, synovial fluid and sperm.

I STAND STEADY ON MY OWN TWO FEET

SOLAR PLEXUS CHAKRA – Note E♭ – transitional point between the lumbar and the thoracic spine

E♭ supports the Solar Plexus Chakra. This vibration bridges the characteristics and attributes of the Sacral Chakra note D which is related to relationship and partnership and the Solar Plexus Chakra note E which is related to individual and self.

This semi tone bridges our connection with others as to how we feel about our self-esteem, our self-worth and ourselves. In order to have a strong relationship with others, we have to have a strong relationship with ourselves first. It is important to grasp the concept that we fit into this world as perfectly as a flower fits in a bouquet. This self-acceptance supports us in our physical health. E♭ is the vibration most called for as it supports the note E of the Solar Plexus Chakra. The Solar Plexus Chakra needs to be strong for the energy to jump into the Heart Chakra, as there is no semi tone between the Solar Plexus Chakra and the Heart Chakra.

Note E♭ physically supports the small intestine, the liver, the spleen, the stomach, the pancreas, and the digestive system.

I LIKE WHO I AM AS I AM

SOLAR PLEXUS CHAKRA – note E located in the gut

Characteristics of a strong Solar Plexus Chakra are a healthy sense of personal identity and a strong sense of personal power. The Solar Plexus Chakra is all about "me". It is about our self-esteem, our ego, personal power, will, and responsibility and gut intuition.

We need to know who we are, own our personal power and take responsibility for our own lives.

The qualities that represent the Solar Plexus Chakra are almost the opposite of those qualities of the Sacral Chakra. The Solar Plexus Chakra energy is logical instead of artistic, sophisticated instead of innocent, suspicious instead of trusting and responsibility bound instead of free flowing. The Sacral Chakra follows the right brain identity whereas the Solar Plexus Chakra thinks like the left brain.

Someone with a balanced Solar Plexus Chakra would have true peace and inner harmony with all of life because they have taken full responsibility of their own life and have allowed others to take responsibility of their own lives. They typically have a warm personality and are responsible, reliable, and have the ability to meet any challenges.

Note E physically supports the small intestine, liver, digestive system, stomach, spleen, gall bladder, autonomic nervous system, muscles and the lower back.

HEART CHAKRA – Note F located in the chest

I LOVE LIFE

The characteristics of a balanced Heart Chakra is acting out of love and compassion and recognizing that the most powerful energy we have is love. The Heart Chakra is all about unity, peace, and unconditional love; hope, forgiveness, compassion and generosity. As the Heart Chakra opens so does the ability to connect with the higher self. It radiates love and forgiveness. Someone with a balanced Heart Chakra radiates warmth, sincerity and happiness and they have a strong connection to all of life. They love and have compassion and a sincere willingness to help. They put their heart into all that they do and you can feel their love unconditionally as they recognize the gifts in everyone.

Note F physically supports the heart, blood, circulation, lower lungs, ribcage, skin and upper back.

Chapter 6

HEART CHAKRA – Note F♯ transitional point between the thoracic and the cervical spine

F♯ supports the Heart Chakra. This vibration bridges the characteristics and attributes of the Heart Chakra "note F", which is related to compassion and unconditional love and the fifth chakra "note G" which is related to the freedom of expression.

This semitone takes information from the heart and moves it into the throat for expression. This vibration supports us in finding our calling in life and establishing ourself in the world. This vibration helps us go after what we want and to have a positive attitude about our accomplishments. With the support of this vibration we are supported by others and are supported by the universe and things happen as they should without the push and without the individual power to accomplish what we think we need to do. F♯ allows us to be in the place of community when our work is seen as an integral part of the whole. Simply said, we are in the zone. Our will is aligned with that of the universe.

Note F♯ physically supports the upper back, upper lungs, throat and neck.

WHAT I HAVE TO SAY IS IMPORTANT

THROAT CHAKRA – Note G located at the throat

The characteristic of a balanced Throat Chakra is the ability to communicate openly with personal expression. The Throat Chakra is the expression of the spoken word for all of the chakras. Through the Throat Chakra we express everything that is alive within us such as our laughing, crying, our feelings of love and happiness, anxiety and aggressiveness, our intention and desires as well as our ideas, knowledge and perception of the inner worlds.

Someone with a balanced Throat Chakra would be reliable and trustworthy. Once they made a commitment they would speak their truth, keep their word and follow through with their promises. Someone with a strong Throat Chakra has independence, freedom, self-determination and will trust their inner guidance.

Note G physically supports the jaw, neck, throat, voice and airways.

THROAT CHAKRA - Note G♯ transitional point between the cervical spine and the skull

I CAN EASILY EXPRESS MY INNER THOUGHTS AND EMOTIONS

G♯ supports the Throat Chakra. This vibration bridges the characteristics and attributes of the Throat Chakra "note G" which relates to the freedom of expression and the Brow Chakra "note A" which relates to inner direction. This vibration gives us the ability to express ourselves in accordance with our life's journey. It supports us in our personal growth by helping us to awaken to our spiritual consciousness.

G♯ is in balance when an individual is successful and well suited to his work and fulfilling his task in life. Taking the chance to go after your heart's desire in the path of your life will support the health of the Throat Chakra.

Note G♯ physically supports the tension in the back of the skull, helps with headaches, confusion, memory, and left and right brain integration.

BROW CHAKRA – Note A location is at the forehead

I CAN RELY ON MY INTUITION

The characteristics of a balanced Brow Chakra are the use of mental power, connecting with the process of manifestation. The Brow Chakra enables us to connect with the energy of the world beyond our five senses and teaches us to go beyond the superficial appearances and find our deeper truths and then cultivate our resources of creativity and wisdom. Through the Brow Chakra we are able to open ourselves to universal creative energy, which allows us to direct ourselves towards fulfilling our life's purpose.

Someone with a strong Brow Chakra is open to new information about their life's purpose, and trusts their intuitive abilities. These people have developed deep level of understanding, intuition, imagination, wisdom, understanding and enlightenment. Their ego and soul spirit are balanced. They are able to create their life and manifest their dreams to their highest good.

Note A physically supports the face, ears, eyes, sinus, and nervous system.

I CAN LET GO OF ANYTHING THAT NO LONGER SERVES ME

BROW CHAKRA – Note B♭ transitional point where the top of the head meets the etheric

B♭ supports the Brow Chakra. This vibration bridges the characteristics and attributes of the Brow Chakra "note A" which relates to inner direction and "note B" which relates to spiritual connection. The importance of this semitone is to prepare us for the next transition and that is into the spiritual realm, which signifies the completion of the cycle of life.

B♭ is the transition between the attachment to the physical identity and to the identification of the self as a divine spark. This transition point cannot be activated until the other vibrational frequencies are aligned. When B♭ is used in that crucial time, that time when all the other vibrations are in line, then the vibration is absolutely necessary to complete the transition to the next level of manifestation.

Note B♭ physically supports the nervous system.

I KNOW WHY I AM HERE

CROWN CHAKRA – Note B location - top of the head

Characteristics of a balanced Crown Chakra, is being connected wholly with the universe, self and God. Life is flowing freely and there is a deep sense of peace.

Through the Crown Chakra, we get our divine inspiration and our divine creativity. This is the chakra where everything comes together and we get the big picture. This is where all the information from all the charkas merges. When this chakra is balanced, there is a sense of peace, serenity, knowing and a connection with the universe.

Someone with a strong Crown Chakra is dedicated to their life path. These people have a soul connection with God and are able to access knowledge from this higher intelligence.

Note B physically supports the brain and the central nervous system.

Aura-Joy

Aura-Joy is a vibrational rescue remedy created to support the auric field. It coherently impacts all the layers of the auric field that creates the egg-like shape of our body bubble. It strengthens the interface of the physical and etheric bodies. It assists with centering the being in their energy field. It powerfully assists those whom are experiencing the negative impact from physical or emotional trauma. It boosts confidence so that the life-force can begin to heal the core energy and at the same time build durability in the netting of the auric field. *Aura-Joy* resonates with the core energy source of the being, healing inside and out, and establishing coherent resonance

Aura-Joy can be used anywhere at any time for anything. Use it as a pick-me-up remedy, when feeling out of sorts. If there is emotional turmoil or trauma, *Aura-Joy* helps to positively shift the emotions. It has been used successfully as a grief remedy. Practitioners use *Aura-Joy* in their therapy rooms to create an inviting energy space for each of their clients. It is also used to help stabilize the new energy for a client after having a treatment.

Aura-Joy is a unique vibrational therapy in that it carries the imprint of twelve notes, the seven whole notes that correspond to the seven main charkas and the five semitones that serve as vibrational bridges for the whole notes. *Aura-Joy* is a full spectrum vibrational medicine restoring balance to the body as it embraces the seven aspects of healing vibration found in Sound, Color, Aroma, Crystals and Gems, Ancient Symbols, Sacred Geometry and Positive Word Affirmations. When these seven aspects of vibrational healing are harnessed together and brought into our lives through *Aura-Joy*, they bring joy, vitality, balance and a renewed zest for life.

Aware or unaware, visible or invisible, vibrational remedies impact us powerfully; for in these aspects we have the true essence of our being.

Every individual that works to raise their vibration and comes into a clear and balanced frequency is contributing to the alignment and uplifting of this world forever. Time has come in this world when these adjustments into atonement are imminent.

Sound
The most effective and simple means of balancing the body is through the use of sound. Life is sound and sound brings life to earth. Sound can be used to interact with other energies and often enhances or amplifies the energies with which it is blended. Sound helps to restore balance, alleviate pain and accelerate healing in the body. *Aura-Joy* consists of all twelve notes.

Colour
Sound and colour have a lot in common in that they resonate closely with one another. Life is colour. All minerals, plants and animals are colourful. Each organ has a specific colour. Each colour has intelligence and polarity, knows its functional role and works selectively. *Aura-Joy* consists of all twelve colours relating to the twelve notes.

Crystals and Gems
The ability of the crystals to absorb and refract the light is what gives the stones their color. The healing comes from the ability to absorb and refract the light available in the crystals. Gems and crystals also hold magnetic force fields, which carry vibrational information that can resonate as a healing vibration for our bodies. Healing information also comes from the geometric pattern of the crystalline formation of these stones. *Aura-Joy* consists of seventeen crystal vibrations.

Sacred Geometry
The body receives healing information intuitively from geometric angles. The vibration of the five platonic shapes is included in the *Aura-Joy* Sound Essence.

Symbology
The chakra symbols carry ancient information that are subconsciously picked up to heal the body. The vibration of the seven chakra symbols is included in the *Aura-Joy* Sound Essence.

Aroma
Essential oils are taken from the life force of a plant and the smell is used to positively affect every level of our being. Aromatherapy supports the body physically, emotionally, mentally, and spiritually. Using essential oils in conjunction with meridian and chakra work is an optimum way of linking plant energy with spiritual growth. The aroma of *Aura-Joy* is a blend of bay, cajeput, coriander, geranium, lavender, lemon, lemongrass, lily of the valley, marjoram, orange, rose, rosemary, sandalwood, thyme, and ylang ylang.

Affirmations
Positive word affirmations offer the body the power of thought. We are what we think.
AURA JOY.

Infinity

Infinity is a vibrational remedy used to support the figure eight energy systems of the entire body both inside and outside the body. Not only will it help integrate the meridians and chakra systems but it will also support us in connecting our divine nature with our human experience for positive soul growth.

Infinity is a vibrational remedy that helps us prepare for higher consciousness. The combination of sound, gem and flower essences makes this vibration unique in opening up to the new energies available for spiritual growth. The four noted chord, C, Eb, F and A when played on the piano goes on to infinity. All the flower essences chosen for this remedy are in complete coherence for consciousness expansion. The use of Amethyst and Yellow Topaz in combination offers again a figure eight model, Amethyst working on the subconscious release and Yellow Topaz allowing for conscious awareness.

Through the pattern of the figure eight, the loops intersecting in the middle creates a focal point for healing in all four dimensions: side to side / front to back / up and down / diagonal to diagonal.

The up and down dimension connects heaven to earth in our association with our spirituality and our physical being and the intersection point is the human mind.

The side-to-side dimension relates to the positive and negative in association with our interaction with friends, family and culture and the intersection point is our heart center.

The back to front dimension represents the past and the future and the intersection point is the present, being in the moment.

The diagonal-to-diagonal dimension represents time and space in association with human history and divine potential and the intersection point is the soul.

The four figure eights together creating a flower image offer us the potential of living in the present moment in our heart center. Living each moment with loving acceptance, benevolently indifferent, in harmony and peace.

The smaller four figure eight imposed on the larger four figure eights implies the unity of nature. It depicts the relationship of the microcosm to the macrocosm. I am one with the universe and the universe is one with me. I am in God and God is in me.

Note "F"

This note is related to the Heart Chakra. The heart chakra is responsible for loving unconditionally. This is the place of arrival. This is where we want to be to make change in the universe. Emotionally this is the place of expansiveness, joy and endurance. The F note awakens compassion and supports us in expressing higher love and healing energies. The arms reach out and receive the divine, which gives us our sense of connection to life, nature and brotherhood.

Note "A"

This note is related to the Brow Chakra, which activates the lessons that lead us to wisdom. The note A supports everyone in expressing their individual value, for each person needs to feel that their unique combination of their physical being is useful. This is where all the gifts and abilities that one embodies come together as an offering for service for higher good.

Note "C"

The note "C" is the most primal note, announcing the creation of the universe.; the dawning of time. It is the note related to the base chakra, which is the beginning of our existence. The Note C brings about a release of fear and anxiety resulting from the disconnection of self with others. The note C is important for grounding; it is the foundation of life energy within the body.

Note "E♭"

This note is where we are, as beings in this universe, at this time. This note is between the sacral chakra and the solar plexus chakra. It is the bridge between relationships and individuality. This note is responsible for the transition from being in partnership and being individualistic. The Solar Plexus Chakra is all about self. It is about Self-Esteem, Self-Confidence and Self Power. Once we fully love ourselves we can love others.

Soul Ray 4
Restores balance and stability of the electrical system on each pertinent level. This remedy addresses the electrical system on each of those levels (physical, emotional, mental and spiritual) as an independently functioning system.

Yellow Topaz
Clarifies intention within oneself is to gain access to inner knowledge and wisdom. Experience the joy of "going with the flow".

Amethyst
It facilitates light seeping into darkness. It adjusts emotional blocks, working only on the subconscious. It adjusts the subtle body's frequencies to the new energetic state.

Sonia
Stabilizes and supports the CSF (cerebral spinal fluid) pulse after it has completed its shift to accommodate the expansion.

Poplar
It supports the healer in transmitting healing energies. Poplar assists in attuning to nature and consequently to the divine. It guides in conscious choice making.

Sage
Drawing wisdom from life's experience. Reviewing and surveying one's life purpose from a higher perspective.

Heather
Inner tranquility. Emotional self-sufficiency.

How to Use Chakra, Aura-Joy, and Infinity Sound Essences

These contain the vibration of colour, sound, crystal, gem, sacred geometry, ancient symbology, positive word vibration, with essential oils added.
The chakra misters are used **externally only** for misting the aura, chakras, or a room.
The misters are ready to use as follows:

- Mist the body and feel the shift
- Mist the air and walk into the mist
- Mist the chakra location that needs the balance
- Pour a capful into the tub
- Mist the hands and wave the hands in aura
- Mist the hands and use figure eight energy to relieve discomfort
- Mist the hands and hold ESR points
- Mist the hands and trace the meridians
- Mist the hands and rub the spinal reflex points
- Mist the hands and hold acupressure holding points
- Mist the hands and hold neuro-vascular holding points
- Mist the hands and rub neuro-emotional points
- Mist the hands an rub the neuro-lymphatic points
- Mist the hand and apply to associated points
- Mist the foot in a reflexology treatment
- Mist the room for many to enjoy
- Use Note C root chakra mist for family gatherings
- Use Note D sacral chakra mist for a romantic evening or a creative session
- Use Note E solar plexus chakra mist in the dining room at dinner for digestion purposes
- Use Note F heart chakra mist in the home if there is virus or bronchial or cold symptoms
- Use Note G throat chakra mist in the conference room for clear communication
- Use Note A brow chakra mist in the bedroom for dreaming and dream recall
- Use Note B crown chakra mist at any church or center for prayer or meditation

For external use only

Sound Essence Protocol

This Energy System balance is gentle, non-invasive, fast and efficient. In less than five minutes you can balance your entire Energy System, for a perfect start of your day.

This Energy Balance can also be done as the final touch after any kind of bodywork such as massage, reflexology, reiki, or energy kinesiology. It raises the body's vibration, giving the treatment a longer holding time, which allows the practitioner to upgrade the client's performance rather than just maintaining.

It supports us in maintaining the positive shift out of the old familiar undesirable pattern.

By using self-monitoring see page 331 or partner monitoring see pg 334 we can assess our biocomputer. The "no" response is used to determine the imbalanced meridian, chakra, auric field or figure eight pattern. In the Sound Essence Balancing Protocol, the "no" response is used to indicate the midline of the three dimensions, side to side, up and down, front and back, for the auric field.

Meridian Integrity

To assess the integrity of the meridians, superimpose the Five-element model over the navel with central and governing meridians (Yin/Yang couple) allocated to the center of the navel. See diagram on page 76.

Start with Yin/Yang couple in the middle of the navel and then touch with two fingers around the navel starting at the top with Ministerial Fire, Earth, Metal, Water, Wood, and ending at the same place as you started at the top of the navel with Sovereign Fire.

Touch each element's location and body pendulum or muscle monitor each location, slowly, one at a time moving through the circle until you get a "no" response. This is considered a stress response determining which of the Meridian Vitalizers is needed to support the meridian system of the body. Mist the indicated Meridian Vitalizer above and in front of the body and walk into the falling mist. Reassess the stressed location around the navel. It should now hold strong. Retest all the around the navel following the five-element pattern and continue the process until there are no longer any "no" or stress responses.

Chakra Integrity

To assess the integrity of the Chakras, touch each chakra location starting from the Root Chakra, Sacral Chakra, Solar Plexus Chakra, Heart Chakra, Throat Chakra, Brow Chakra, and Crown Chakra. See diagram on page 125. Stop at the first "no" or stress response. If the stress response is the Root Chakra or the Crown Chakra mist the body. If the stressed response indicates the middle charkas, Sacral Chakra, Solar Plexus Chakra, Heart Chakra, Throat Chakra, Brow Chakra, then touch the chakra on the front and back of the body. If the stressed response comes from the front of the body location use the whole note misters. If the stressed response comes from touching the charkas in the back of the body use the semi-tone mister related to that chakra. Simply, find the matching Chakra Sound Essence mister and mist above and in front of the body. Retest until there are no longer any "no" or stress responses.

Auric Field Integrity
The third aspect of the Energy Balancing System is to check the balance of the auric field by testing the three planes, front to back/ left to right/up to down, assessing for a stressed response. Mist above and in front of the person with Aura-Joy and have them step into the falling mist. This seals the entire auric energy field around the body and holds the balancing of the charkas and meridians.

Figure Eight Pattern
Simply mist Infinity above the head. This restores the figure eight pattern weaving our physical self with our soul self.

Sound Essence Protocol Step by Step

1. Ask permission.
2. Check for a clear circuit.
3. Check for meridian integrity, hydration, switching.
4. Set goal for the balance.
5. Find emotion related to the goal.
6. Pretest in relation to the goal.
7. Pretest activity in relation to the goal.

Meridian/ Element Balance
8. (optional) Engage meridian mode El 2c (thumbnail against inside second knuckle of the little finger) and test indicator muscle.
9. Test 5 elements in a clockwise direction around the navel and central and governing in the center looking for an unlocked IM or a "no" response.
10. Find issue in relation to element.
11. Mist the Meridian Vitalizer Sound Essence in front and above the body and have the client walk into the falling mist.
12. Retest elements and repeat steps 8-11 until El 2c is clear.

Chakra Balance

13. (optional) Engage chakra mode ST 10 (thumbnail goes over the nail of the pointer finger) and test indicator muscle.
14. Test 7 chakras in the front of the body starting at the Root Chakra looking for an unlocked indicator muscle. If the indicator muscle unlocks on the sacral, solar plexus, heart, throat or brow chakra location, test for front or back imbalance. If there is front imbalance choose the whole note misters, if there is back imbalance, choose the semitone misters.
15. Find issue in relation to chakra.
16. Mist in front and above the body with the appropriate Chakra Balancer and have the client walk into the falling mist.
17. Retest the chakras and repeat steps 13-16 until the chakra mode ST 10 is clear.

Auric Balance

18. (optional) Engage auric field mode EL 5c (thumbnail against the outer top joint of the baby finger).
19. Test auric field:
    Check the three planes:
    S/S midline – centerline of the body
    U/D midline - waist
    F/B midline - side seam
20. Find positive affirmation.
21. Mist in front and above the body with the Aura Joy mister and have the client walk into the falling mist while partner repeats positive affirmation.
22. Recheck the mode EL 5c.

Figure Eight Balance

23. (optional) Engage Figure Eight energy mode EL 7½ a. (Thumbnail against the inner middle joint of baby finger)
24. Test Figure Eight Pattern. (Use hand to make 8 pattern in front of body in both directions.)
25. Mist with Infinity in front and above the body and have the client walk into the falling mist.
26. Recheck the mode EL 7½ a.
27. Finish balance by rechecking goal, emotion, pretests, and pretest activities.
28. Celebrate!

PART 2

Sound Essence and the Energy Systems of the Body

Chapter 7

Meridians & Five Elements

YIN-YANG

FIRE

EARTH

METAL

WATER

WOOD

Introduction

Traditional Chinese Medicine recognizes that everything influences everything else. This holistic approach to health recognizes both intrinsic and extrinsic interactions. Intrinsic interaction is how the organs and systems function inside the body. The extrinsic interaction is how the environment affects the body. Practitioners of Traditional Chinese Medicine recognize the natural forces of energy, which regulate life. They called this chi. Chi is the breath of life. It is what creates and nourishes the human spirit to give us energy. Chi is the force of nature that moves energy through all matter.

The Traditional Chinese Meridian Theory recognizes two types of chi or energy sources for the body. The first energy source comes from our food, the nourishment that we take into the body, which eventually flows through the blood stream. The second energy source is the life force that flows through the meridians.

Meridians are energy pathways that interface the outside of the body to the inside of the body. The meridians are the most physical level of the four energy system levels, which consist of meridians, chakras, auras, and figure eights. Meridians affect both the physical body and the energy body. The meridians are closely linked to the nervous system and the nerve pathways that feed every organ and part of the body, yet they also control the flow of chi in the etheric body. Balancing the meridians, balances the whole body both the physical and the etheric body. We can balance the physical part of the meridian chi with food and herbs and etheric part of the meridian chi with vibration such as sound.

The life force that travels through the body circulates in a 24-hour cycle. There are fourteen meridians and twelve that are associated with organs and functions of the body. The life force chi affects each meridian for two hours. Each meridian has a fortification phase of two hours everyday. The meridians determine our daily cycle. The Large Intestine meridian operates at peak potential between 5am and 7am eliminating waste as we rise. We eat breakfast at peak time for the Stomach meridian between 7am-9am; this should be our largest meal of the day. 9am to 11am just around coffee time is the Spleen meridian time when the blood is being made, this is often the time when our blood sugar level drops and we need sweets. The Heart meridian works the hardest between 11am and 1pm; this is the best time for a jog. The Small Intestine meridian assimilates our digestion between 1pm and 3pm, our blood moves out of our extremities and is focused on the small intestine and we feel lethargic. 3pm to 5pm is Bladder meridian time when we start to wind down our day and, voiding the collective waste of the day. 5pm to7pm is Kidney meridian time, balancing us between our workday and home life. The Kidney meridian is known to be the storehouse for our chi, our life energy. Circulation/Sex meridian time is between 7pm and 9pm as it supports the circulation of the blood and lymphatic. Hormones are at peak function, distributing heat throughout the body between 9pm and 11pm representing the Triple Warmer meridian. The Gall Bladder meridian operates at full potential between 11pm and 1am concentrating bile salts and metaphysically digesting the events of the day. The Liver meridian is working its hardest between 1am and 3am, it is working while we are sleeping. Finally the Lung meridian is at its full potential between 3am and 5am bringing us connection to the world as we breathe in life energy. Every meridian has a starting and finishing point. The end point of one meridian is linked to the beginning point of the next meridian creating an endless cycle of free-flowing energy.

The meridian system is a closed system so if the energy ever gets blocked, one meridian will be under energy and another will be over energy. This energy blockage is expressed as imbalance such as pain, discomfort and disease in the body. A healthy body depends on maintaining these free-flowing energy pathways.

To further understand the Traditional Chinese Medicine Theory, we can visit the yin and yang theory, which takes us directly into the Five Element Theory.

Yin and yang are opposite forces but complementary and interdependent. They exist simultaneously and can influence each other beneficially. Yang imbalances and problems can be relieved by yin energy and yin imbalances can be overcome by yang energy. Yin force is seen as passive, cold, receptive, feminine and internal. The yang force is active, hot, productive, masculine and external.

Each yin meridian is coupled with a yang meridian constituting an element. There are five elements representing nature within the context of the Five Element Theory.

The Fire Element is divided into Sovereign Fire and Ministerial Fire. Sovereign Fire consists of the Heart Meridian and Small Intestine Meridian, and Ministerial Fire consists of the Circulation/Sex Meridian and the Triple Warmer Meridian. The Earth Element consists of the Spleen and Stomach Meridians. The Metal Element consists of the Lung and Large Intestine Meridians. The Water Element consists of the Kidney and Bladder Meridians, and the Wood Element consists of the Liver and Gall Bladder Meridians.

By using the five elements to organize the meridians, we are delving deeper into the holographic viewpoint of the Chinese Meridian System. The five elements have themes, which help us to better understand what in nature would support the internal organs.

These elemental themes include tastes, smells, sounds, seasons, climates, emotions, stages in life, personality traits, etc.

FIRE CREATES EARTH

The red **Fire element** contains Heart, Small Intestine, Triple Warmer, and Circulation/Sex meridians. The Fire element radiates light and warmth. The fire energy supports communication and relationships and allows one the freedom to seek happiness and love. The emotion of the Fire element is joy and its sound is laughter, without the Fire element the other elements would not exist.

The Heart meridian is like a king that rules the whole domain of body and mind and spirit. The Heart meridian unites all the meridians so that there is co-ordination of energy throughout all of the meridian system. If the Heart meridian is healthy, the spirit of the person is also liberated and healthy.

The Small Intestine meridian helps us to assimilate thoughts and feelings.

The Circulation/Sex meridian protects the heart against emotional, physical and spiritual insult.

The Triple Warmer meridian represents three energy centers on the body, which seem to correspond with the second, third and fourth chakras. It serves the endocrine system to regulate heat and energy.

EARTH CREATES METAL

The yellow **Earth element** contains the yin Spleen meridian and the yang Stomach meridian. The feeling of earth relates to sympathy and empathy and its sound is singing. The quest is for nourishment, support and understanding.

The Spleen meridian is the body's transport manager, distributing the blood and life force energy throughout the body.

The Stomach meridian is in charge of food digestion and also the digestion of thoughts and feelings.

METAL CREATES WATER

The white **Metal element** contains the yin Lung meridian and the yang Large Intestine meridian. The Metal element is all about letting go of the past and being able to take in and assimilate new life supporting experiences. Its sound is weeping and its emotion is grief.

The Lung meridian governs the respiration and controls the body rhythms. The Lung meridian also controls the absorption of life energy through the breath.

The Large Intestine meridian is responsible for elimination as it carries out the impurities of the body, mind and spirit.

WATER CREATES WOOD

The blue **Water element** contains the yin Kidney meridian and the yang Bladder meridian. There is no force greater in nature than water. The Water element governs our will and our chi, along with our willingness to sustain life. Its sound is groaning and its emotion is fear.

The Kidney meridian is the storehouse for our vital being; our chi. This meridian controls the water and the fluid balance of the body.

The Bladder meridian is responsible for the storage of water. It stores fluids and regulates the reservoirs of water and fluids in the body.

WOOD CREATES FIRE

The green **Wood element** contains the yin Liver meridian and the yang Gall Bladder meridian. The Wood element is said to connect heaven and earth, like a tree rooted in the ground with its branches rising toward heaven; trees are strong and enduring while at the same time flexible and bending. The Wood element is a source of creativity and its sound is shouting and the emotion is anger.

The Liver meridian is a detoxifier for the mind and the body and provides clarity and order to the other meridians.

The Gall Bladder meridian is in charge of choice making.

This is the twelve meridians organized in the five element system. Sound Essence offers two more meridians, the Central and Governing Meridians as a coupled item.

The Central Meridian is associated with the brain and the central nervous system. The Governing Meridian is associated with the spine and the autonomic nervous system. Combined in the pattern of yin and yang, they together offer success and support.

The human essence is a holistic energy system consisting of both intrinsic and extrinsic interactions. Food and herbs support the integrity of the meridian system as does sound and colour. There are also many body touching techniques that fully embrace the concepts of meridian therapy, which include Acupuncture, Shiatsu, Jin Shin Do and Kinesiology. By restoring balance in the meridians, the body creates homeostasis and self-corrects many of its problems.

Restoring balance and homeostasis is the concept supported by the Meridian Sound Essences. The Meridian Sound Essences support the physical aspect of the meridian with the vibration of herbs and supports the etheric aspect of the meridian with the vibration of sound. The magical effects of the Meridian Sound Essences come from tapping into the dualistic nature of the meridians. The formulas for theses essences balance the meridians with the homeopathic signature of the herb that resonates with the intrinsic component of the chi and blend it with the sound vibration related to the specific meridian that resonates with the extrinsic component of chi. The meridian is getting a complete harmony of balanced vibration that promotes it in health and stability.

The next few pages in this manual are designed to help the user of the Meridian Sound Essences to understand how these essences affect the body; physically, emotionally or spiritually.

Each element is explained with an overview of the elemental theme and then divided into the related meridians. The meridian pages are designed to offer the reader insight into the cause of meridian blockage creating imbalance or sickness in the body. Blockage of meridian flow can come from simple physical complications with the body or emotional stagnation or lack of spiritual connection. Physical complications can come from accidents or stress. Emotions are supposed to move through our body allowing us experiences in this world. If an emotion gets stuck because we hang on to it for too long, it can cause imbalance in the body. Likewise, if we are not true to our life purpose we cause disharmony in our vibratory field, which also causes imbalance in the body.

The meridian pages offer the reader the key components of each meridian and also the information from the plant energies used in the vibrational remedies to gather insight on the cause of imbalance. Using the Meridian Sound Essences will support the body in raising the vibration for consistent harmony, thus allowing the body to adjust into alignment. When the body aligns itself it can also heal itself, we just need to support it with healthy vibrations and thoughts.

FIVE ELEMENT THEORY DIAGRAM

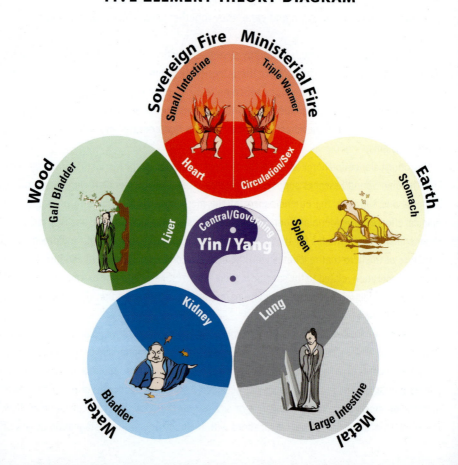

Yin Yang Couple
Success/Support

I have all that I need.

Overview

The concept of yin and yang is likely the most important concept in the theory of Chinese Medicine. It uniquely expresses the ebb and flow of life and life force and all of nature. Yin and yang are considered opposing yet complementary forces, which profoundly express the interdependence of everything in the context of positive and negative. In this concept of movement from light to dark; from sunshine to shadow; from the rising and falling of tides; and the changing of the seasons, there is the simple explanation of all of life. One of the dualistic forces does not exist without the other. As the day moves into night there is always a glimpse of light as in the moon of the night.

Yin and yang are complementary and interdependent aspects of the single unifying aspect of *chi*. These natural forces are always moving, constantly transforming and forever changing. *Chi* is another word for life force which is a reflection of our health and vitality. By promoting physical health in the body through the use of homeopathy and sound, we will also promote the vitality in our *chi*. Our ultimate goal is to achieve balance physically, emotionally, and spiritually. Sometimes we are too yin and sometimes we are too yang. The yin force is seen as passive, cold, receptive, feminine, internal, constantly working, solid, and dark. The yang force is active, hot, productive, masculine, external, intermittently working, hollow and light. Both of these forces contain a small amount of the other. These opposite forces interact in order to create balance in the body. Balance is the primary message derived from the yin and yang theory. The balancing factor in the body doesn't just pertain to organs and meridians systems. It also helps to explain our moods and mood

ASSOCIATED MERIDIANS
CENTRAL AND GOVERNING

PHYSICAL COMPONENT
Brain and Spine

EMOTIONAL COMPONENT
Success/Support

METAPHYSICAL COMPONENT
Central Meridian – Proper creative expression in all avenues

Governing Meridian – Ability to govern life

swings. If joy and sorrow are opposite yet complementary emotions then one could not experience joy to its fullest if one had never experienced sorrow and the reverse is true. Today in society we try not to express our negative emotions yet there is great value in negative emotions as they play an integral role in keeping us emotionally healthy. The purpose of experiencing a negative emotion is to make us aware of what we are doing and thinking and to assess whether we are congruent with our life's purpose. Emotions play a large role in the state of our health, finding the balance of yin and yang emotions is another component in maintaining a healthy *chi*.

The fundamental cause of distress or imbalance in the body comes from our resistance to the natural flow of universal energy. This resistance results in stagnation and depletion of life force energy, which causes sickness and distress. We need to constantly monitor our sense of being in sync with the rhythm and flow of life.

Meridians & Five Elements
Yin Yang Couple

The Central meridian
Place both hands on your pubic bone and bring them straight up over the front of your body to your bottom lip.

The Brain
The brain is housed in the skull and is part of the central nervous system, continuous with the spinal cord. The brain functions as the primary receiver, organizer and distributor of information for the body. It has two (right and left) halves called "hemispheres."

Functions
Governs all the yin meridians

The Central Meridian is related to the brain and the central nervous system. It supports the body with co-ordination both physically and emotionally, allowing one to handle more than one thing at a time. It supports the eyes.

Herbs
Gingko Biloba – *Ginko biloba*
Gingko Biloba carries and activates the original memory. It reminds us of our primary purpose. It supports those who are on a spiritual quest and are doing planetary work.

Meridian Sound Essence
Central - Primary Purpose
The Central meridian governs all the other meridians. It supports conscious awareness and represents our connection with our source. The Central Meridian Sound Essence can be used to revitalize sexuality, the procreation capacity and the divine joy as in knowing one's place and having all you need to manifest abundance.

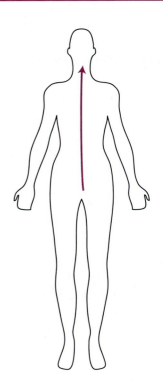

Central Meridian Issues

Physically
Central Nervous system
Brain
Eyes
Esophagus
Reproductive system
Hormonal system
Menstruation difficulties
Sexual dysfunction
Hernia

Mentally
Memory
Consciousness
Ability to think

Emotionally
Self-respect
Success

Spiritually
Connected with nature
Grounded

Central Meridian Issues

Herbs
Catnip
Chamomile
Feverfew
Gingko Biloba
Gota Kola
Ginger
Hops
Lemon Balm
Oatstraw
Skullcap
St John's Wort
Valerian
Wood Betany

Bach Flower Essences
Larch
Rock Rose

Pacific Essences
Indian Pipe
Hookers Onion
Nootka Rose
Whale

Affirmations

1. I am successful.
2. I have a strong healthy brain.
3. I have strong healthy eyes.
4. I have good focus.
5. I achieve my goals.
6. I handle myself well in all situations.
7. I am creative.
8. I express myself clearly and appropriately.
9. It is easy for me to concentrate.
10. I am in control of my destiny.

MERIDIANS & FIVE ELEMENTS
YIN YANG COUPLE

THE GOVERNING MERIDIAN

Place one hand at your tailbone and trace straight up your spine and have the other hand meet it and trace the meridian over the top of your head, over your nose, and to your top lip.

THE SPINE

The spine is a series of bones known as the vertebral column, which surrounds and protects the spinal cord. Each of these bones is connected by a number of ligaments and provides support for the upper body. The vertebral column provides attachment points for the ribs and the muscles of the back. The spine consists of 26 bones and has 5 regions and each has varying characteristics. The cervical spine has 7 bones, the thoracic has 12 bones, the lumbar spine has 5 bones, the sacrum has five fused bones, and the coccyx has four fused bones.

FUNCTIONS

Governs all the yang meridians

The Governing Meridian is related to the spine, skeleton and the autonomic nervous system, which controls involuntary bodily functions. It offers physical support to the skeleton and energetic support to all of the meridians.

HERBS

Valerian – *Valerian officinalis*
Valerian is comforting and soothing like the womb of a mother. It helps to calm and soothe someone in trauma or distress.

MERIDIAN SOUND ESSENCE

Governing – Soothing
The Governing meridian's key focus is choice as it supports subconscious clearing. Free will is the first and greatest gift of our creator. The enhancement or the balance of this meridian using the Governing Meridian Sound Essence allows for the capability of a decision

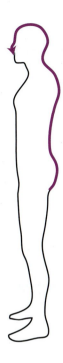

GOVERNING MERIDIAN ISSUES

PHYSICALLY
Autonomic Nervous System
Skeletal system
Spine
Brain
Face
Ears
Anus

MENTALLY
Memory
Clear thinking

EMOTIONALLY
Feeling supported
Trusting
Unbalanced

SPIRITUALLY
Connected with self and higher self

Chapter 7

Governing Meridian Issues

Herbs
Catnip
Chamomile
Feverfew
Ginko Biloba
Gota Kola
Ginger
Hops
Lemon Balm
Oatstraw
Scullcap
St. John's Wort
Valerian
Wood Betany

Bach Flower Essences
Holly
Chestnut Bud

Pacific Essences
Douglas Aster
Hooker's Onion
Nootka Rose
Sea Horse
Whale

without doubt or self-recrimination. It supports the feeling of knowing. It is the essence of the warrior.

Affirmations

1. I accept myself as I am.
2. I have a healthy flexible spine.
3. I have healthy ears.
4. I am fully supported.
5. I have flexibility.
6. I am motivated for the right reasons.
7. I listen and respond appropriately.
8. It is easy for me to encourage others and myself.
9. I know the truth.
10. It is easy for me to support myself in work that I love.

Sovereign Fire Couple

Love /Hate

*I am filled with joy and gratitude
as I am learning from my experience.*

Overview

Fire in the Five Element Theory is associated with summer. Summer is a time of the most intense heat. Fire is associated with the colour red, which is definitely a predominant sight in the heat of the summer when the forests are ablaze. If the face shows red, it is a sign that the heart is involved. Jovial fellows often have a red hue to their face. Joy or lack of joy, are the emotions that have the greatest effect on the Fire element.

The Fire element consists of four meridians divided into Sovereign and Ministerial Fire. Sovereign Fire is the Heart Meridian and Small Intestine Meridian. Ministerial Fire is the Circulation/Sex Meridian and the Triple Warmer Meridian. The two Yin Meridians are the Heart and Circulation/Sex Meridians. The two Yang Meridians are the Small Intestine and the Triple Warmer Meridians.

The sound associated with this joyous element is laughter. The sense organ for the Fire element is the tongue. If ever there is a roughness or pimples on or at the end of the tongue it is a warning to take care of your heart. What is in your heart that you need to express?

The Fire element is expressed through the blood of the body, the taste is bitter and the smell is burnt or scorched.

When the Heart Meridian is balanced and functioning well, it is easier for us to experience joy in our lives. Depleted heart energy may cause heart disease, palpitations, angina pectoris, and overall tension and fatigue. Excess energy in the heart may cause a sensation of tension and tightness in the heart and chest area .

Eastern Philosophy suggests that the heart is the master of the voice, meaning that the heart controls the use of the voice. When we are in love we sing, when we are angry we scream, when we are sad we cry and when we

ASSOCIATED MERIDIANS
HEART AND SMALL INTESTINE

PHYSICAL COMPONENT
Heart and Small Intestine

EMOTIONAL COMPONENT
Love

METAPHYSICAL COMPONENT
Inner joy

Chapter 7

COLOUR	Red
SEASON	Summer
SOUND	Laughing/Giggling
NOTE	'G'
TASTE	Bitter
ODOR	Scorched
CONDITIONS	Heat
CONSCIOUSNESS	Spirit, self-awareness, "I am" consciousness
ACTIVITY	Yin – Wisdom / Yang – Intellect
SENSE	Taste
ACTION	Sight
TISSUES	Blood Vessels
FLUID	Sweat

PHYSICAL	Heart and Circulation
EMOTIONAL	Excess
MENTAL	Idealism
SPIRITUAL	Expression

are content we hum. Joy in the voice can be heard as a laughing quality. A person may be discussing a very mundane topic, but if the heart is strong and dominant, there is still a happy bounce in the words, indicating a strong happy nature.

The small intestine is responsible for taking nutrition out of food and making it available to the bloodstream. A weak small intestine condition contributes to other types of digestive disorders including constipation and appendicitis. In women, small intestine disorders leads to chronic menstrual problems, including premenstrual syndrome, and ovarian pain and cysts. Those with a weakened small intestine tend to think too much, suffer from anxiety, and tend to control emotions with their minds, experience a lack of joy and sometimes, deep sadness.

Excess small intestine energy contributes to poor circulation in the lower organs; such people may have cold hands and feet, and chronic constipation that can alternate with diarrhea. People with excessive Small Intestine energy tend to have strong determination and an ability to finish what they begin. They are restless, overworked and eat too quickly. They withhold their emotions usually to their own detriment and have trouble relaxing. They are highly ambitious but often fail to appreciate their accomplishments.

Meridians & Five Elements
Sovereign Fire Couple

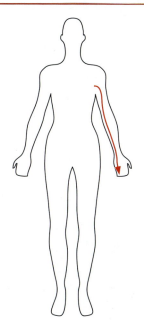

Heart Meridian (11 a.m. to 1 p.m.)

Place your open hand underneath the opposite armpit in alignment with your little finger and trace straight down inside the arm, over the palm and outside to the little finger. Do both sides.

The Heart

The heart is a cone-shaped muscle about the size of a fist and is located a little to the left of the midline of the chest. It receives blood through the veins and beats approximately 100,000 times per day to circulate the blood throughout the body.

The Heart Meridian is said to rule the blood and blood vessels, so when we assess the heart meridian, we are assessing the heart, blood flow and blood vessels. According to Traditional Chinese Medicine, the Heart Meridian unites all the meridians so that there is coordination of energy throughout all of the meridian system. If the Heart Meridian is healthy, the spirit of the person is also liberated and healthy. Imbalances in the Heart Meridian show up as heart palpitations, forgetfulness, pale tongues, tiredness, night sweats, or hot hands and feet.

Functions

The Heart Meridian provides the propulsive force for circulating the blood throughout the vascular system of the body.

Sound

The heart tone activates and regulates the rhythm of the body, the physical and emotional pulse. It is useful for physical defects of the heart and any kind of heart sickness on an emotional level. This tone is exceptionally powerful for teenagers.

Heart Meridian Issues

Physically
Circulation of blood
Complexion
Cold hands and feet
Speech
Sleep disorders
Nervous disorders due to anxiety and/or agitation
Shock, trauma, loss of consciousness

Mentally
Memory
Consciousness
Ability to think
Intuition

Emotionally
Enthusiasm, passion, spontaneity
Apathy
Exhaustion
Depression and mood swings

Spiritually
Seeks expansion of consciousness
Seeks heartfelt connection with others or God

Heart Meridian Issues

Herbs
Cayenne
Hawthorn
Motherwort

Bach Flower Essences
Holly
Sweet Chestnut
Vervain
White Chestnut

Pacific Essences
Diatom
Dolphin
Fireweed
Hooker's Onion
Hootka Rose
Jellyfish
Lily of the Valley
Periwinkle
Salal

Herbs

Motherwort – *Leoncrus Cardiaea*
Motherwort helps us to enjoy freedom in new thought. Motherwort is in the realm of communication. It allows the transmission of knowledge, of ancient wisdom, of the joining of the intuitive with the scientific.

Heart Meridian Sound Essence

Heart – Transmission of Knowledge

The Heart has to do with the electrical functioning of your pump. The electrical fibrillations are easily disrupted so the Heart Meridian Sound Essence serves to regulate and reinforce the tissues and the electrical conductivity.

Affirmations

1. I love who I am.
2. I have a strong healthy heart.
3. I like what I do.
4. I like how I look.
5. I move with grace and ease.
6. My timing is always appropriate.
7. I love others as they are.
8. I am loved.
9. I am grateful.
10. I give freely.

MERIDIANS & FIVE ELEMENTS
SOVEREIGN FIRE COUPLE

SMALL INTESTINE MERIDIAN (1 P.M. TO 3 P.M.)

Start at the outside tip of the little finger, go straight up the outside of the arm to your shoulder, drop back on your shoulder blade, go up the side of the neck, go over to your cheekbone, and back to the opening of your ear. Do both sides.

THE SMALL INTESTINE

The small intestine receives food and liquid from the stomach and continues the digestion process by sending the waste to the large intestine and the purer nutrients to the spleen. The Small Intestine Meridian assimilates not only nutrition but also thought and emotions. It has the ability to take in and utilize information effectively on all levels – physically, emotionally, mentally and spiritually. It sorts the pure from the impure and discards the non-useful. The Small Intestine Meridian purifies nutrition and thought for the Heart Meridian to regulate.

FUNCTIONS

Receives food mass from stomach, bile from liver and gall bladder, and pancreatic juice from the pancreas.
Absorption of simple sugars, amino acids, fatty acids and carbohydrates.

SOUND

The vibratory tone for small intestine is primarily useful as a cleanser. It purifies the system through removing the all excess and allowing integration of what is necessary. This tone is the activator of the capacity for discernment on all levels. Particularly useful for decision making, when a specific choice must be made.

HERBS

Slippery Elm – *Ulmus fulva*
Slippery Elm's keyword is adaptability. It gives the strength and ability to move as necessary. Slippery Elm supports anyone after any kind of large trauma or hormonal shift.

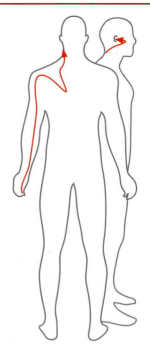

SMALL INTESTINE MERIDIAN ISSUES

PHYSICALLY
Bowel disorders
Ulcers
Neck and shoulder pain
Hearing

MENTALLY
Power of discernment
Ability to make choices
Sort things out – can be obsessive

EMOTIONALLY
Transformer of emotions
Receive new feelings with ease
Forgives and forgets

SPIRITUALLY
Devotion to spiritual truth

Small Intestine Meridian Issues

Herbs
Aloe Vera
Buckthorn
Cascara Sagrada
Flaxseed
Slippery Elm
Strawberry

Bach Flower Essences
Beech
Chestnut Bud
Holly
Star of Bethlehem
White Chestnut
Willow

Pacific Essences
Barnacle
Goatsbeard
Hookers Onion
Nootka Rose
Salal
Sea Lettuce

It helps to regain balance and aligns the whole system into a new position.

Small Intestine Meridian Sound Essence

Small Intestine – Assimilation

The Small Intestine Meridian Sound Essence will create an interface that allows only the information that is beneficial to be assimilated, it acts like a filter or a grid that is intelligently discerning, one that is constantly opening and closing to ideas, emotions or food.

Affirmations

1. I am a student of life and learn from all of life's experiences.
2. I have a strong healthy small intestine.
3. I eliminate toxins efficiently.
4. I appropriately express my emotions.
5. I am loved and accepted.
6. I love and accept others.
7. I have good judgment.
8. I think logically.
9. I respect others and their mistakes.
10. I give equally.

Ministerial Fire Couple

Love /Hate

*I am in the rhythm of life,
getting better every day.*

Meridian & Five elements
Ministerial Fire Couple

Overview

Fire in the Five Element Theory is associated with summer. Summer is a time of the most intense heat. Fire is associated with the colour red, which is definitely a predominant sight in the heat of the summer when the forests are ablaze. If the face shows red, it is a sign that the heart is involved. Jovial fellows often have a red hue to their face. Joy or lack of joy, are the emotions that have the greatest effect on the Fire element.

The Fire element consists of four meridians divided into Sovereign and Ministerial Fire. Sovereign Fire is the Heart Meridian and Small Intestine Meridian. Ministerial Fire is the Circulation/Sex Meridian and the Triple Warmer Meridian. The two Yin Meridians are the Heart and Circulation/Sex Meridians. The two Yang Meridians are the Small Intestine and the Triple Warmer Meridians.

The sound associated with this joyous element is laughter. The sense organ for the Fire element is the tongue. If ever there is a roughness or pimples on or at the end of the tongue it is a warning to take care of your heart. What is in your heart that you need to express?

The Fire element is expressed through the blood of the body, the taste is bitter and the smell is burnt or scorched.

The Triple Warmer Meridian is not related to an organ, but is related to a collection of functions. The burners are the Upper Burner, the Middle Burner and the Lower Burner. The Upper Burner is situated from the diaphragm upwards and includes the heart, lungs, pericardium and throat and head. The Middle Burner is located from the diaphragm to the umbilicus and includes the stomach, spleen and gall bladder. The Lower Burner is located below the umbilicus and includes the liver, kidneys, intes-

Associated Meridians
CIRCULATION/SEX AND TRIPLE WARMER

Physical Component
Circulation, lymphatic system and hormonal function

Emotional Component
Love

Metaphysical Component
Communication and growth in relationships

COLOUR	Red
SEASON	Summer
SOUND	Laughing/Giggling
NOTE	'G'
TASTE	Bitter
ODOR	Scorched
CONDITIONS	Heat
CONSCIOUSNESS	Spirit, self-awareness, "I am" consciousness
ACTIVITY	Yin – Wisdom, knowing, deep synthesis, ("knowing") of life
	Yang – Intellect, awareness, discernment
SENSE	Taste
ACTION	Sight
TISSUES	Blood Vessels
FLUID	Sweat

PHYSICAL	Heart and Circulation
EMOTIONAL	Excess
MENTAL	Idealism
SPIRITUAL	Expression

tines, and bladder.

Symptoms that may be associated with obstruction in the Triple Warmer Meridian may include: pain in the lateral aspect of the arm and elbow, pain around the circumference of the ear, ringing in the ears, congested and sore throat, abdominal distention, swelling in the cheek, pain in the shoulder, and edema.

The Circulation/Sex Meridian is closely related to the heart. It functions as an external covering of the heart and protects it from attacks by exterior pathogenic factors. Symptoms of an imbalanced Circulation/Sex Meridian may include palpitations, mental restlessness, flushed face, mental disturbance, stifling feeling in the chest, spasms in the arms, swollen feeling in the armpit or sensation of heat in the palms. The Circulation/Sex Meridian influences a person's relations with other people.

Circulation/Sex Meridian
(7 p.m. to 9 p.m.)

Place the fingers of one hand at the outside of the opposite nipple, come up over the shoulder, go down the middle of the inside arm and off the middle finger. Do both sides.

The Circulation/Sex Meridian

This meridian relates to the chest area protecting the heart. Balancing the Heart Meridian also helps to balance the Circulation/Sex Meridian. The pericardium is a loose-fitting membrane containing an outer layer of tough connective tissue and an inner layer of serous tissue, which is a delicate membrane.

Between these two layers is a space called the pericardial cavity which contains pericardial fluid.

The Circulation/Sex Meridian or what is sometimes called the Pericardium Meridian is traditionally associated with the circulation of the blood in the body, the lubrication of the sexual organs, and a protection of the heart, both physical and emotionally. Typically, imbalance of the heart will show up first in the Circulation/Sex Meridian and will eventually manifest in the Heart Meridian. The Circulation/Sex Meridian has the capacity to balance emotions and integrate heart and mind in sexual relationships. The Circulation/Sex Meridian protects the heart against injury and insult emotionally, physically and spiritually.

Functions

Prevents over-distention of the heart
Provides a tough, protective membrane around the heart
Anchors the heart in the media sternum

Sound

Activating the circulation/sex meridian with tone encourages expansion, growth and outreach. It is useful for stepping into new fields of endeavor with confidence. To be used to help release any kind of systemic blockages

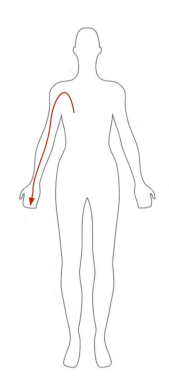

Circ/Sex Meridian Issues

Physically
Urination
The back, spinal column, and neck
Bones and teeth
Vision and hearing
Occipital headaches
Leg and knee pain

Mentally
Lack of fluidity
Hindsight
Living in the past

Emotionally
Jealousy
Holding on to grudges
Phobias

Spiritually
Aspiration to lofty heights
Will
Resoluteness

Circ/Sex Meridian Issues

Herbs
Cayenne
Hawthorn
Motherwort

Bach Flower Essences
Holly
Sweet Chestnut
Vervain
White Chestnut

Pacific Essences
Alum Root
Harvest Lily
Hooker's Onion
Nootka Rose
Ox-Eye Daisy
Pink Seaweed
Purple Magnolia
Sea Horse
Sea Turtle

such as plaque buildup in the blood vessels resulting from high cholesterol. It is a powerful stimulant for those experiencing any kind of lethargy; physical emotional, spiritual. Even those in a coma will benefit greatly from the circulation/sex tone.

Herbs

Sarsaparilla – *Aralia nudicaulis*

Sarsaparilla's keyword is instinct. It is a tonic for those coming into self-knowledge. Sarsaparilla is for those who need to learn to trust themselves and to rely on their own instincts.

Circulation/Sex Meridian Sound Essence

Circulation/Sex – Trust in Own Instincts

The Circulation/Sex Sound Essence supports us in transformation. Life is a process of accumulation; accumulation of experience and reaction, which builds up in responsive ability and leaves a residue. The Circulation/Sex Meridian Essence has the capacity for cleaning and clearing this residue through the pro-creative and circulatory systems. It cleans first allowing room for growth and expansion.

Affirmations

1. I love who I am.
2. I have a strong healthy heart.
3. I like what I do.
4. I like how I look.
5. I move with grace and ease.
6. My timing is always appropriate.
7. I love others as they are.
8. I am loved.
9. I am grateful.
10. I give freely.

Triple Warmer Meridian
(9 p.m. to 11 p.m.)

Start at the ring finger on the outside of the hand, trace straight up the arm, over the elbow to beneath your ear, follow your ear around and behind, ending on the temple at the outside corner of the eyebrow. Do both sides.

The Triple Warmer Meridian

The Triple Warmer is physically nonexistent. It correlates the functioning of the three main functions of the body as described and determined through Eastern Philosophy.

Functions

INTAKE- The energy required for the lungs and the heart to circulate oxygen and blood – Upper Burner

ASSIMILATE - The energy required for digestion and absorption – Middle Burner

ELIMINATE - The energy required for elimination of waste – Lower Burner

The Triple Warmer Meridian serves the endocrine system to regulate heat, energy and emotions in the body. It is the meridian that coordinates the function of the respiratory (intake), digestive (assimilation), and elimination (discharge). It is also associated with how we coordinate our family and social relationship dynamics. Keeping the Triple Warmer Meridian healthy supports us in staying connected with our intuition.

Sound

Activating the Triple Warmer Meridian correlates all the information systems of the body. The tone promotes integration and communication between systems on all electrical and hormonal levels. This tone is most useful for all transition times, either the major ones experienced during a life time such as birth, puberty, marriage, menopause and death, or day to day transitions. Use this remedy for any kind of situation that requires extreme adaptation.

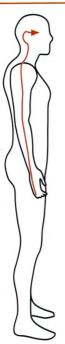

Triple Warmer Meridian Issues

Physically
Disturbances related to respiration and circulation – Upper Burner
Disturbances related to digestion and absorption – Middle Burner
Disturbances related to elimination and re-production – Lower Burner

Mentally
Unclear thinking
Anxiety

Emotionally
Jealousy
Holding on to grudges
Phobias
Depression
Low self esteem
Unbalanced

Spiritually
Not feeling balanced on all four levels

Chapter 7

Triple Warmer Meridian Issues

Herbs
Aloe Vera
Buckthorn
Cascara Sagrada
Flaxseed
Slippery Elm
Strawberry

Bach Flower Essences
Beech
Chestnut Bud
Holly
Star of Bethlehem
White Chestnut
Willow

Pacific Essences
Harvest Lily
Hooker's Onion
Moon Snail
Nootka Rose
Orange Honeysuckle
Poplar
Rainbow Kelp
Viburnum

Herbs

Sassafras – *Laurus sassafras*
Sassafras's keywords are encouragement with empathy. Sassafras supports those working in the healing arts. It is the trusted mentor for coaches.

Triple Warmer Meridian Sound Essence – Encouragement

The Triple Warmer is the meridian that facilitates the coordinated action of all 520 hormones in the body. The hormonal system is constantly adjusting to accommodate shifts in the internal and external environment. Without coordination, these hormones send out mismatched messages or signals to various organs and systems. The Triple Warmer Meridian Sound Essence provides a constant ray of light bringing the hormones into alignment so that they can function in a coordinated manner maintaining balance.

Affirmations

1. I am a student of life and learn from all of life's experiences.
2. I have a strong healthy small intestine.
3. I eliminate toxins efficiently.
4. I appropriately express my emotions.
5. I am loved and accepted.
6. I love and accept others.
7. I have good judgment.
8. I think logically.
9. I respect others and their mistakes.
10. I give equally.

Earth Couple
Sympathy / Empathy

I am content and blessed and have confidence in all that I do.

Overview
The Element Earth is related to late summer when produce is at its peak and ripens to its ultimate sweetness. It is the time of the year for the golden yellow of the wheat fields in the prairies. Earth is the center around which the other elements revolve. The Earth Meridians are related to the organs of the stomach and spleen which are located in the centre of the body. All nourishment comes from the earth; the trees are rooted in the soil and the water is filtered through the soil. The Earth element keeps us centered, allowing us to change direction without losing balance.

The sense of the Earth element is taste and its sensing organ is the mouth. The taste associated with this element is sweet. Sweet cravings or sweet tastes in the mouth may indicate an imbalance in the Earth element.

Someone with an imbalance in the Earth element may have an "apple" sweet body odor.

The sound associated with the Earth element is singing. The emotional theme for this element is sympathy and empathy. The Earth element houses the yin Spleen meridian and the yang Stomach Meridian.

The function of the Spleen Meridian is to transform the nutrition from the digestive process into life force energy and transport this energy through the blood stream. The state of the spleen is one of the most important factors in determining the amount of physical health and energy a person has. A person who has blocked spleen energy will feel tired, the muscles may be weak, and in severe cases could atrophy. If the Spleen Meridian is out of balance, there may be an impairment in the sense of taste or the presence of an abnormal taste in the mouth; lack of appetite and the lips may be pale and dry.

ASSOCIATED MERIDIANS
STOMACH AND SPLEEN

PHYSICAL COMPONENT
Stomach and Spleen functions

EMOTIONAL COMPONENT
Sympathy

METAPHYSICAL COMPONENT
Reflection

COLOUR	Yellow
SEASON	Late Summer
SOUND	Singing/ Humming
NOTE	'C'
TASTE	Sweet
ODOR	Fragrant
CONDITIONS	Wind
CONSCIOUSNESS	Essence, The primary sense of presence of the body
ACTIVITY	Yin – Subconscious mind, intuitive process Yang – Conscious mind, conscious thinking
SENSE	Touch
ACTION	Thought
TISSUES	Flesh / Fat
FLUID	Saliva

PHYSICAL	Digestion and Absorption of Nutrients
EMOTIONAL	Sympathy
MENTAL	Grounding
SPIRITUAL	Contentment/Needs

The Spleen is the residence of thought. It influences our capacity for thinking, studying, concentrating, focusing and memorizing. People who have an extraordinary memory in their work or field of study are demonstrating this capacity of the spleen.

The work of the Stomach Meridian is to digest the foods we intake. The stomach along with the spleen is responsible for transporting food essences to the whole body, especially the limbs. If the Stomach Meridian is balanced the person will feel strong and vital.

Spleen Meridian (9 a.m. to 11 a.m.)

Start at the outside corners of each big toe and go straight up the inside of your legs, flaring out at your hips, up the side of your rib cage, to the arm crease, then down the side to the bottom of the rib cage. Do both sides.

The Spleen

The spleen is a sac-like organ made up of sponge-like lymphatic tissue. It is located behind and beneath the stomach in the left upper quadrant of the abdomen.

The spleen in Traditional Chinese Medicine is considered an important digestive organ. Its main function is to transform food into blood. The spleen extracts nutrients from the food we eat and makes it into blood and sends this healthy blood to the lungs.

The Spleen Meridian travels from the feet to the torso and is considered responsible for ruling the upward movement of water and blood. If the spleen does not efficiently transport the blood and water to the lungs, the blood can stagnate, showing up as symptoms such as abdominal pain, hemorrhoids, bloating or diarrhea.

The spleen also controls blood flow and many of the blood functions and if there is imbalance, bleeding disorders may appear. The spleen regulates the flow of blood to the mouth, muscles and flesh. If the spleen is healthy, the lips will be red and moist and the muscles will be strong. The Spleen Meridian also controls the sense of taste.

In Traditional Chinese Medicine, the integrity of the Spleen Meridian is a direct representation of a person's vital energy. It regulates blood quality and moves the nourishment from food and thought throughout the body. If there is an imbalance in the Spleen Meridian, there is not enough energy circulating through the body.

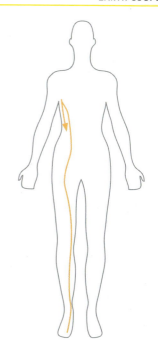

Spleen Meridian Issues

Physically
Inability to transform nutrients into a strong physical body
Weak muscles
Bruising and bleeding disorders
Weight problems
Water retention, diarrhea, lots of mucous
Lymphatic system
Menstrual cycle
Immune system

Mentally
Foggy thinking
Lack of mental clarity

Emotionally
Sympathy – feels all the pain of the earth
Psychic and emotional sponge
Over protectiveness
Needy

Spiritually
Seeks nourishment
Seeks harmony with others

Spleen Meridian Issues

Herbs
Buchu
Calendula
Chapparal
Cleavers
Dandelion
Devil's Club
Echinacea
Juniper Berries
Licorice
Mullein
Parsley
Stevia
Usnea
Uva-Ursi

Bach Flower Essences
Gorse
Vine

Pacific Essences
Dolphin
Goatsbeard
Pipsissewa
Sea Turtle
Silver Birch
Viburnum
Urchin
Wall Flower

Functions
Production of blood cells
Blood storage
Blood filtration to remove impurities

Sound
The vibratory rate that stimulates the spleen meridian also regulates blood chemistry. Any imbalance of blood sugar, immune factors or hormones can be regulated with application of this vibration. Activating this meridian with sound reestablishes a balanced state when there is a stress response or adrenalin overload. This tone is useful for blood sugar imbalances, in supporting children to meet new challenges in school or anyone facing new situations.

Herbs
Dandelion – *Taraxacum officinale*
Dandelion's key word is integrity. Dandelion is adaptable and works with other herbs to enhance them. Dandelion is a powerful cleanser on all levels. Metaphysically, dandelion operates like a magnet bringing in clarity of vision, focus and determination. It allows all extraneous things to fall away. Dandelion gives clarity of purpose and focus to all circumstances.

Nettle – *Urtica dioica*
Stinging Nettle has the capacity to penetrate and infuse. Stinging Nettle allows you to be guided to the next place and then supports you and gives you energy to be in that new place. On a mental level it is used for studying for exams. It aids in getting to the point and retaining information.

Usnea – *Usnea Barbata*
Usnea's keyword is clairvoyance. Usnea gives one trust in their higher consciousness. Usnea supports all the extrasensory perceptions and heightens any kind of clairvoyance.

Spleen Meridian
Sound Essence – Integrity

The Spleen Meridian regulates body chemistry. The Spleen Meridian Sound Essence offers the capacity for enthusiasm and regulation. It helps the meridian to be consistently fueled to maintain consistent speed to maintain optimum energy levels for all the body's regulatory mechanisms, including blood sugar levels.

Affirmations

1. I can relax and all will be well.
2. I have a strong, healthy spleen.
3. I have a strong, healthy pancreas.
4. I have confidence in all that I do.
5. I am self-assured.
6. I am free to make mistakes.
7. I am free to explore and grow.
8. It is easy for me to allow others to take care of themselves.
9. I have faith.
10. I have more than enough.

Chapter 7

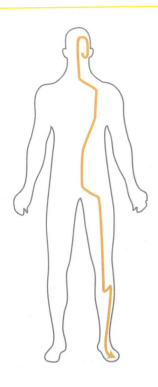

Stomach Meridian Issues

Physically
Indigestion, gas, bloating, nausea and vomiting
Lack of physical energy to perform activity
Eating disorders such as bulimia and or anorexia

Mentally
Ungrounded "spaced out"
Disconnected thoughts
Repetitive thoughts leading nowhere, inability to focus
Thinking too much

Emotionally
Worry
Discontent

Spiritually
Doubt and uncertainty

Stomach meridian (7 a.m. to 9 a.m.)

Place both hands under your eyes, drop straight down to the jaw, circle up around the face to your forehead, drop straight down through the eyes to the collarbone, over the chest, in at the waist and out at the hips, down the leg (outside the knee) and out to the second toe. Do both sides.

The Stomach

The stomach is a dilated, sac-like, distensible portion of the alimentary canal below the esophagus and below the diaphragm to the right of the spleen, partly under the liver.

The stomach is responsible for digesting the food intake. As it breaks down these substances it sends the undigested foods to the intestines and the purer substances to the spleen. The Stomach Meridian and the Spleen Meridian are related as the Earth element. If the stomach's balance is impaired it will manifest as stomachache, nausea, distention, bloating and possibly vomiting.

The location of the Stomach Meridian in the body is the center of the body and it passes by all the sense organs such as the mouth, eyes, ears and nose. The Stomach Meridian has a direct connection with the senses and is affected by emotions. Also the reverse is true; if there is an imbalance in the Stomach Meridian, many of the other meridians may be affected. The Stomach Meridian in Traditional Chinese Medicine is called the sea of nourishment. The stomach digests the food we intake but also the thoughts we take in. This is why we get "gut hunches" as the stomach serves as a frontline detector for any stress from food, thought or emotion.

Functions

Organ of digestion
Regulates the passage of food to the remainder of the gut
Acts as a reservoir

Its acid kills microbes present in foods
It is important in the acid-base equilibrium of the body

Sound

Stimulating the Stomach Meridian with sound empowers one's ability to say "no". When there is too much information, any kind of sensory and emotional overload or physical burdens are just too much, use this activator for Stomach Meridian. It empowers one to set boundaries and strengthen limits. Assimilation of food of any kind can only take place in a safe environment. The vibratory tone of stomach helps create that safe space. This is useful for all conditions for when the system is overwhelmed. Caution: overuse of this tone creates a hermit, too much isolation.

Herbs

Wormwood – *Atemisia absinthium*
Wormwood's key word is discernment. Wormwood in very small doses is useful for those who are struggling with decision-making. Wormwood enhances the breath and is useful for asthmatics and those that are stuck in sorrow.

Stomach Meridian
Sound Essence – Discernment

The Stomach Meridian Sound Essence facilitates reception on all levels. It transports safe substance or thought through the system but if the substance or thought is harmful, the Stomach Meridian escorts it harmlessly out of the system. The Stomach Meridian Sound Essence facilitates the wisdom to discern and decide how to best handle the substance, thought, or situation.

Chapter 7

Stomach Meridian Issues

Herbs
Aloe Vera
Buckthorn
Cascara Sagrada
Flaxseed
Slippery Elm
Strawberry

Bach Flower Essences
Beech
Chestnut Bud
Holly
Star of Bethlehem
White Chestnut
Willow

Pacific Essences
Grape Hyacinth
Grass Widow
Hermit Crab
Hooker's Onion
Narcissus
Nootka Rose
Red Huckle Berry
Sea Lettuce
Sea Palm
Sponge
Wall Flower
Wind Flowery

Affirmations

1. I am a student of life and learn from all of life's experiences.
2. I have a strong, healthy small intestine.
3. I eliminate toxins efficiently.
4. I appropriately express my emotions.
5. I am loved and accepted.
6. I love and accept others.
7. I have good judgment.
8. I think logically.
9. I respect the choices of others.
10. I give equally.

Metal Couple
Guilt/Grief/Regret

*I release all that no longer serves me
to embrace positive change in my life.*

Overview

Metal in the Five Element Theory is associated with autumn. Autumn is the time of the year that we make preparations for winter by storing food and securing shelter. The Metal element represents the mineral ores, salts, crystals and gemstones of the inner earth. These function by creating structure and communication. Metal and crystals are used for electrical wire and computer chips. The Chinese liken the electrical wiring and the crystals of the computer messaging to our nervous system and the brain.

In traditional Eastern philosophy Metal energies are expressed as the inner workings and activities of the mind and in developing ideas, writing and speaking.

Metal is associated with the colour white. Whiteness in facial hue may indicate a metal imbalance, mainly noticed in the skin around the eyes and cheeks.

The sense organ for the Metal element is the nose and the associated sense is smell, and the associated smell is putrid. The flavor associated with metal is spicy which opens up the senses, clears the sinuses, and stimulates the lungs; however too much spice can cause imbalance in the lungs. Often a craving for spicy foods or a strong distaste for them may suggest an imbalance in the Metal element.

Metal's body fluid is mucous. Symptoms that indicate a Metal imbalance are mucous related such as runny nose, sinus congestion, coughs and colds.

The skin acts as the third lung, being the body's outer shell, in contact with the air.

The Metal element houses our sources of inspiration for new ideas and is where new emotions take shape. The Metal element governs the interactions between the

ASSOCIATED MERIDIANS
LUNG AND LARGE INTESTINE

PHYSICAL COMPONENT
Lung and Large Intestine

EMOTIONAL COMPONENT
Grief

METAPHYSICAL COMPONENT
Letting go

Colour	White
Season	Autumn
Sound	Weeping/Sobbing
Note	'D'
Taste	Pungent
Odor	Rotten
Conditions	Clear
Consciousness	Animal Instinct; Primary reactions to life
Activity	Yin – Response; Surrender
	Yang – Instinctive reaction
Sense	Smell
Action	Speech
Tissues	Skin/Hair
Fluid	Mucous

Physical	Breathing
Emotional	Control
Mental	Flexibility
Spiritual	Worth

outside and inside of the body. A balanced Metal element gives us the capacity to set limits and to protect our boundaries and to let go of old thought patterns and beliefs which enable us to grow and evolve.

The Metal element personality likes definition, structure, discipline, and organization. The Metal element personality is methodical, efficient and has many principles. This person can easily become overly strict and rigid. Rigidity and a tendency to hold on to ideas and emotions can cause constipation as well as muscular tightness, emotional tension and other restrictions.

The emotions that reflect an imbalance in the Metal element are grief, depression, melancholy, low vitality, low inspiration and sorrow. These emotions come from big losses but if prolonged may cause injury to lungs and/or the large intestine. The sound for the Metal element is crying or weeping which can be a good outlet for sorrow or grief.

The lungs and large intestine are two major elimination organs of the body. Letting go is really the message of the meridians of the Metal element. Letting the abdomen expand fully at every inhalation causes the diaphragm to move, which will move the intestines and eventually ease the constipation. Deep breathing strengthens the lungs. Breathing involves the intake of the new and the elimination of the old. So your deepest attitudes toward living and dying may affect your breathing process and balance of the Metal element. Welcome each breath and each change in your life by looking toward the new experience and the growth it will bring.

Meridian & Five Elements
Metal Couple

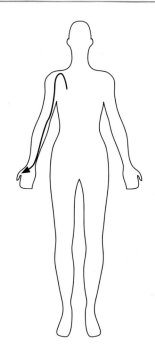

Lung Meridian (3 a.m. to 5 a.m.)
Place one hand on the upper chest just inside the shoulder and move it up over your shoulder, straight down the inside of your arm, through the palm and off your thumb. Do both sides.

The Lungs
The two cone-shaped spongy organs of respiration are contained within the pleural cavity of the thorax.

During inhalation the lungs take in air and send it into the body, while through exhalation the air expels the waste to the outside. The nose and throat are openings to the lungs and are related to the Lung Meridian. If either of these openings are disturbed, symptoms such as coughing, asthma, and sneezing occur.

The lungs also help move water around the body and to the kidneys, and the skin. According to the Five Element Theory, the lungs are said to receive heavenly *chi* through breathing. The lungs control the rate and depth of respiration and therefore they control the absorption of the life energy through the breath.

The Lung Meridian is said to rule the outer body areas such as, skin, body hair, and sweat. The Lung Meridian is important in the resistance to disease and therefore a deficiency in lung *chi* decreases a person's defenses against imbalances such as colds and flus. Getting cold easily and perspiring too little are indications of lung imbalance.

Functions
Bring air and blood into intimate contact so that oxygen can be added to the blood and carbon dioxide can be removed.
Production of sound.
Eliminates excess body heat.

Sound
The tone for the Lung Meridian opens the way for new possibilities. It releases old sorrow and inspires interest in

Lung Meridian Issues
Physically
Breathing disorders
    Asthma, bronchitis, coughing, emphysema
Nose problems – diminished sense of smell
Sinusitis
Dry skin and dry hair
Pallor
First line of defense against external pathogenic factors
Affects the voice and quality of speaking

Mentally
Sadness and worry
Inability to receive

Emotionally
Jealousy
Holding on to grudges
Phobias

Spiritually
Inability to live life with exuberance

Lung Meridian Issues

Herbs
Coltsfoot
Comfrey
Elderberry
Elecampagne
Ephedra
Flaxseed
Horehound
Licorice
Lobelia
Marshmallow
Mullein
Slippery Elm

Bach Flower Essences
Honeysuckle
Rock Water

Pacific Essences
Arbutus
Bluebell
Death Camas
Fairy Bell
Grape Hyacinth
Hooker's Onion
Indian Pipe
Nootka Rose
Polyanthus
Purple Crocus
Sand Dollar
Sea Horse
Vanilla Leaf

new endeavors. This tone is particularly useful for working with any kind of mental confusion, schizophrenia, dementia or Alzheimer's.

Herbs
Slippery Elm – *Ulmus fulva*
Slippery Elm's keyword is adaptability. It gives the strength and ability to move as necessary. Slippery Elm gives support after any kind of large trauma or hormonal shift. It helps to regain balance and to bring the whole system back into alignment into a new position.

Lung Meridian Sound Essence
Lung – Enthusiasm
The Lung Meridian Sound Essence is essential for enthusiasm, the capacity to embrace each moment. It is vital for us to actively reach out for the future, yet have the capacity to let go of the past. Let bygones be bygones. The Lung Meridian Sound Essence is invaluable in bringing one into the present moment.

Affirmations
1. I am humble with nature.
2. I accept myself exactly as I am.
3. I have strong healthy lungs.
4. My breath is deep and efficient.
5. I respect the opinion of others.
6. I enjoy being in the company of others.
7. I hear what others have to say.
8. It is easy for me to establish deep personal relationships.
9. I accept others as they are.
10. I appreciate all that I have.

Meridian & Five Elements
Metal Couple

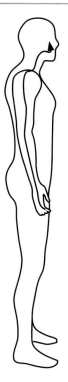

Large Intestine Meridian (5 a.m. to 7 a.m.)

Place the open fingers of one hand at the end of the pointer finger of the opposite hand, trace straight up the outside of the arm to the shoulder, over the shoulder, cross the neck to beneath the nose and end at the flare of your nose. Do both sides.

The Large Intestine

The large intestine extends from the ileum (small intestine) to the anus and consists of the cecum, colon and rectum.

The large intestine is where the final digestion occurs, as it processes any remaining foods and fluids from the small intestine. The Large Intestine Meridian is traditionally associated with elimination. Letting go is the theme of a healthy Large Intestine Meridian. A Large Intestine Meridian imbalance may show up as mental constipation such as constant negativity. Physical problems that may occur in the large intestine are bloating, diarrhea and constipation.

Functions

The re-absorption of fluid from the intestinal contents into the blood stream.
Expulsion of solid waste from the body.

Sound

Activating the Large Intestine Meridian with sound relieves the body of excess weight whether it be physical, emotional or spiritual. This is a most powerful release mechanism for the body. It must be used cautiously because overuse can create excessive loss. If used as a weight loss system, use it with Spleen Meridian sound because the blood balance must be maintained in the body.

Large Intestine Meridian Issues

Physically
Bowels and elimination
Gums and teeth
Face and mouth
Shoulder and neck injuries
Frontal headaches

Mentally
Rigid: black and white thinking
Inability to eliminate old mental habits
Controlled and controlling
Analytical

Emotionally
Lack of spontaneity
Pompous, arrogant
Needs to be right
Melancholy, sadness
Inability to let go

Spiritually
Seeks the absolute
Seeks perfect authority outside of self

Chapter 7

Large Intestine Meridian Issues

Herbs
Buckthorn
Cascara Sagrada
Chaparral
Fennel
Flaxseed
Goldenseal
Marshmallow
Oregon Grape
Psyllium
Slippery Elm

Bach Flower Essences
Crab Apple
Rock Water

Pacific Essences
Camellia
Grass Widow
Hooker's Onion
Nootka Rose
Polyanthus
Starfish
Vanilla Leaf

Herbs
Slippery Elm – *Ulmus fulva*
Slippery Elm's keyword is adaptability. It gives the strength and ability to move as necessary. Slippery Elm gives support after any kind of large trauma or hormonal shift. It helps to regain balance and to brings the whole system back into alignment into a new position.

Large Intestine Meridian Sound Essence – Letting Go
The Large Intestine has to do with receiving and letting go on a more fundamental level. The large intestine is a key to the integration of hydration or moisture the body. Whereas the lungs take in the air, the large intestine removes moisture in the body. The matter that enters into the large intestine is dehydrated. The Large Intestine Meridian Sound Essence facilitates ease of transition on all levels; physical, emotional, mental, and spiritual.

Affirmations
1. I joyfully release the past to allow for change.
2. I have a strong, healthy colon.
3. It is easy for me to eliminate waste.
4. I am free to learn.
5. I move with ease and grace.
6. It is easy for me to express myself.
7. My relationships are open and free.
8. I am free.
9. I have peace.
10. I have wealth.

Water Couple

Fear/Anxiety

I love to be alive and in charge of my own destiny.

Overview

Within the Five Element System, winter is related to the element Water. There has been the same amount of water on the planet since its beginning. Energy cannot be created or destroyed; only transformed. Water is in the air, on and within the earth, and constitutes a major part of all living matter. Water has the ability to be everywhere but nowhere. Water is the deep and hidden aspect within all living things. Water is the essential medium of the body, through which all things pass. This fluid is important for functions such as the circulation of blood which carries heat and nourishment throughout the body; the lymphatic flow, which helps to process and eliminate wastes and provides your ability to fight off infections and other foreign agents; and for the flow of urine, saliva, perspiration, tears and sexual fluids.

Water can be warm and loving or it can be cold and frightening. It is nourishing, refreshing, and invigorating. Both the human body and the planet earth are approximately 80% water and the properties of sea water to human plasma are almost identical. Water is the circulatory system of the earth. Clouds, mountain snow, lakes, rivers, streams and the oceans are all part of this water circulation. Water refers to the deepest aspects of growth that takes place in the recesses of the earth.

Winter is the season in which the water element is most dominant. The bladder and kidneys, which deal with the body's water, are the organs associated with this element. Winter's power is deep and cold. The kidneys are nourished by cold climate; however extreme coldness or wetness can injure them. Keep yourself warm and dry, particularly in winter, as cold, wet days can bring out a deep stiffness or pain, especially in the back.

Associated Meridians

KIDNEY AND BLADDER

Physical Component
Kidney and bladder functions

Emotional Component
Fear

Metaphysical Component
Overcoming fear and anger

Chapter 7

Colour	Blue
Season	Winter
Sound	Groaning/Moaning
Note	'A'
Taste	Salty
Odor	Putrid
Conditions	Cold
Consciousness	Willpower; will to live; survival; procreation
Activity	Yin – Passive reproduction; sensuality
	Yang – Active reproduction; sexuality
Sense	Hearing
Action	Listening
Tissues	Bones/Teeth
Fluid	Urine

Physical	Fluid, Electrolyte Balance
Emotional	Timidity
Mental	Covertness
Spiritual	Trust

The taste associated with the Water element is salty. The majority of water on the planet is salty. Even our body's fluid contains many mineral salts. Craving or disliking salt may indicate a water imbalance. Eating too much salt creates a craving for water and may injure the kidneys.

The emotional imbalance associated with the water energy is fear and the sound associated with this element is groaning. Fear can be either a cause or a consequence of a water imbalance. An illness affecting the bladder or kidneys may generate a fearful feeling; and fear can itself injure these organs, according to the Five Element System. The ears are the sense organ associated with the Water element. Its sense is hearing. Water is the receptive element, which listens to sound and is open to energy input.

It is said that the kidneys govern the storage of the life force in the bones and marrow. People with bone problems may have a Water element imbalance, while a healthy Water element keeps the bones healthy and strong.

Meridian & Five Elements
Water Couple

Kidney Meridian (5 p.m. to 7 p.m.)

Place your fingers under the ball of each foot and bring your fingers up to the inside of each foot, circle behind the inside of each ankle bone, and go straight up the front of the body onto the chest to the K27 points; beneath the clavicle at the top of the sternum. Do both sides.

The Kidneys

The kidneys are two bean-shaped organs that lie just below the diaphragm and posterior abdominal wall on either side of the lumbar region of the spine.

In Traditional Chinese Medicine, the kidneys are said to store *chi*. The kidneys are responsible for the life force and vitality of the entire body. They need to be healthy to produce reproductive energy and contribute to the nurturing of the fetus. The kidneys regulate the body's water balance and temperature. All of the body's life regulating processes is related to the kidneys. A general lack of energy in the body often indicates a Kidney Meridian imbalance.

The Kidney Meridian rules the Water element, which means all the fluids of the body including perspiration, skin moisture, and urine. The kidneys filter the water from the digestive process and send the purified water to the lungs and the wastewater to the bladder.

The Kidney Meridian also rules marrow, which in turn rules the bones. It has been noticed that stiffness of the lower spine, weak legs and knees, and soft, brittle bones are related to the Kidney Meridian. The Kidney Meridian also seems to control the health of teeth, hair and ears.

According to the Five Element Theory, the kidneys and the adrenals are connected.

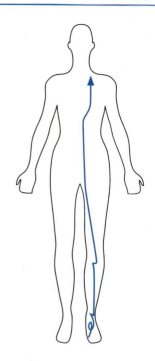

Kidney Meridian Issues

Physically
Formation of urine
Hormones
Stiff joints
Brain
Reproduction, growth and development
Physical energy, stamina
Edema

Mentally
Alertness
Ability to perceive
Critical

Emotionally
Fear
Phobias
Secretiveness

Spiritually
Gravitates towards symbols
Worshipping hidden (unseen) gods
Will to persevere on chosen path

Chapter 7

HERBS
Cleavers
Cornsilk
Juniper Berries
Marshmallow
Parsley
Pippsisewa
Uva-Ursi

BACH FLOWER ESSENCES
Aspen
Elm
Hornbeam
Mimulus
Oak
Olive
Pine
Red Chestnut
Rock Rose

PACIFIC ESSENCES
Bluebell
Blue Camas
Candystick
Coral
Death Camas
Douglas Aster
Easter Lily
Fuchsia
Hooker's Onion
Nootka Rose
Ox-Eye Daisy
Pipsissewa
Snowberry
Snowdrop
Surfgrass

FUNCTIONS
Filter blood.
Produce and excrete urine to the bladder.
Regulate the water, electrolyte and acid-base balance.
Stimulate the production of the red blood cells.
Regulate composition and pH-value of tissue fluid.
Produce enzyme rennin which controls blood pressure.

SOUND
The vibratory tone for the Kidney meridian regulates the inner breath of the body. The tone regulates the internal rhythm, the opening and closing of the physical, emotional, or spiritual bodies. Regulated kidney function is like the ebb and flow of tides. Imbalance either dams the waters or creates a flood, freezing in fear or running in hysteria.

HERBS

Black Cohosh – *Cimicifuga Racemosa*
Black Cohosh's keyword is rejuvenation, especially after trauma. It gives one backbone, strength and ability to persevere. It must be used sparingly as too much may induce inflexibility.

Gravel Root – *Eupatorium Purpureum*
Gravel Root's keyword is patience and is wonderful for those who seek wisdom and patience. It gives mental clarity and patience to communicate precisely.

Juniper Berries – *Juniperis species*
Juniper Berries' key words are: trust, stalwart, and dependable. It transmits surety and helps one to rebuild trust in the face of fear.

Uva–Ursi Bearberry – *Arctostaphylos uva ursi*
Uva-ursi's keyword is empowerment. Uva-ursi gives one the power to walk into life and into the wisdom of self-discovery. It supports those that are ready to em-

brace their power, to fully express themselves and live up to their true potential. It helps to integrate the fruits of life's experience and gives certainty to the direction and action to be taken.

Kidney Meridian Sound Essence
Kidney – Patience and Trust

The Kidney Meridian Sound Essence facilitates the process of transforming reflexive instinct into conscious thought where choice becomes a possibility. The Kidney Meridian Sound Essence is a filter and purifier for our emotions and this facilitates clarification on all levels. It supports us in our reactions to circumstances through conscious choice rather than through the fight-and-flight instinct.

Affirmations

1. I enjoy being alive.
2. I have strong healthy kidneys.
3. My body fluids and minerals are regulated optimally.
4. It is easy for me to consume the adequate amount of water each day.
5. Challenges motivate me.
6. It is easy to take risks.
7. I learn from my mistakes.
8. What I start is always finished.
9. I am loved and accepted to all those that are important to me.
10. I relish in life's blessings.
11. I allow myself to receive

Chapter 7

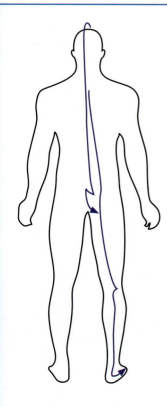

Bladder Meridian Issues

Physically
Urination
The back, spinal column and neck
Bones and teeth
Vision and hearing
Occipital headaches
Leg and knee pain

Mentally
Lack of fluidity
Hindsight
Living in the past

Emotionally
Jealousy
Holding on to grudges
Phobias

Spiritually
Aspiration to lofty heights
Will
Resoluteness

Bladder Meridian (3 p.m. to 5 p.m.)

Place both hands between your eyebrows; go up over the head and down the back of your head and neck. Remove your hands from your neck; reach them back underneath and as high as you can stretch onto your spine. Trace your hands down either side of your spine to below your waist, jog in and up toward the waist, and then in and around the curve of your bottom. Then start again on either side at the top of your spine farther out from the first tracing and go straight down to the back of your knees, in at the knees down to the floor, and off your little toes.

The Bladder

The bladder is a muscular, membranous, distensible reservoir for the urine that is produced by the kidneys.

The Bladder Meridian is the longest and most yang of all the meridians. The function of the bladder is to store and eliminate fluid waste from the body. It is responsible for fluid balance and body energy. It is closely related to the kidney. In Traditional Chinese Medicine it has been taught that if you keep the Bladder Meridian in harmony, you keep the whole body harmonized. Adaptability and flexibility are associated with the Bladder Meridian. Bladder disharmonies can manifest as fever, painful and frequent urination, thirst, dry mouth, lower back pain, or bed-wetting.

Functions

Storage of urine

Sound

Stimulating the Bladder Meridian with sound activates all points and meridians. It is the universal connector and integrator. In the same way that Central and Governing Meridian stimulates the vertical or divine plane, the bladder meridian activates the horizontal or material plane. This is the best systemic tonic. If a practitioner has only one Sound Essence or tone, use the Water Sound Essence.

Meridian & Five elements
Water Couple

Herbs
Parsley – *Petroselinum sativum*
Parsley's keyword is circumspect. It is useful for those who are overly enthusiastic and can get carried away. It will help these people to gather in their energy and become more circumspect and contemplative. Parsley's attitude is like a shy smile under a big hat.

Bladder Meridian
Sound Essence – Circumspect
The Bladder Meridian has to do with the issues of control and release. Control and release of emotions in the Kidney and the Bladder Meridians are similar in that they are products of civilization. Working with releasing emotions in these two meridians can be very helpful when working with animals or severely handicapped people. The Bladder Meridian Sound Essence will not bring consciousness or awareness, but will facilitate release of negative emotions, which opens space for consciousness or enlightenment.

Affirmations
1. I am in full charge of my life.
2. I have a strong, healthy bladder.
3. I have full control over my elimination.
4. I am in charge of my emotions.
5. I encourage others.
6. I am free to be me.
7. I am worthy of respect.
8. I respect others.
9. I have patience.
10. I make wise investments.

Bladder Meridian Issues
Herbs
Buchu
Cornsilk
Dandelion
Parsley
Plantain
Uva-Ursi

Bach Flower Essences
Aspen
Centaury
Cerato
Larch
Limulus
Olive
Rock Rose

Pacific Essences
Blue Camas
Brown Kelp
Candystick
Easter Lily
Fuchsia
Hooker's Onion
Nootka Rose
Salmonberry
Snowberry
Snowdrop
Sponge
Yellow Pond Lily

Wood Couple
Anger/Rage

The choices I make support growth and beneficial change to me and the universe.

Overview

Wood in the Five Element Theory is associated with spring; a time of new beginnings. Spring is the time of the year that we prepare for a new year of growth. The Wood element represents growth of nature such as roots, limbs and leaves of trees, and plants. The Wood element also represents the growing structures of our body such as the spine, limbs and joints.

Wood is associated with the colour green, which is also the predominant colour of spring. Green as a facial hue particularly around the eyes and on top of the cheeks indicates a wood imbalance in the body. Emotions such as anger, rage and wrath can put emotional strain on the liver. Suppressed anger may also injure the liver and gall bladder since any suppressed emotions can breed disease. The meridians associated with the Wood element are the liver and the gall bladder and the sound associated with this element is shouting, which is a most appropriate emotional expression for anger. However, one does not need to be angry to shout. If we listen to Mediterranean cultures talk, it is easy to witness passionate communication by means of shouting. It is important for us to express all the sounds of the five elements, which are: shouting, singing, crying, laughing and groaning.

The sense organs for the Wood element are the eyes. Sight is the sense and tears are the fluid. The eyes are connected with the liver; therefore vision can be strengthened by supporting the meridians of the Wood element.

Tissues of the Wood element are the muscles, ligaments and tendons; the parts that hold us together and that give us strength and flexibility. Muscle fatigue and

Associated Meridians
LIVER AND GALL BLADDER

Physical Component
Liver and Gall Bladder functions

Emotional Component
Anger

Metaphysical Component
Proper expression of willpower

Chapter 7

Colour	Green
Season	Spring
Sound	Shouting/Uttering
Note	'E'
Taste	Sour
Odor	Rancid
Conditions	Rain
Consciousness	Soul; the storage of all experiences
Activity	Yin – Planning; metabolic activity and life adaption Yang – Decisions; the catalyst for all actions
Sense	Sight
Action	Countenance
Tissues	Muscles/Tendons
Fluid	Tears

Physical	Flexible
Emotional	Volatility
Mental	Judgement
Spiritual	Purpose

weakness are two possible difficulties associated with a wood imbalance. Sour flavor is associated with the Wood element. A person who craves sour and vinegary foods indicates a Wood element imbalance.

The Wood element gives the ability or capacity for control. If a person with a Wood element imbalance is met with challenge or request for change, they may respond by trying to control either their behavior or the situation. When in harmony, the energy of the Wood element is directed and deliberate with a clear sense of vision. According to the Five Element Theory, the Wood element gives the spiritual faculty of life; the liver is the home of the soul. This element in balance gives us the inspiration and desire for life.

Liver Meridian (1 a.m. to 3 a.m.)

Place your fingers on the insides (lateral side) of your big toes, and trace straight up inside the legs, flaring out at your hips, up the sides of your rib cage, and back to underneath your ribs, in a hollow directly below but in line with your nipples.

The Liver

The liver is the largest organ in the body. It is situated on the right side beneath the diaphragm; level with the bottom of the sternum. It covers the stomach, duodenum and right kidney. It is the first organ to receive blood from the intestines where the blood has absorbed the final products of digestion. The liver is integral for proper digestion. Imbalances manifest as belching, gas, nausea and diarrhea.

The liver stores and disperses the blood evenly and smoothly throughout the body. Heavy menstrual flows often mean that the liver is not storing blood properly.

The Liver Meridian is responsible for the functions of the tendons, nails and ligaments; so if there are brittle nails or weak tendons or cracking of joints, support the liver to transport the blood to these areas. According to the Five Element Theory, the strength of the eyes are related to the Liver Meridian.

The liver is a detoxifier for the mind and body and provides clarity and order to the other meridians. If the Liver Meridian is strong and healthy, there will be a feeling of good spirits and well-being. Frustration, because of a lack of planning or follow through is a possible reflection of liver imbalance. The liver is said to house the "soul" therefore it is important to keep the Liver Meridian balanced when aspiring to deep levels of consciousness.

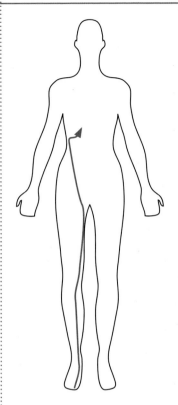

Liver Meridian Issues

Physically
Muscles and tendons
One-sided headaches
Eye Problems
Paralysis

Mentally
Inability to make decisions
Vacillation

Emotionally
Judgemental
Resentment
Bitterness
Opinionated
Controlled

Spiritually
Seeks life purpose
Utilitarian

Liver Meridian Issues

Herbs
Burdock
Calendula
Dandelion
Goldenseal
Milk Thistle
Oregon Grape
Red Clover
Stinging Nettle
Wood Betany
Yellow Dock

Bach Flower Essences
Agrimony
Impatience
Mustard
Pine
Rock Rose
Vervain
Walnut
Water Violet
Wild Oat
Wild Rose

Pacific Essences
Anemone
Arbutus
Blue Lupin
Chiton
Hooker's Onion
Nootka Rose
Pearly Everlasting
Plantain
Pipsissewa
Twin Flower
Weigela

Functions
Detoxification.
Stores vitamins A, B12, D, E and K.
Plays role in regulation of blood volume.
One of the main sources of body heat.
Manufactures cholesterol.
Controls the flow of bile.

Sound
Activating the Liver Meridian instills a sense of control on all levels. This tone is useful for those who are swinging between the poles of fear and anger and require stability. It is particularly useful for males in crisis.

Herbs

Catnip – *Nepetac cataria*
Catnip is a cosmic joker, light-hearted and powerfully charismatic. Catnip enhances the possibilities of the moment, bringing everything into a tingly, brighter, livelier place. It is useful for both ends of the emotional spectrum, depression or hyperactivity as it brings both into an appreciative state.

Crampbark – *Viburnum opulus*
Crampbark's keyword is grounding. It is useful for vitalizing the root and sacral chakra energy, and is particularly useful in reconnecting any kind of birth or creative issue. When there has been trauma that disconnects one from the physical, Crampbark helps to ground us and keep us firmly rooted.

Fennel – *Foeniculum valgare*
Fennel is a clarifier of thought. It can be useful if one is feeling foggy or confused. It calms the tendency towards tangential thinking for those who are mentally disturbed. Fennel is wonderful if your nerves have been frayed or frazzled. It creates an emotional buffer that you can coast on.

Ginger – *Zingiber officinale*
Ginger is so many things on all levels. All the characteristics known about it on a physical level apply to it on a metaphysical level. It is like a good host that can anticipate and provide for all your needs. Ginger is like walking with your wealthy big brother who is able to help provide for you, to sustain you and protect you.

Oregon Grape – *Berberis aquifolium*
Oregon Grape's key word is communication. The root, flowers and fruit all have the capacity to give you a different perspective in stuck situations. Oregon Grape helps with the integration of new information.

Peppermint – *Mentha piperita*
Peppermint's key word is graciousness. It is the good hostess who can uplift people and soothes any tension. Peppermint is energizing but also soothing like a dip in a cool stream in the summer. It benefits anyone in need of refreshment.

Wild Yam – *Dioscorea villosa*
Wild Yam's keyword is synergy. It is also a very powerful energizer. It is useful for people in a leadership role and for people who need to keep many balls in the air.

Liver Meridian
Sound Essence - Graciousness

The Liver Meridian manages stress of all kinds. Chemical, emotional or spiritual toxins are integrated into the liver. Change on any level including shifting our consciousness can cause stress in the body. The Liver Meridian Sound Essence protects the liver by acting as a cushion in defense of any internal or external changes.

Affirmations

1. I welcome change into my life.
2. I have a strong healthy liver.
3. My body eliminates toxins effectively.
4. It is easy for me to express my emotions appropriately.
5. I adapt to change easily.
6. I have flexibility.
7. I easily integrate new ideas.
8. I have relationships that beneficially blossom.
9. I have good discernment.
10. I attract good fortune into my life.

Gall Bladder Meridian
(11 p.m. to 1 a.m.)

Place the fingers of both hands on the outside of your eyebrows, drop to the opening of your ears, take your fingers straight up about two inches, circle forward with your fingers, and drop back behind the ears. Go forward again over to your forehead, back over the top of your head, and around your shoulders. Leave your shoulders, take your hands to the sides of your rib cage, go forward on the rib cage, half circle backwards on the waist, forward on the hips, straight down the sides of the leg and off the outside of the little toe.

The Gall Bladder

The gall bladder is a pear-shaped sac on the undersurface of the right lobe of the liver.

The gall bladder stores bile from the liver and sends it to the intestines when needed for digestion. As the gall bladder and the liver are closely related, it is impossible to influence one without the other. The Gall Bladder Meridian is the second largest meridian of the body and extends from head to toe. Imbalances of the gall bladder are extensive, ranging from headaches to gout. The condition of the Gall Bladder Meridian has a direct correlation with decision making. Imbalances with the gall bladder manifest as a painful chest, a bitter taste in the mouth, sometimes gall stones, constipation, vertigo, unclear thinking and problems with vision.

Functions

Storage site for bile.
Acts to concentrate the bile by removing water content.

Sound

Gall bladder stimulation with sound is a system stabilizer. It is particularly useful when the body is challenged by viral or bacterial infections. It is also valuable for any kind of skin disorder that involves eruptive conditions

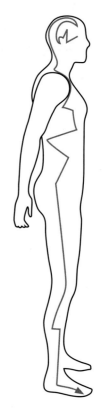

Gall Bladder Meridian Issues

Physically
Muscles and tendons
One-sided headaches
Eye Problems
Paralysis

Mentally
Inability to make decisions
Vacillation

Emotionally
Judgmental
Resentment
Bitterness
Opinionated
Controlled

Spiritually
Seeks life purpose
Utilitarian

GALL BLADDER MERIDIAN ISSUES

HERBS
Blessed Thistle
Cascara Sagrada
Dandelion
St John's Wort

BACH FLOWER ESSENCES
Centaury
Impatience
Rock Rose
Scleranthus
Walnut
Water Violet

PACIFIC ESSENCES
Chickweed
Forsythia
Hooker's Onion
Mussel
Nootka Rose
Pearly Everlasting
Plantain
Poison Hemlock
Red Huckleberry
Staghorn Algae
Twin Flower
Weigela

such as blisters or cold sores. It also activates lymphatic drainage.

HERBS
Oregon Grape - *Berberis aquifolium*
Oregon Grape's key word is communication. The root, flowers and fruit all have the capacity to give you a different perspective in stuck situations. Oregon Grape helps with the integration of new information.

GALL BLADDER MERIDIAN SOUND ESSENCE - Communication
The Gall Bladder Meridian has to do with support; the ability to provide what is appropriate when necessary. An imbalance in the Gall Bladder Meridian is a sense of being out of step or out of time. No other systems can function optimally without the appropriate support of the Gall Bladder. It has the ability to provide what is necessary when needed. The Gall Bladder Sound Essence is the support for the entire system.

AFFIRMATIONS
1. I make choices that are beneficial to me and the universe.
2. I have a strong healthy gall bladder.
3. I make smart decisions.
4. I make healthy choices.
5. I choose to work on personal growth.
6. I attract positive experiences.
7. I attract positive people.
8. I choose relationships that support me in my growth.
9. I choose the truth.
10. My finances are stable.

Chapter 8

Chakras
Exploring Vibrational Healing Through our Seven Senses

Introduction

If a picture is worth a thousand words then a symbol must be worth a million words. The symbols of the chakras when we listen with our eyes gives us a profound understanding of their value and how they are important in keeping our bodies balanced and healthy. A symbol is able to expand our mind and let ideas incarnate into newly formed patterns. A symbol can feel and mean the same thing to people of different cultures and through the ages of generational change. Symbols hold their knowledge through the test of time.

The chakras are symbolic representations of the many faucets of our being. The chakras are allocated to colours, notes, geometric shapes (yantras), sounds (mantras), elements, animal symbols, Sanskrit letters and nature purposes. Each chakra is represented with a different number of petals, which are thought to represent the vibrational expression of each chakra. The chakra symbols are succinct in expressing the essential qualities of each chakra.

Each chakra is commonly assigned a specific colour similar to the rainbow colours, red, orange, yellow, green, blue, indigo and violet. The colours represent the relative vibration of the chakras, moving from the slowest vibration at the root chakra to the most rapid vibration at the crown chakra. The colours themselves offer symbolic colour in our life such as red is strong and forceful, orange is less aggressive but nevertheless fiery. Yellow is solar and warming, green is cool and promotes natural growth, blue is the colour of healing, indigo is expansive, violet is associated with spiritual aspiration. The same holds true for the harmonic scale representation of the chakras. Note C relating to the colour red and the root chakra is the longest wavelength vibration and the note B relating to the colour violet and the crown chakra is the shortest wavelength. Sound and colour are very close in vibration and can offer the body similar healing affects. The yantras or geometric shapes inside of the chakra symbol also offer the body healing information.

Each chakra is also assigned to an element. This links the qualities of the chakra to the qualities represented by the elements. The elements are an ancient holographic representation of the universe.

The yantra of the base chakra signifies elemental earth. The crescent moon, the yantra of the sacral chakra signifies elemental water. The triangle of the solar plexus chakra signifies elemental fire. The hexagon of the heart chakra or the Star of David signifies the element of air and bridges the elemental chakras and the spiritual chakras. The throat has a circular yantra related to the element ether, which I would like to believe relates to sound, the brow does not have a yantra but relates to colour and light and the crown chakra is not traditionally described in terms of colour or yantras but relates to thought.

The element earth related to the base chakra does not exactly refer to mother earth. It refers to the qualities of a person, which may be considered earthy such as someone with the attributes of practicality, survival, organization and structure. The Earth is slow to change and it needs to be manipulated. The element Water related to the sacral chakra refers to the qualities of a person, which may be considered fluid in nature such as someone with the characteristics of reflection, movement, flow and depth. Water is shapeless yet dynamic. There is a close connection between all water and the influence of the moon. The element Fire relates to the solar plexus chakra and refers to the qualities of a person considered to be fiery in nature with the characteristics of action, change, expansion and passion. Fire is difficult to confine because it is expansive and volatile. Fire has the power to shift energy from one state to another.

The element Air relates to the heart chakra and refers to the qualities of a person considered to be airy such as pervasion, omnipresence, and invisibility. Air cannot be seen, we cannot touch air yet it touches us, similar to love we cannot touch love but love touches us. Air is always moving, it is unlimited and shared by everyone. Spirit or Ether is represented by the throat chakra. This chakra refers to the qualities that help to manifest thoughts into action. It represents negative time and space. It represents mystery.

The brow chakra has representation in the light element referring to the inner light of the third eye.

The crown chakra has representation through thought, as it is our connection to our higher source.

Chakras are energy centres that are located slightly off of the physical body and have been described as spinning wheels of colour. The chakras connect our auric field which consists of the light bodies with the meridians. The auric field expresses, receives and assimilates life-force energy and transmits this energy to the chakras, which filter the information and direct it to the meridians, which connect to the organs and glands.

Life-force energy continually flows up and down our body. Every chakra centre processes this life-force energy differently, depending on the emotional theme of the filtering process. The chakras process daily events of our life. For example if the life-force energy flows through us and is processed through a chakra in love and trust, the colour of the chakra will be pure and bright and we feel fabulous and empowered. Now if the life-force energy is filtered through a chakra in fear and doubt, then the colour of that chakra will be dull and muddy and we will feel lousy and hurt.

The light bodies of the auric field directly influence how each chakra processes our life-energy and reacts to each experience. Our light bodies influence the life-force energy flowing through us and this expression is in the functioning of our chakras. Therefore, a change in thought or vibration can instantly shift the expression of the chakra. Each chakra has a specific tone, colour, frequency and function. When the chakras are functioning normally, they will be open, spinning appropriately and the colour will be pure and clear. When chakras become blocked, the life-force energy becomes blocked leading to pain and discomfort and eventually disease.

It is through the symbology of the chakras that we get the clue that these energy centres need to be maintained and revitalized by way of vibration. These revitalizing vibrations come from sound, colour and thought and more such as sacred geometry, crystals and gems, aromatherapy, homeopathy, flower, tree, sea and gem essences, herbs and food.

The Chakra Sound Essences embrace the seven aspects of healing vibrations, which are found in: Sound, Colour, Crystals and Gems, Positive Word Affirmations, Sacred Geometry, Symbols and Aroma. These seven aspects of healing vibrations interact with the physical and energetic body to produce full spectrum vibrational healing for chakra balancing. Aware or unaware, visible or invisible, these vibrational remedies impact us powerfully. This is because in these seven aspects are found the true essence of our being.

This chapter offers the reader exploration into the many aspects of the chakras and the ability to gather insight on balancing their body. Each Chakra is related to a special sense and this is highlighted throughout the chapter. The entire magic of balancing the chakras is vibrationally supporting the seven senses related to the seven chakras.

Root Chakra	Smell	Aromatherapy
Sacral Chakra	Taste	Food, Herbs, Homeopathy, Flower, Sea, Gem and Sound Essences
Solar Plexus Chakra	Sight	Symbology and Sacred Geometry
Heart Chakra	Feel	Healing Touch and Crystals and Gems
Throat Chakra	Sound	Music and Yantras
Brow Chakra	Light and Colour	Colour Therapy
Crown Chakra	Thought	Prayer, Mantras and Positive Word Affirmations

By using the various therapies that support the senses related to the charkas enables the filters of charkas to be healthy and pure which promotes feeling fabulous and empowered.

Root Chakra

Vitality/Courage/Self-Confidence

*I am rooted in life and in myself.
I am safe, stable, and secure.*

ALL IS ONE

The Root Chakra is at the base of the spine and spins over the pelvis and sexual organs. It offers its support by carrying the life force up our body and down our legs. This chakra is a channel for bringing in the energies from the earth. It is literally our grounding force keeping us connected to mother earth. It has been said that to dance from your root chakra is to dance with the earth.

The Root Chakra is our foundation. It gives us our drive for the basics of life like food, shelter and the need to be part of a group or tribe. Tribe is used to describe our family and neighbors no matter what culture we live. Each tribe has its own belief systems that it imparts unto its members; be it cultural beliefs or expectations, religious beliefs and strategies, or superstitions. These belief systems are deeply ingrained into us and reside in the Root Chakra. Sometimes these beliefs serve us and at other times they hinder us in our growth. It is when there is confusion that imbalances occur in the Root Chakra.

The Root Chakra is linked to the basic of survival responses that come from fear of personal injury or tribal threat. This connection of the Root Chakra to survival and the fight or flight response is the reason that the adrenal glands are directly related to this energy center.

The Root Chakra also serves as the foundation for all the higher chakras as it is the source of the life force.

The Root Chakra speaks to us about honor, loyalty, justice, abundance and security. It keeps us linked to our primal belief systems and helps us stay connected to the "we are one" attitude that we will need to employ to keep this universe healthy.

Characteristics of a balanced Root Chakra are a strong and determined feeling that life is good. There is a belief

COLOUR
Red

COMPLIMENTARY COLOUR
Green

SOUND
Note C

SENSE
Smell

LOCATION
Base of Spine

BASIC PRINCIPLE
To be here and to have

ASSOCIATED GLANDS
Adrenals

ASSOCIATED MERIDIANS
Circulation/Sex

EMOTIONAL COMPONENT
Fear

PHYSICAL COMPONENT
Spinal column, legs, feet, bones, teeth and large intestine

that dreams will easily manifest and there is worthiness of abundance and prosperity in all areas of life. A strong Root Chakra is essential for grounding and focus. It anchors us in the flow of life and is the foundation for everything we do in our life. A strong Root Chakra gives us a positive approach and outlook on life.

Insufficient Root Chakra Energy
Feeling disconnected from the body
Financial difficulty
Fearful, anxious and restless
Poor focus and discipline
Poor boundaries
Disorganized
Lack of stamina

Excess Root Chakra Energy
Obesity and overeating
Hoarding and greed
Sluggish and lazy
Fear of change
Rigid boundaries
Addiction to security

Harmonious Function of the Root Chakra
Good health
Comfortable in the body
Well grounded
Sense of trust in the world
Vitality
Sense of safety and security
Stability
Prosperity

Physical Imbalances
Poor circulation
Varicose veins
Lazy feeling
Sore back
Dry skin and hair
Hard to move bowel
Pale blotchy skin
Belching, burping and gas
Constipated
Diarrhea
Headaches

Emotional Imbalances
Lack of commitment
Operating out of fear
Unfinished business with parents
Abuse or neglect in childhood
Not able to stand up for oneself or provide life's necessities
Need for safety or security in the world
Inability to keep a job or permanent living situation
Limiting psychological programming (i.e.; You're stupid)

ISSUES

ROOTS
Like the plants, we also need roots in the earth to grow and become nourished. Our roots represent where we come from; this includes the earth, the womb, our ancestors and tribes or cultures and our personal families. Our roots are seen as the way our system plugs into the larger system such as the planet. Getting back to our roots brings us into the collective consciousness and brings us home to earth.

GROUNDING
Grounding keeps us connected to time and space and helps us to interact with our environment. It gives us support and strength and centering. When we are grounded we are present and living life in the moment; there is a sense of support and security. We are connected to our true self and operate inside of healthy boundaries. We are true to ourselves and express ourselves appropriately allowing our own true potential to shine.

NOURISHMENT
We need nourishment in many forms. Our bodies need nourishment physically, emotionally and spiritually. Nourishment, either biochemically, emotionally or spiritually is our most basic form of support for the survival of our multi-dimensional body.

TRUST
Trust is the basic issue of the first chakra. Trust is the foundation from which security and stability arise. Where there is trust there is a sense of well-being which allows us to connect, bond, and share the world with others optimistically.

HEALTH
The Root Chakra needs to be healthy for the rest of the body to be healthy. The Root Chakra is the foundation for the entire chakra system. Fear will weaken the root chakra so it is important for us to feel safe, secure and supported to enjoy the health of our bodies and to enjoy life.

- Roots
- Grounding
- Nourishment
- Trust
- Health
- Shelter
- Family
- Prosperity
- Appropriate boundaries

Shelter

Home is the sanctuary in where we revitalize ourself with our family. This shelter should be safe and secure in order to nourish us.

Family

Our families, their past and present beliefs, have a tremendous impact on our journey. We hold these issues and belief in the Root Chakra. Detaching, freeing ourselves from the negative emotional energies and accepting the family heritage is crucial to being able to find self-acceptance and reclaim our spirit and power. Grounding our spirit also comes from focusing on the positive, life-giving and life-sustaining qualities in our family backgrounds.

Our journey to wholeness involves unplugging from the group consciousness of the family so that we are able to evolve at our own rate. This takes reclaiming or discovering the essence and strength of our spirit and our power, incorporating the positive beliefs that are helpful to us as we journey through personal growth and health.

Family is integral for survival. We need to be fed, held and cared for over many years until we are capable of sustaining ourselves. It is by being a part of the family and how the family accepts touching and holding that we determine our grounding and our boundaries. Touching and holding are important issues that give us our sense of security. This family is then part of our being and support system. As we grow older and complete our journey through personal growth and health we again need the family for caretaking and survival. The tribe is an important foundation of our well-being.

Prosperity

The Root Chakra is associated with scarcity or abundance beliefs and issues. Were beliefs of scarcity developed by you because you were refused certain things you desired and lack of money was given as the reason? Were you told to be grateful for what you had because you had more than the starving children in the world? Perhaps you developed a belief that you did not deserve to ask for what you wanted.

We initially need to meet the basic needs of survival and nourishment and self-preservation. Once we have achieved security and stability we then have the freedom to expand beyond survival consciousness and into prosperity consciousness. Prosperity gives us our independence enabling us to support ourselves independently of the tribe or family. We need this independence to determine our future.

Appropriate Boundaries

Boundaries are necessary to keep us grounded so as not to lose our attention on matters and to stay present in the moment.

CHAPTER 8

COLOUR

Red

- The colour red warms and revitalizes and awakens the Life Force, vitality and courage.
- Red is the most passionate of all colours because of its primitive association with blood and fire.
- Red is the longest wave length and has the lowest rate of vibration of the visible spectrum.

PHYSICALLY

- Red delivers the energy, which is needed for building and strengthening the body. It stimulates vitality and energy throughout the body. Red supports the adrenal system and the circulation of blood and helps in the manufacture of hemoglobin for new red blood cells.
- Red raises blood pressure and promotes heat in the body.
- Red stimulates the nervous system and excites the cerebrospinal nerves and the sympathetic nervous system, which is why it helps various forms of numbness and paralysis. Red stimulates the sensory nerves therefore it benefits deficiencies of smell, sight, hearing, taste and touch.
- Red energizes muscles and aids mobility in joints and positively affects impotence and frigidity.

EMOTIONALLY

- Motivation, stimulation, activity and will are keywords for red.
- Red is synonymous with passion and physical love. Red brings new life and new beginnings. Red is associated with warmth and excitement, with initiative and willingness to act and with the pioneering spirit that lifts us up. Persistence, physical strength, drive and power are typical red traits.
- Friendliness and forgiveness are beautiful qualities of this colour as are prosperity and gratitude.

SPIRITUALLY

- Red in its highest expression helps us to reach our fullest potential.

FOOD
Beets
Cherries
Eggplant
Meat
Radishes
Red Cabbage
Red Onions
Red Peppers
Salmon
Spinach
Strawberries
Watercress
Watermelon
Yams

HERBS
Buchu
Cayenne
Dulse
Licorice
Marshmallow
Meadowsweet
Mugwort
Sarsaparilla
Strawberry
Valerian

SOUND

Note 'C'

PHYSICAL ASPECTS
Note C is located at the area of the coccyx at the base of the spine. It is tied to the functions of the circulatory system, the reproductive system, the functions of the lower extremities and pelvic floor muscles. It is our basic life-force center. It influences the activities of the testicles and ovaries, the legs and feet and the pelvic area of the body.

EMOTIONAL ASPECTS
The balancing of the Root Chakra with the note C brings about a release of fear and anxiety resulting from disconnection with one's center of gravity and the disconnection of self with others. The note C supports the body in all survival issues and in being able to relate to others. With the aid of this essence, people will feel their common humanity and this note is particularly valuable for those people who are experiencing the effects of depression if the source of depression comes from being disconnected. This note allows people to get into their own feeling center and promotes their ability to have a common feeling with others.

SPIRITUAL ASPECTS
This is our center for life-promoting energy. Spirit flows similarly to an electrical current and for spirit to function in this world it must be grounded. The note C is an important tool for grounding. There is no such thing as being a spiritual person if one has no grounding. It is the seat of the kundalini within the body.

BACH FLOWER ESSENCES
Agrimony
Aspen
Centaury
Cherry Plum
Chestnut Bud
Clematis
Crabapple
Elm
Gentian
Gorse
Honeysuckle
Mimulus
Olive
Rock Rose
Star of Bethlehem
Wild Rose

PACIFIC ESSENCES
Blue Lupin
Brown Kelp
Chickweed
Hooker's Onion
Indian Pipe
Narcissus
Nootka Rose
Polyanthus
Seahorse
Snowdrop
"Staghorn" Algae
Twin Flower

Essential Oils
Benzoin
Black Pepper
Cinnamon Leaf
Clove Bud
Juniper Berry
Myrrh
Sandalwood
Spikenard
Spruce, Black
Vanilla
Vetivert
Ylang Ylang

PLANT FORM – ESSENTIAL OILS

Vetivert

Vetivert is a deep smoky earthy-woody smelling oil made from the roots of this grass. Being a root-oil, Vetivert is very grounding to the body, mind and spirit. The name Vetivert means "oil of tranquility."

Physically
- The oil has been used by the Ayurvedics for heat stroke, fevers and headaches. Vetivert is used to strengthen the red blood cells and promotes oxygen throughout the body. Vetivert has been used to alleviate symptoms of rheumatism, arthritis, and muscular aches such as muscle pains, sprains and joint and muscle stiffness. In the reproductive system it is used to promote fertilization of the female egg.

Mentally
- Valued mostly for its sedative qualities, Vetivert helps with extreme nervousness and helps the mind to cope with stress. Vetivert helps the mind stay connected with the body and emotions. It helps with postpartum depression.

Emotionally
- Vetivert is well known for its strengthening, grounding, regenerating and aphrodisiac properties.

Spiritually
- Vetivert helps to keep the body grounded during meditation.

Ylang Ylang

Ylang Ylang is wonderfully exotic, an intensely sweet and enticing flowery fragrance derived from the blossoms of the Ylang Ylang tree. In fact in Malayan, Ylang Ylang means the flower of flowers. It has been told that in Indonesia people would spread these delicate and sweet smelling flower petals on the bed of a newly married couple.

PHYSICALLY
- Ylang Ylang helps to balance blood pressure and breathing. It relaxes muscles and relieves heart palpitations and hyperventilation. It is noted for helping with premenstrual tension and depression

MENTALLY
- Ylang Ylang has been known to aid in stress reduction. Known for its unique calming abilities, it is especially useful when there is nervous tension, restlessness, irritability, anxiety, fear, or anger. As an essential oil it has been considered an aphrodisiac and aids in the treatment of frigidity and impotence.

EMOTIONALLY
- Ylang Ylang is often considered to have antidepressant qualities. It helps one to reach out to others and share without losing one's own personal power. Ylang Ylang helps to develop self love and be in touch with one's body.

SPIRITUALLY
- Ylang Ylang has warm and intoxicating effects useful for strengthening the inner being.

GEMSTONES
Bloodstone

Garnet

Hematite

Red Agate

Red Jasper

Red Tiger's Eye

Ruby

Opal

Topaz

MINERAL FORM – CRYSTALS AND GEMSTONES

Red Jasper

Jasper is known as the supreme nurturer. Jasper grounds energy, aligns chakras and is considered the "Stone of Health". As red jasper is the stone associated with the Root Chakra it acts as a grounding stone and aids in the acceptance of physical reality and encourages and sustains vitality.

PHYSICALLY

- Jasper in relation to the Root Chakra stimulates energy and circulation. It helps imbalances related to the sexual organs, digestive and intestinal problems. Jasper strengthens the immune system and is said to have a detoxifying and anti-inflammatory effect.

MENTALLY

- Jasper aids in quick thinking and organizational abilities. It encourages forthrightness and honesty and the ability to see projects through to completion and also the ability to take on unpleasant tasks. Jasper encourages the imagination and assists in transforming ideas into actions.

EMOTIONALLY

- Jasper allows the ability for self protection. It promotes will power and endurance, and gives us the courage to stand tall and ready for conflict.

SPIRITUALLY

- Red Jasper is the most dynamic for stimulating determination in regards to personal achievement. Jasper offers tranquility, wholeness, protection, and grounding.

Rose Quartz

Rose quartz contributes love to all the essences and holds the vibration of all the information components. Rose quartz has a soft and silky vibration, bringing a wonderful, powerful loving energy. Rose quartz bestows a calming, cooling energy, which supports all of the chakras to remove negativity and to reinstate the loving gentle forces of self-love. It brings us patience and the knowing there is no need for haste, bringing calmness and clarity to the emotions and restoring harmony to the mind. It has been known as the "stone of gentle love".

PHYSICALLY
- Rose quartz stimulates blood circulation in the tissues. This stone fortifies the heart and sexual organs, helps with sexual problems and encourages fertility.

MENTALLY
- Rose quartz is used to help us make decisions and frees us from worry.

EMOTIONALLY
- Rose quartz helps us with empathy, and sensitivity. It encourages self-love, a strong heart, romance and the ability to love.

SPIRITUALLY
- Rose quartz supports all the chakras and holds the vibration it is given.

AFFIRMATIONS

1. I love my body and trust in its wisdom.
2. I nurture my body each and every day.
3. I take full responsibility for my life.
4. I have respect for all living things.
5. I have a feeling of belonging.
6. I have abundance and prosperity in all areas of my life.
7. I deserve the best that life has to offer.
8. My needs are always met.
9. I am safe and secure at all times.
10. Life is good.
11. I have a strong foundation in my life.
12. The earth supports me and meets my needs.
13. I am responsible for the quality of my life.
14. It is safe for me to enjoy my life now.
15. I have a right to express myself and manifest my dreams.
16. I have a code of honor.
17. I have integrity.
18. I have healthy human relationships.
19. I have roots.
20. I have the support I need.
21. I have a sense of community.
22. I have stability.
23. I have two feet firmly planted on the ground.
24. I have a feeling of belonging.
25. I have nourishment and shelter.
26. I say "yes" to life.

Aromatherapy

Aromatherapy is the art of using pure essential oils to affect the health of the body. Essential oils are remarkable substances which, positively affect every level of our being. Aromatherapy supports our bodies physically, emotionally, mentally and spiritually. They are truly considered a holistic therapy affecting us on all levels.

Essential oils are the life force of the plant. The plant's most potent energy is in its essential oil stored in tiny pockets of the leaf, bark, flower, or root. The plant uses its essential oil in times of crisis, drought, cold or disease, or any hardship.

Every plant has its own signature, its own identity, its own unique quality and its personalized gift of aroma. The gift is in its message as every plant has its own message. For example lavender says "relax a bit", jasmine whispers "be good to yourself", eucalyptus would say "go ahead and breath a little deeper".

Aromatherapy is a universal therapy meaning we collect these flower energies from all over the world. For example, France offers us lavender, England brings us peppermint and thyme, North America is known for its supply of orange and lemon fragrance, Canada is known for its pine and cedarwood, and sandalwood comes from India.

Every plant is connected to the energy of the country in which it is harvested, because of soil conditions, atmospheric conditions, and moisture zones. Every plant carries the energy of the people in the country from which it has been harvested. So as we collect aromatherapies from all over the world we are effectually connecting to the universal group consciousness.

As humans in this world, even though we live in urban centers and cities there is still a primitive need to relate to nature. Even without our knowing, we innately carry an internal connection to the earth regardless of environmental conditions and technology. Because we are sitting in office and moving in automobiles from garage to garage, without stepping outside, as a human race we are becoming less connected to the environment. Our primitive bodies need to stay connected to the earth from which we gather our nurturing energy. Bringing aromatherapy into our lives helps us to restore that innate drive to connect with nature.

Scent is another form of communication. Think about salmon returning to their spawning ground by way of the imprint of the smell of the river. Smell will draw the salmon to their roots even if the river is polluted. Scent is picked up by a special part of the brain. It is considered one of the most primitive parts of the brain. It is believed that the "scent brain" works on a lock and key type receptor. Every smell that is recorded in our brain has a special function. Smell has an incredible ability to link us to past experiences. Smell has the longest recall of all of the senses. Years can pass and a scent can, in an instant, bring us back to a time we may have had completely forgotten.

Physically

Essential oils not only have a special effect on the mind, and the central nervous system relating to emotions, they also react with the body on a purely physical level. When applied directly on the body, they are in contact with one of the largest organs, the skin. The oils penetrate the skin and are distributed to every cell in the body within minutes, thus affecting the organs and glands of our bodies. The external application of essential oils supports our bodies and challenges our physical imbalances. The healing attributes of an essential oil go directly to the place in the body where it is most needed. At this physical level, essential oils work with the biochemistry of the body.

Mentally

Essential oils affect the brain in two ways; one is through direct absorption and the other way is through the olfactory system, which is your sense of smell that starts with your nose and ends inside of the brain at the limbic system. Smell is the only sensory system to transport into the limbic system, which makes it our most primitive sense. This primitive sense is expressed in the Root Chakra.

The limbic system is the most primal of brain function and is in charge of processing memory, emotions, sexual drive and hunger. It controls the hormones and regulates bodily rhythms; such as heart rate and body temperature, respiration, blood circulation, and metabolism.

When you smell something, you don't think, you immediately react. Smell accesses the limbic brain, which is the connection between the voluntary and involuntary nervous system and helps us to integrate right and left brain and is the seat of our emotions.

From the mere sense of smell we know whether there is danger and whether to fight or flee. It is the sense of smell that gives you all kinds of sensations on how to react, for example the smell of fire could mean supper is ready or the home is burning down depending on the intensity of the smell and we can detect this immediately and respond appropriately without conscious thought.

Aromatherapy has been proven to directly affect the central nervous system by strengthening it and calming the nerves allowing the mind to better cope with stress.

EMOTIONALLY

Emotions themselves are stored in the body organs, glands and systems. Feelings are taken in through the chakras, and then transferred into the meridian system, which consists of energy channels that run over and through the body. Since each organ has a vibrational frequency, as do emotions, the emotions will settle in an area with a corresponding frequency. Disease occurs when the body's vibrational frequency drops below a certain point. Essential oils can raise the body's frequency because they vibrate at a high frequency and transfer that frequency to the body. An example from Dr. Young's book entitled *Aromatherapy – An Essential*

Beginning demonstrates how effective aromatherapy is.

A 26 year old man whose frequency was 66 Hz held a cup of coffee. Within 3 seconds, his frequency dropped to 58 Hz. He removed the coffee and inhaled an aroma of essential oils, and it took only 21 seconds for his frequency to go up

A 24 year old man whose frequency was 66 Hz, took a small drink of coffee. Within 3 seconds, his frequency dropped to 52 Hz. He removed the coffee, but no essential oils were used. It took 3 days for his frequency to go up.

Dr. Young's book, *Aromatherapy: An Essential Beginning*, shared these vibrational values.

Healthy Body from Head to Foot	62-78 Hz	Processed/ canned food	0 Hz
Cold Symptoms	58 Hz	Fresh Produce	up to 15 Hz
Flu Symptoms	57 Hz	Dry Herbs	12 – 22 Hz
Candida	55 Hz	Fresh Herbs	20 – 27 Hz
Epstein Bar	52 Hz	Essential Oils	52 – 320 Hz
Cancer	42 Hz		

SPIRITUALLY

Essential oils have been used in religious celebrations and rituals for thousands of years. The three wise men gave baby Jesus the gift of essential oils. Oils were used in the tombs of Egypt to preserve the mummies. Essential oils are famous for their meditative use by monks. These are only a few ways in which essential oils were first used. Traditional cultures thought fragrances were gifts from the gods and linked the human realm to the gods. Essential oils' link with the spirit and soul helps us grasp our life purpose and get the meaning of life existence. Using these oils in conjunction with meridian and chakra work is one way of linking this herbal plant energy with spiritual and soulful growth.

Sacral Chakra

Happiness Confidence Resourcefulness

*I open myself to others naturally.
Creative and sexual energy have the
power to create and transform.*

HONOR ONE ANOTHER

The second chakra extends from the top of the pelvic bone to the navel. As the navel is the cord of life in the embryonic stage of life, this cord seems to continue in an energetic manner connecting us to our pure creative energies that truly nourish our beings.

The Sacral Chakra is considered a sacred vessel of imagination and creative juices.

The Sacral Chakra is our emotional center. It is associated with relationships, creativity, pleasure, body image and sexuality. The essence of the second chakra is being comfortable in our bodies, with our sexuality and allowing us the opportunity to rest and relax and be comfortable.

The Sacral Chakra is associated with the water element and controls the body fluids. It controls all the urinary fluids and the function of the kidneys and bladder and also the fluids regulated by the sexual organs.

The Sacral Chakra is the energy associated with sexuality and the expression of sensual emotion. Whereas the first chakra is basic to survival; the second chakra allows the soul to embrace the body. On the spiritual level the sacral chakra lets us experience liberation and free-flowing feelings which make us willing to see life as original and new. It is governed by faith and trust in the larger picture.

Characteristics of someone with a strong Sacral Chakra are the ability to respond kindly to nature. To be solely connected to nature, animals, humans, self and the spiritual world. They exude sensuality and peacefulness and are nurturing, focused, capable, spiritually aware and emotionally responsive.

COLOUR
Orange

COMPLIMENTARY COLOUR
Blue

SOUND
Note D and C#

SENSE
Taste

LOCATION
Lower abdomen

BASIC PRINCIPLE
To feel and have pleasure

ASSOCIATED GLANDS
Ovaries and gonads

ASSOCIATED MERIDIANS
Bladder, kidney, large intestine

EMOTIONAL COMPONENT
Guilt

PHYSICAL COMPONENT
Pelvic area, reproductive organs, kidneys and bladder. All liquids such as: blood, lymph, gastric juices, cerebral spinal fluid, mucus, and sperm

INSUFFICIENT SACRAL CHAKRA ENERGY:
Poor social skills
Excessive boundaries
Frigidity
Fear of sex
Denial of pleasure
Fear of change
Lack of compassion and excitement

EXCESS SACRAL CHAKRA ENERGY:
Sexual acting out
Sexual addiction
Addiction to pleasure
Emotionally sensitive
Poor boundaries
Obsessive attachment

HARMONIOUS FUNCTION OF THE SACRAL CHAKRA:
Graceful movement
Ability to experience pleasure
Ability to change
Ability to nurture self and others
Being creative
Enthusiasm for life

PHYSICAL IMBALANCES:
Frequent and painful urination
Pain in the lower back
Swollen hands and feet
Burning urine
False sense of needing to urinate
Puffed and bloated
Pain in the leg and groin
Cough or sneeze and lose water
Gout symptoms
Menstruation difficulties
Depressed
Mood swings

EMOTIONAL IMBALANCES:
Unable to get along with others
Worrying what other people think of you
Enjoying and values social status
Following the crowd
Power seeking

ISSUES

MOVEMENT
Unlike the first chakra where stability and security are the focus, the second chakra focuses on achieving the opposite - letting go, flow, movement, feeling and yielding. Through movement and change, awareness is encouraged. The inertia of the root chakra is overcome through this movement, which helps us get in touch, and heightens the total awareness of all of our senses.

SENSATION
Sight, sound, touch, taste, and hearing are the filters between the internal and the external world. These senses are about our physical, tangible interactions in the world. These senses give us the feedback on our constantly changing world by which we form our basic belief systems, coping strategies, and thought processes. The senses allow us to differentiate between pleasure and pain, move forward or backward, react or retract.

EMOTIONS
The senses bring in the raw data and the feelings are the reaction to the information. Emotions are the way we organize our feelings. Emotions are expressed in the sacral chakra by movement. We move when we are angry and excited; we sigh or cry when sad; we bounce and laugh when we are joyous and happy.

SEXUALITY
Sexuality is the ultimate expression of the sacral chakra, which embodies the issues of movement, sensation, pleasure, emotions and polarity. To be fully enriched by the second chakra is to experience our right to feel and our right to healthy sexuality.

DESIRE
Desire is a necessary impulse, fueling movement and change. We need the "movement" for desire as it assists us in embracing change and keeping us involved in life. Spiritual disciplines disapprove of desire, teaching that desire traps and distracts us from our spiritual path. We

---

Movement
Sensation
Emotions
Sexuality
Desire
Pleasure
Change
Flow
Need
The Shadow
Guilt
Duality

are taught that God, enlightenment, or peace is found only by denying our desires. But seeking God is also a desire, a yearning, and a need. Without the aspiration and the desire, we would not put forth enough effort to attain what it is we are seeking. It is through desire that we get the energy, inspiration, and seed for the will. We need to stay in touch with our feelings to know our desires and by knowing our deepest desires may we follow and stay true to our life path.

Pleasure

The basic principle of the second chakra is to have pleasure and to allow the free flow of energy throughout the body. Pleasure invites us to extend and expand and to embrace all of our senses. Pleasure gives us the experience of being fully alive, taking in life to its fullest. Enjoying the simplest of the earth's gifts such as enjoying the sound of waves and dolphins or watching the sunset over the mountains. Pleasure invites us to relax which helps us to release stress. When there is enough pleasure and there is no stress, we can enthusiastically take in new ideas or take on new projects, which broadens our awareness again.

Change

The Root Chakra is all about grounding, stability, holding on. The Sacral Chakra is all about change, movement, shifting and letting go.

Flow

Flow is yet another expression of movement of the Sacral Chakra. When the Sacral Chakra is open, emotions and feelings are able to flow through freely and appropriately.

The Shadow/ Duality

The number two as related to the second chakra is associated with duality and polarity. It is the work of the Sacral Chakra to recognize and reclaim the shadow side of ourself. To embrace the body as whole; inside and outside, feminine and masculine, mind and body. If we ignore the shadow we become polarized and we attract the exact opposite of what we express. It makes us extremely uncomfortable to be around someone expressing our shadow self, but until we embrace it we will be confronted by it all the time. It will show up in our children, spouse or boss. If we suppress our feelings and live life benevolently indifferent and stoic we will have little tolerance for others who are needy, crying or strongly expressive with their emotions. It will always be in our face until we embrace the duality of ourselves. This is the work of the number two - the Sacral Chakra.

Guilt

Guilt helps us to define boundaries. Guilt can be used as a feedback mechanism and helps us to discern right from wrong.

Chapter 8

Food
Apricots
Carrots
Mandarins
Mangos
Melons
Papayas
Peaches
Oranges
Orange Peppers

Herbs
Crampbark
Ginger
Gota Kola
Hawthorn
Hops
Meadowsweet
Parsley
Psyllium
Sassafras
Scullcap
Valerian
Yarrow
Yellowdock

COLOUR

Orange

The orange colour supplies us with a stimulating, renewing energy and freeing us from rigid emotional patterns. It encourages our self-esteem and heightens the joy we get from sensual pleasure.

PHYSICALLY

- Orange is the colour of success. People who like orange, love life.
- Orange is the basic health colour bringing joy, health, vitality and creativity into our lives. Orange stimulates the blood and circulatory process and also affects the mental, nervous and respiratory systems.
- It is the colour of calcium and hence assists the encouragement of breast milk, healthy hair, nails, bones and teeth.
- Oranges helps to balance spleen, kidney and reproductive organs. It affects the physiological functioning of the stomach, pancreas, bladder and lungs and relieves ulcers and gallstones. Constipation, intestinal cramps or spastic colon can be significantly relieved by the use of the colour orange.
- Orange also supports the respiratory system and encourages deep rhythmic breathing.

EMOTIONALLY

- Orange brings the "Kiss of life": good health, vitality, creativity and joy as well as confidence, courage, buoyancy, spontaneity and a positive attitude to life. Orange promotes enthusiasm, compassion, communicates movement and enterprise. Orange is a blissful energy that greatly strengthens the willpower.

SPIRITUALLY

- Orange allows us to share ourselves and to be able to relate to others.

SACRAL CHAKRA

SOUND

Note C♯ – Birthing

Physical Aspects
The location of the C♯ semitone on the body is where the sacrum meets the lumbar spine; where the solid meets the moveable. This vibration is good for those that have had difficulty in giving birth or being born.

Emotional Aspects
C♯ helps individuals to embrace their sexuality. It helps those who want to embrace life but feel held back with the burdens of their emotions. It helps them to express their emotions appropriately yet without reservation.

This frequency is most valuable for those that have experienced difficulty giving birth, especially for those that have had Cesarean sections. It is necessary for males who have undergone any kind of sexual shock and need to establish their own grounding place for the will.

Spiritual Aspects
C♯ is the bridge between the C note which is related to foundation and family and the D note which relates to movement and a relationship with one other. This bridge moves us out of the family tribe and into a dance with a partner in life. C♯ is related to the womb of the female and the "hara" of the male; both powerful energy centers the former slightly more physical.

Bach Flower Essences
Agrimony
Beech
Centaury
Cherry Plum
Chestnut
Chicory
Crab Apple
Heather
Holly
Impatience
Mimulus
Pine
Rock Water
Vine
Water Violet
Willow

Pacific Essences
Candystick
Death Camas
Dolphin
Fuchsia
Hooker's Onion
Moonsnail
Mussel
Narcissus
Nootka Rose
Orange Honeysuckle
Periwinkle
Pink Seaweed
Plantain
Seahorse

Note D

Physical Aspects

This center is tied to the function of the adrenal glands. It is also a major influence on the reproductive system and the entire muscular system of the body. It influences the elimination system, the activities of the spleen, bladder, pancreas, and kidneys. It is the center for physical integrity and balance.

Emotional Aspects

Comfort is the key word that relates to the note D. Being comfortable in one's own skin, that feeling of being at home in one's body. It gives one the sense of contentment; I'm okay, you're okay. It gives the ability to receive and give acceptance. A balanced sacral chakra is a place where we dance the dance of life.

Spiritual Aspects

This is a center that influences sensation and emotion. The note D awakens the desire to blossom. Once the grounding connection is made then comes the response to grow and then to begin the journey that ultimately leads to spiritual completion. The note D initiates the gathering of the forces.

PLANT FORM - ESSENTIAL OILS

Cedarwood

Cedarwood was traditionally used by American Indians to enhance their potential for spiritual connection and communication. The American Indians believed the Cedarwood trees acted like a wooded canvas protecting the animals and bringing them rejuvenation. Cedarwood has a deep woody, balsamic, yet very pleasant fragrance.

PHYSICALLY
- Cedarwood supports the respiratory system and helps conditions of bronchitis and tuberculosis. It also supports the urinary system and helps conditions of cystitis, urinary infections and water retention. Cedarwood helps skin and hair disorders such as acne, psoriasis, cellulite, dandruff and hair loss.

MENTALLY
- Cedarwood helps to balance nervous tension and anxious states. It benefits the mind with its calming and soothing action.

EMOTIONALLY
- Cedarwood keeps the body balanced.

SPIRITUALLY
- Cedarwood has historically been used for psychic work, yoga and meditation rituals.

ESSENTIAL OILS
Carrot Seed
Cedarwood
Geranium
Mandarin
Melissa
Neroli
Nutmeg
Orange
Petitgrain
Tangerine

Geranium

Geranium is the "flower of constancy" which delivers a cozy, sweet minty scent. This oil, extracted from the leaves of the geranium plant, offers romantic, relaxing and clarifying effects.

Physically
- Geranium supports the digestive, liver, urinary, circulatory and nervous systems. Geranium assists the body in balancing the liver and gallbladder, digestion, gastric ulcers, kidney and urinary stones, and water retention. Geranium is an excellent hormonal balancer and helps with premenstrual symptoms and menopause.

Mentally
- It helps to relieve tension and anxiety and lifts the spirits, dispelling melancholy and depression or over-excitement.

Emotionally
- This balancing effect on the emotions reduces mood swings and can be put to good effect when treating premenstrual symptoms and menopausal issues. Geranium is perfect to put you in a good mood, induce sleep, relax or energize.

Spiritually
- Geranium helps release creative blocks and supports growth by opening the heart to universal love.

Petitgrain

Petitgrain is a fresh, wood, orange scent that is stabilizing and reassuring. Petitgrain, which is French for small grains or fruits, is derived from fresh leaves and young branches of the bitter orange tree.

PHYSICALLY
- It relaxes muscle spasms and it calms the stomach and digestion, is good for stress related to irritable bowel syndrome. Petitgrain cleanses and tones the skin.

MENTALLY
- Petitgrain is a fabulous stress reliever and helps with restful sleep. It calms racing thoughts and promotes inner communication.

EMOTIONALLY
- Petitgrain is good for all stress. It calms anger and panic. It relieves feelings of betrayal, sadness, pessimism, trauma and disharmony. It allows us space and time for inner healing.

SPIRITUALLY
- Petitgrain revitalizes the spirit. It balances and restores the energy in the aura. It fills one with inner strength and awareness of divine love.

Tangerine

This delicate and sweet oil comes from the peel of the tangerine. The aroma of tangerine is cheery, joyous and uplifting.

Physically
- Tangerine acts as a toner for the digestive, circulatory and lymphatic systems. This oil assists with water retention, constipation, diarrhea, flatulence, intestinal spasms, and tired and aching limbs and circulation. It specifically assists organ function such as the liver, gallbladder, stomach and intestines. Tangerine aids muscle spasms, premenstrual symptoms and insomnia.

Mentally
- Tangerine is best known for its antidepressant qualities. It is soothing to the psyche and calming to the nerves. It helps clear irritability and lowers anxiety.

Emotionally
- Tangerine is fabulous to offset moodiness and anxiety. It helps shift anger, sadness and depression and lightens fatigue.

Spiritually
- Tangerine instills joy and youthfulness.

MINERAL FORM – CRYSTALS AND GEMSTONES

Carnelian

This orange stone is said to expand our consciousness of love and the more love we give the more will be returned to us. It is the "lion king stone" introducing the acceptance of the cycle of life. Carnelian motivates and creates the energy necessary to accomplish tasks. Carnelian is the colour of joy and when we are joyful we have the energy to take on the world.

PHYSICALLY
- Carnelian is superb in stimulating the metabolism by increasing the absorption of vitamins and minerals into the small intestine and thus improving the quality of blood. It influences the female reproductive organs to increase fertility. Helps low back pain problems and imbalances such as rheumatism and arthritis.

MENTALLY
- Carnelian sharpens the mind to solve problems efficiently and quickly. It definitely helps improve analytical abilities and clarifies perception. Carnelian supports positive life choices and promotes business success.

EMOTIONALLY
- Carnelian lifts the emotions and bestows everyday courage for life's ups and downs.

SPIRITUALLY
- Carnelian grounds and anchors one into the present. Carnelian nurtures the community spirit and it helps us become willing to help and be a productive participant of the group.

GEMSTONES
Carnelian
Copper
Coral
Goldstone
Tiger's Eye

Goldstone

Gold stone is a man-made stone. It is an attempt to make stone that would contain gold. It is has the healing properties of natural glass and is yellowy brown with a glittering appearance. It is uplifting and helpful to the Solar Plexus Chakra; bridging from the Sacral Chakra and used in the E♭ Sound Essence remedy.

Physically
- Gold stone strengthens the nervous system and purifies and energizes the entire physical body. It helps with tissue regeneration.

Mentally
- Goldstone is a powerful mind balancer, and allows one to accept love and open the mind. This aids in personal illumination, openness and honesty.

Emotionally
- Goldstone is calming and refreshing and is good for relaxation and sharing.

Spiritually
- Goldstone raises the vibration rate and awareness of the user. It energizes and releases energy in the body. It is a transmitter stone.

Rose Quartz

Rose quartz contributes love to all the essences and holds the vibration of all the information components. Rose quartz has a soft and silky vibration, bringing a wonderful, powerful, loving energy. Rose quartz bestows a calming, cooling energy that supports all of the chakras. It removes negativity and reinstates the loving gentle forces of self-love. It brings us patience and the knowing there is no need for haste, bringing calmness and clarity to the emotions and restoring harmony to the mind. It has been known as the "stone of gentle love".

PHYSICALLY
- Rose quartz stimulates blood circulation in the tissues. This stone fortifies the heart and sexual organs, helps with sexual problems and encourages fertility.

MENTALLY
- Rose quartz is used to help us make decisions and frees us from worry.

EMOTIONALLY
- Rose quartz helps us with empathy, and sensitivity. It encourages self-love, a strong heart, romance and the ability to love.

SPIRITUALLY
- Rose quartz supports all the chakras and holds the vibration it is given.

AFFIRMATIONS

1. I open myself to others naturally.
2. Creative and sexual energy has the ability to create and transform.
3. I love myself exactly as I am.
4. I move easily and effortlessly.
5. I deserve pleasure in my life.
6. I feel good when I am in control of my life.
7. I unconditionally love and approve of myself at all times.
8. I am enough, what I do is enough, what I have is enough and who I am is enough.
9. I trust the process of life.
10. I trust in my own perfection.
11. I feel pleasure when I pamper myself.
12. I feel pleasure during lovemaking.
13. I feel pleasure when I am touched.
14. I feel pleasure when I relax.
15. I feel good when I remain flexible.
16. I feel good when I allow others to control their lives.
17. I feel good when I am in control of my own life.
18. I feel joy when I am able to let go of every detail.
19. I feel joy when I laugh.
20. I feel joy when I dance and sing.
21. I feel joy when I just let things be.
22. I feel a sense of well being when I take care of myself.
23. I feel a sense of well being when I look and feel good.
24. I feel unconditionally loved and approve of myself at all times.
25. I allow pleasure, sweetness and sensuality into my life.
26. I allow abundance and prosperity into my life.
27. I give myself permission to totally enjoy my sexuality.
28. I trust in the Infinite Intelligence to give me exactly what I need for my growth and development.
29. I open myself up to beauty, joy and harmony of the Universe and I enjoy it.

TASTES

Food

Food really has the lowest vibrational frequency compared to the other remedies. Food is considered nourishment for the body on the physical and biochemical aspect of the body. Food grown in soil closest to your home will better nourish your body compared to food grown afar. The food grown in your garden, in your backyard has the loving care of your hands and heart; it carries your vibration and will nourish you more than any other food you could purchase. Of course live food is the best for you. It could be considered heart food. Something gathered the day that you eat it has much more nourishment for your body. It is the nutrients in the fresh food that aid in the digestion of the body; fresh food has enzymes and fiber that support your system. The food that we get from grocery stores has had to be transported and is less than fresh; some of our food from this source is adulterated with growth hormone, sprays to keep pests off the food or to ripen the food as it is being transported.

It is important for our body systems to eat food of the season. Have you ever craved greens in the spring? This is our innate cyclical wisdom for eating foods in season. In tune with nature and mother earth we too are cyclical and have an inner rhythm that matches the seasons of the year. We should eat greens in the spring and berries in the summer and field produce in the late summer and autumn and root vegetables in the winter. Have you ever noticed that our feasting celebrations occur in the harvest season just before winter?

Herbs

Herbs were made for humans to balance their bodies. Herbs have historically been thought of as medicine from the earth. Eating the whole herb has a holistic effect on our bodies. The chemical constituents in herbs are perfectly formulated for our bodies to assimilate the healing attributes of the herb. Side effects are rare when we eat the herb in its entirety. Every plant has its own signature and its own nutritive value for the human body. Herbs can be eaten as food or made into a tea for consumption. Tinctures are one of the ways to get the healing properties from the herbs straight into our bloodstream. Tinctures are made, by placing the herb into a macerate of alcohol. Some of the chemicals of the herb are water soluble and some are alcohol soluble, so by allowing the herbs to sit in a 40% solution of alcohol for a lunar cycle allows the healing chemicals to dissolve into the macerate. Once this is done, the tincture can be used for up to 10 years. Tinctures are taken as drops in water and absorbed directly into the blood stream where the body carries them to organs and glands as needed.

Homeopathy

Homeopathy is a bridge between allopathic medicine and vibrational medicine. Homeopathy is the next step into vibrational remedies from herbs. Herbs work physiologically with the biochemistry of the body. Homeopathy has no trace of the biochemical in its remedy, thus works on the energy of the imprint of the herb.

The discovery of homeopathy is credited to Samuel Hahnemann (1755-1843), who created cures based on the principle of " like cures like". Homeopathic remedies often vibrationally duplicate the physical disease in the person to push that imbalance out of the body. This simply means that if a person came in contact with a herb and had a reaction such as with an onion and got a runny nose and tearful eyes then symptoms of someone who had a runny nose and tearful eyes could be cured with the homeopathic remedy of onion. Homeopathic remedies come in different dilutions each having its own purpose. Less is more is the theory of homeopathy so what might be considered high concentration of the herb, like 1 drop in 10 is really the lowest dose compared to 1 drop in100. The farther away the dose is from the chemical component of the dilution; the stronger the dose.

Homeopathic remedies have their grading system related to the metric system so 1 drop in 10 is considered

---

The Hierarchy of Vibrational Medicine
Homeopathy
Gem Essences
Flower Essences
Sound Essences

a 1X dose, and 1 drop in 100 is considered a 1C dose and this is done sequentially in the workings of homeopathy. For example 3x dose means that 1 drop of the herb was added to 9 drops of water and then 1 drop from this mixture was added to another 9 drops of water and I drop from this mixture was added to another 9 drops making this formulation somewhat exponential. The same holds true for the 1C formulation. The "C" depicts 1 drop in 99 drops of water. In the theory of homeopathy then a 1X formulation is useful for recent injuries such as a bruise or sprain and a 1C formulation is useful for an accident or trauma that is years old. The greater the potency, (remember less is more with homeopathy), the further back the remedy will go in repairing the illness. The belief system of homeopathic healing is that the body will recognize the signature of the herb in vibrational form.

GEM, FLOWER, SEA AND SOUND ESSENCES

Gem, Flower, Sea and Sound Essences are energy medicines and resonate at higher frequencies than homeopathy. They work on the body in a completely different dimension, hence do not interfere with any other form of medicine, whether it be herbs, food, homeopathy or allopathic. These energy medicines affect our body in the etheric template.

- These remedies assist our understanding of the imbalance we are experiencing.
- They restore balance emotionally, mentally and spiritually thus physiologically.
- They support us in embracing new levels of awareness, which helps us to move through our physical, emotional and spiritual imbalances.
- They come from nature and thus help us to attune to our natural rhythms.
- These energy medicines are catalysts for transformation of emotional, mental and spiritual levels, thus repercussing upon the physical level. They work from the outside of our physical body inwards on an energy level.

The first documented use of flower essences was by Hildegard Von Bingen, Sept 16, 1098 - Sept. 17, 1179. Hildegard was a German magistra, monastic leader, mystic, author and composer of music. In the sixteenth century, Swiss doctor/alchemist Paracelsus experimented with flower essences. Flower essences were rediscovered in Britain, in the early 1930's by Dr. Edward Bach, a homeopathic physician. He believed that sickness came from attitudes and how we viewed life. Dr. Bach felt that a healer's focus should be directed towards the ills of the heart and spirit of a person. Working with a patient in this manner often prevented the manifestation of the emotions into physical disease. He noticed that patients with particular physical ailments had similar attitudes. For example, someone that constantly expresses criticism may experience the symptoms of arthritis; someone that felt that he was overlooked or that he never had enough would develop symptoms of thyroid problems, etc. He also believed that nature had the answer for our sicknesses and diseases. Dr. Bach prepared medicines from the dew of flowers and tree leaves and witnessed the negative mind states of his patients altering. As the mind or belief system shifted the physical body began to restore, creating integrated, mind/body health. It has been stated that Dr. Bach could place the bloom of the flower on his tongue and would then experience how the flower would correct the state of mind. Dr. Bach's work on flower essences is being continued world-wide.

Since the 1930's, flower essences have been made throughout the world, and like food and herbs, it seems that the flowers in your neighborhood are the ones that have the more potent effect on your well-being. Different geographical areas have different themes as each culture has its own issues. As geographical location has a bearing on the theme of the flower essences so does the historical time in which they have been created have an effect on us.

The flower essences of Dr. Bach were discovered in England in the 1930's, a time when there was depression and a sense of heaviness in the culture. Compare this to the 1960's in California when the issues for our culture at this time was "finding ourselves" and the "meaning of relationships", now compare this to the late 1980's and early 1990's when our culture and many of the "new worlds" such as Canada, Alaska, New Zealand and Australia are seeking higher awareness and understanding of spirituality. Some believe there are flower essences that have yet to be discovered because humans have not yet raised their consciousness enough to benefit from the vibration of these undiscovered flowers.

The flower essences of Dr. Bach support us on a fundamental level. His remedies support core level issues relating to survival. The remedies from California, The Flower Essence Society remedies support us with relationship issues. They support us with our interactions with others.

The remedies developed in the 1980's globally support us in our spiritual growth.

Some of the flower essence producers are:
- Sabina Pettitt: Pacific Essences *(sea, shell and flower essences)*
- Steve Johnson: Alaskan Essences *(essences from the vegetation of winterland)*
- Mary Garbely: New Zealand Flower Essences (full range of essences from the New Zealand landscape)
- Ian White: Australian Bush Essences (essences from the unique vegetation found only in this part of the world)
- Machelle Smallwright: Perelandra Essences (rose, vegetable, and natural essences)

1999 was the inception of the Sound Essences, just in time to prepare us for the speeding up of time in the 21st century. This energy medicine brings human consciousness into another realm of healing, these capture the incredible healing vibrations of sound to align the body. Sound Essences work exceptionally well, blended with flower essences. So as we raise our consciousness and our vibrations we have the energies of the earth to support us in all that we do; we only need to listen.

To categorize all the essences into the meridians and the chakras is not the focus of this book, however, I feel strongly that the flower and sea essences support our energy balance.

I have chosen to mention the Bach and Pacific Essences in this manual simply because I know these essences best. Practitioners all over the world have their favorite. The point of categorizing the various essences into meridians and chakras is to empower the reader with essence knowledge. I love finding a flower remedy specific for a client and blending it with the Sound Essence to tailor the remedy specifically for the client at that time.

Unlike medicinal herbology, flower essences do not use the physical material of the plant. They use the individual imprint of the plant's signature. The plants expression of itself is in its flower.

Much of the plant's energy is used to produce the expression of its self, and this is known as the flower. The flower carries a vibrational imprint unique to the plant. This imprint is transferred to water, which is called flower essence. When we take a flower essence remedy this vibrational imprint is transferred to us. If the vibration is a match, our bodies use it to support our internal and external energy systems. Vibrational remedies are benign in the sense that they only work if the vibrations match. Because they work on a completely different dimension on the body they cannot interfere with other herbal remedies, aromatherapy or allopathic therapy.

As flower essences give their imprint by way of their personality of the plant from the deva of the flower, Gem Essences give their imprint in the formation of the crystalline structure. It is the geometry of the crystal or gem that offers information to our energy body. Gem essences do not contain the energy of the life force as the Flower Essences but operate on the principle of resonance of geometrics. Each crystal has a unique molecular structure that gives it its characteristics and this is the signature of the crystal or gemstone. It is the vibration in this molecular structure that resonates with the human body that offers resonance of harmony.

Gemstones and gem essences function in the realm of vibrational therapy between flower essences and homeopathy. Sound Essences function in the realm of vibrational therapy above flower and gem essences.

It has been noted that sound and music are the most simple and effective means of restoring vitality and balance. Chakras totally resonate with sound.

Sound Essences carry the imprint of the wavelength vibration of specific notes. Every note has a healing resonance with each chakra. The Sound Essences are essences that have captured the messages of the vibration of each of the seven whole notes affecting the seven major chakras and the five semitones working as chakra bridges, offering the body healing on the physical, emotional, mental and spiritual levels. Historically, composers knew how to elicit emotions in the body by using certain keys. It is undisputed that music can heal the body.

There are as many indications for Flower and Gem and Sound Essences as there are flowers, gems and notes. Each flower, gem and note has its own personality and vibrational frequency and its own life energy pattern; hence each has its own unique function and healing effect on us as individuals. To match the person with the correct vibrational medicine is an art form that clearly has a future.

As we start taking responsibility for our own health we will soon recognize the link between psychological make-up and physiological responses of the body. Healing is not just removing the physical discomfort but it is getting the insight of our outlook on life. Vibrational remedies help us to shift attitude and look at our situations differently. In order to shift sickness, we must shift our attitude and for some, change comes with difficulty. The vibrational remedies open the consciousness to the higher self, bypassing personality resistances and blockages and offer the whole body a healing journey.

Traditionally, homeopathy as well as flower, gem and sound essences were taken as drops under the tongue as a direct intake of the vibration. Recently vibrational therapists have been finding that using these remedies in an atomizer, directly affects the auric field. It is my opinion that using the vibrational remedies in an atomizer has the greatest healing effect.

Solar Plexus Chakra

Wisdom / Clarity / Self Esteem

*I accept myself completely.
My personal power is growing stronger everyday.*

HONOR ONE-SELF

The Solar Plexus Chakra is located between the navel and the diaphragm, and it governs more organs than any other chakra. On the right side, it governs the liver and the gall bladder. On the left side, it governs the spleen, stomach and the pancreas. In the middle, it governs the diaphragm and small intestine.

The third chakra is all about our self-esteem, our ego, personal power, will, responsibility and gut intuition. It is in this energy center that we need to know who we are, own our personal power and take responsibility for our own lives.

The Solar Plexus Chakra represents the element of fire and fire stands for light, warmth, energy and activity.

The third chakra represents our sun and our power center. It is through this energy center that we absorb the solar energy that nurtures our aura and vitalizes our body. The Solar Plexus Chakra is the force that maintains our individual identity, our inner sense of who we are.

The qualities that represent third chakra are almost the opposite of those qualities of the second chakra. Third chakra energy is logical instead of artistic, sophisticated instead of innocent, suspicious instead of trusting and responsibility bound instead of free flowing. The second chakra follows the right brain identity whereas the third chakra "thinks" like the left brain.

Characteristics of a strong Solar Plexus Chakra are a healthy sense of personal identity and a strong sense of personal power. You can then take full responsibility of your own life and allow others to take responsibility of their own lives. You can accept yourself completely and have a feeling of true peace and inner harmony with all of life.

COLOUR
Yellow

COMPLIMENTARY COLOUR
Violet

SOUND
Note E and E♭

SENSE
Sight

LOCATION
Solar Plexus

BASIC PRINCIPLE
To act and be an individual

ASSOCIATED GLANDS
Pancreas and Adrenals

ASSOCIATED MERIDIANS
Stomach, Spleen, Small Intestine, Gall Bladder, and Liver

EMOTIONAL COMPONENT
Shame

PHYSICAL COMPONENT
Liver, digestive system, stomach, spleen, gall bladder, autonomic nervous system muscles, and lower back.

Insufficient Solar Plexus Chakra Energy:

Weak willed and easily manipulated
Poor discipline and follow through
Cold emotionally and physically
Victim mentality and blaming others
Unreliable
Poor self-worth

Excess Solar Plexus Chakra Energy:

Need to be right and have the last word
Stubbornness and arrogant
Overly aggressive, domineering and controlling
Manipulative, power hungry and deceitful
Temper tantrums and violent outbursts
Competitive drive and ambition

Harmonious Function of the Solar Plexus Chakra:

Responsible and reliable
Confidence and self-esteem
Spontaneity, playfulness and a sense of humor
Ability to meet challenges
Feeling of peace, balance, and inner harmony
Warm personality

Physical Imbalances:

Ulcers
Liver problems
Gallstones
Gas pains
Indigestion
High blood pressure
Stress
Fatigue
Jaundice
Constipation
Diarrhea
Diabetes
Vomiting
Hypoglycemia
Hypothyroid
Muscle cramps and spasms
Nervous exhaustion
Depression
Duodenum problems
Duodenal ulcer

Emotional Imbalances:

Feeling deprived of recognition
Aloofness
Fearing group power
Confining life to a narrow view
Always planning but never manifesting
Constantly needing change
Judgmental and critical
Mentally bullying

ISSUES

ENERGY/ ACTIVITY
A healthy third chakra exhibits energetic vitality. There is enjoyment and enthusiasm about life. Our sense of personal power gives us hope that we can make things viable for ourselves, and with this positive outlook we are not afraid to venture into the unknown, to take risks, or to make mistakes. When our energy field is strong, we have faith in ourselves and we do not lose our direction when challenged. We enjoy tackling challenges, and grappling with the world and moving ahead in our world and taking on new challenges.

INDIVIDUALISM/AUTONOMY
Individualism begins at the third chakra. We break away from our families and tribes and begin to experience ourselves. With a healthy Solar Plexus Chakra, we develop and nurture our uniqueness and step out of the crowd, no longer needing or striving for approval. It takes individualism to make a difference and to contribute our gifts back to the universe. We first need the courage to be different and then we can make a difference.

WILL
The fuel for your will is what you want and need. Passion is what gives your will strength and direction.

SELF-ESTEEM
Self-esteem comes from within. It is an observation that those who treat themselves well, take care of their bodies and are connected to their feeling and allow themselves pleasure had a higher self-esteem because they felt good. Nurturing themselves gave them energy and confidence. Their sense of self is defined internally rather than by the external environment.

PROACTIVITY
Proactivity is about choosing your actions, rather than controlling or being controlled by them. Proactive people take responsibility for shaping their future, for initiating behavior that will create the situations they want. Being

- Energy
- Activity
- Autonomy
- Authority
- Individuation
- Will
- Self-esteem
- Shame
- Proactivity
- Power

proactive means you are a creative influence on your environment rather than a victim of its circumstances. Proactivity requires initiative and will.

Power

It is the third chakra that allows us to stand in our own power. To have a balanced Solar Plexus Chakra is to stand in our power and to express this power appropriately. Once we stand in our own power, we have the ability to determine our own destiny. It is the power we find in ourselves that we need to break through the barriers we have set for ourselves. All of this adds up to expressing your personal power.

Ego-Identity

Ego is the awareness that we are separate from the tribe and we have the ability to make our own choices and to create our own identity. The first chakra is concerned with our world from the inside, the second chakra with the external world around us and the third chakra blends them both to create how we express ourselves in the outside world.

COLOUR

Yellow

The colour yellow strengthens our nerves and thoughts and also stimulates contact and interaction with others.

Yellow is a creative and inspiring colour. Yellow is sunshine and happiness. Yellow helps with clarity of thought and brings the feeling that everything will be alright.

PHYSICALLY

- Yellow helps to strengthen the nervous system and the muscles, including the heart, creating better circulation. Yellow is best known to stimulate the digestive process such as the action of the liver, gall bladder and the flow of bile; it promotes the secretion of digestive juices, which assist the stomach and intestines, and therefore promotes proper bowel movements. It also assists in the assimilation of better nutrition. Yellow purifies the blood stream and supports the lymphatic system. Yellow is an excellent colour for the relief of inflammatory disorders of the joints and connective tissues and can help alleviate arthritis, rheumatism and gout. Yellow can help diabetics lower their intake of insulin and encourages the natural flow of pancreatic insulin.

EMOTIONALLY

- Yellow is the lightest of all the warm spectrum colours and the colour which most closely resembles the sun
- Yellow brings an air of radiance, brightness, cheerfulness and gaiety.
- Yellow is the colour of intellect and corresponds with knowledge and wisdom, inspiration and open mindedness.

SPIRITUALLY

- Yellow helps to discover the self-sense that includes all other self-senses as well as dissolving the separation between others and ourselves.

FOOD

Bananas
Butter
Corn
Eggs
Grapefruit
Lemons
Melons
Olive Oil
Pineapples
Turnips
Yellow Peppers
Yellow Squash

HERBS

Alfalfa
Cleavers
Coltsfoot
Cornsilk
Dandelion
Elecampagne
Garlic
Lemon Balm
Mullein
Plantain
Stinging Nettle

Bach Flower Essences

Agrimony
Beech
Centaury
Cerato
Cherry Plum
Chicory
Crabapple
Gentian
Holly
Hornbeam
Larch
Mimulus
Oak
Vervain
Vine
Walnut
Wild Rose
Willow

Pacific Essences

Anemone	Pearly Everlasting
Blue Camas	Pink Seaweed
Camellia	Pipsissewa
Coral	Purple Magnolia
Dolphin	Red Huckleberry
Harvest Lily	Sea Lettuce
Hooker's Onion	Snowdrop
Nootka Rose	Urchin
Orange Honeysuckle	Wallflower

SOUND

Note E♭

Moving from nourishment into individuation and transition into puberty.

Physical Aspects

The location of the E♭ semitone on the body is where the lumbar spine meets the thoracic. The spinal vertebrae are getting smaller in size in this location. E♭ by location supports the small intestine, liver, spleen, stomach, pancreas; the digestive system of the body which on a metaphysical level is how we assimilate new ideas and digest life's circumstances.

Emotional Aspects

This vibration is good for those who have had difficulty moving into puberty. This vibration supports individuals with issues surrounding the transition between nurturing and independence. It supports those who have distanced themselves from family.

E♭ is the vibration most called for as it supports the whole note E of the Solar Plexus Chakra. The Solar Plexus Chakra needs to be strong for the energy to jump into the Heart Chakra, as there is no semitone between the Solar Plexus Chakra and the Heart Chakra. E♭ is the most commonly needed vibration.

Spiritual Aspects

E♭ is the bridge between the Sacral Chakra and the Solar Plexus Chakra, moving from relationships and partnerships into individualism and self. This semitone bridges our connection with others into how we feel about our self-esteem, our self-worth, and ourselves. In order to have strong relationships with others, we have to have a good relationship with ourselves first. It is important to grasp the concept that we fit into this world as perfectly as a flower in a bouquet. This self-acceptance supports us in our physical health.

Note E

PHYSICAL ASPECTS

This center is linked to the solar plexus area of the physical body. This includes the digestive system, the adrenals, the stomach, the liver, and the gall bladder. It assists the body on its assimilation of nutrients. It is also linked to the functions of the left hemisphere of the brain.

EMOTIONAL ASPECTS

This note is most useful for those people that have difficulties in making decisions. It helps people to discern. It supports the choosing of what is going to be taken in and what is going to be let go. It takes one to the conclusion of decisions by bringing them to resolustion.

SPIRITUAL ASPECTS

Spiritually, note E is the seat of goodness as we begin to choose, we are becoming closer to the guiding vibration that leads to the light. If I have the power to choose, how do I know what is the right choice, the good choice, the best choice?

Essential Oils

Bergamot
Birch
Citronella
Coriander
Ginger
Fennel
Grapefruit
Lemon
Lemongrass
Litsea Cubeba
Rosemary

PLANT FORM – ESSENTIAL OILS

Bergamot

Bergamot oil comes from the fruit of the bergamot tree. Bergamot oil is light, delicate and refreshing, somewhat citrus-like orange and lemon with slight floral overtones.

Physically
- Bergamot is useful for cold sores and infectious disease, bronchitis, fever, tonsillitis, sore throat, vaginal candida. Bergamot helps with gallstones and intestinal parasites.

Mentally
- Bergamot is like a sedative yet it is uplifting and is excellent for anxiety, depression and nervous tension.

Emotionally
- Bergamot has a combined cooling and refreshing quality and helps to soothe anger and frustration.

Spiritually
- Bergamot has a sedating effect that can still the mind which allows us to access our intuition.

Grapefruit

Grapefruit oil comes from deep inside of the grapefruit peel. Its aroma is sweet, sharp and refreshing.

PHYSICALLY
- Grapefruit truly supports the digestive system helping with dyspepsia, digestive complaints, liver disorders, gallstones, eating disorders and obesity. It helps the body digest fats. Grapefruit also helps with cellulite, muscle fatigue, colds and the flu.

MENTALLY
- Grapefruit may have a balancing effect on the central nervous system and has a reputation for stabilizing depression. It helps to open the person to new ideas and possibilities.

EMOTIONALLY
- Grapefruit has an overall uplifting and reviving quality. It helps ease grief caused by emotional violence and helps one cope with resentment and envy.

SPIRITUALLY
- Grapefruit has euphoric and hypnotic qualities.

Lemongrass

Lemongrass, grown in the tropics is refreshing and stimulating. It acts as a sedative for the central nervous system.

PHYSICALLY
- Lemongrass helps with muscular aches and pains, poor circulation, varicose veins and muscle tone. This oil helps bladder infection, water retention, kidney disorders and aids the lymphatic, respiratory and parasympathetic system.

MENTALLY
- Lemongrass lessens stress, lowers nervous exhaustion and lightens mental fatigue. This oil is a mental stimulant helping with focus and concentration.

EMOTIONALLY
- Lemongrass serves as a tonic for the nerves and helps to establish personal power.

SPIRITUALLY
- Lemongrass brings wisdom and inspiration into one's affairs. It promotes wise judgment.

Rosemary

Rosemary, the flower of loyalty, is a strong fresh, clear, and woody aroma made from the spiky leaves of the Mediterranean shrub-like herb. The name is derived from the Latin "ias maus' meaning dew of the sea. The use of rosemary has a very rich history used for festive occasions in many European traditions to symbolize signs of love and faithfulness.

Physically
- Rosemary has a positive effect on the digestive system, is helpful for indigestion, colitis and constipation. It is also good for hepatic disorders as it is a liver and gall bladder tonic. The circulatory system also benefits from the oil, as it normalizes blood pressure and helps combat hardening of the arteries and varicose veins. Rosemary assists the respiratory system, helping asthma, bronchitis and whooping cough. The other benefits of Rosemary include a positive effect on menstrual cramps, an excellent skin tonic property, a stimulant for the scalp, encouraging hair growth and providing treatment of dandruff and greasy hair.

Mentally
- Rosemary has a stimulating effect on the nerves. It seems to dispel amnesia, lethargy and hysteria. Rosemary restores the mind and is good for headaches due to hypertension.

Emotionally
- Rosemary helps to clear the mind and emotions. It brings the ability to vocalize thoughts and feeling. It helps to build confidence.

Spiritually
- Rosemary helps develop sensitivity to subtle forces and high intuition. It helps us to clear away fears and move forward in trust. Rosemary supports us with a spiritual connection to earth.

Gemstones

Amber
Citrine
Emerald
Gold
Sunstone
Tiger's Eye
Topaz

MINERAL FORM – CRYSTALS AND GEMSTONES

Amber

Amber is a resin that has been fossilized and is usually golden brown. Sometimes there are tiny insects inside the amber stone. Amber was thought to bring good luck to ancient warriors.

Physically

- Amber helps support the urinary system. It has been successful in the treatment of kidney and bladder disorders. It has been used for goiter and other throat disturbances.

Mentally

- Amber dissolves oppositions, which makes us more flexible and adaptable to our circumstances. It has a sunny and bright disposition, which always helps to calm nerves and brings about a lively personality.

Emotionally

- Amber allows good luck, happiness and the sense of being carefree. It strengthens self-belief which cultivates trust and the ability to make choices.

Spiritually

- Amber supports manifesting thought into reality. It helps physical energy to be transferred towards the Heart Chakra and move into unconditional love. Amber supports the Crown Chakra.

Citrine

Citrine is said to be the "Stone of Prosperity" attracting wealth, success, happiness, and generosity. The yellow colour of citrine augments the Solar Plexus Chakra and promotes cheerfulness.

PHYSICALLY
- Citrine stimulates digestion and promotes the Solar Plexus Chakra and digestive organs associated with it. It also promotes the stomach, pancreas, spleen and circulation of the blood.

MENTALLY
- Citrine stimulates mental endurance and focus. It gives us the ability to draw conclusions and fully understand these conclusions.

EMOTIONALLY
- Citrine helps to dissipate negative energy and to promote inner calm. This stone encourages confidence and self-expression. It promotes a radiance from within, culminating in a constant happy, sunny disposition.

SPIRITUALLY
- Citrine opens the Solar Plexus Chakra and helps to stimulate the Crown Chakra.
- Citrine encourages us toward new experiences and the desire for variety. It helps us to see the spice of life.

Tiger's Eye

Tiger's eye promotes the Solar Plexus Chakra by promoting intuitive impressions. It balances the yin and yang energy.

PHYSICALLY
- Tiger's eye slows down the flow of energy in the body so is helpful to calm adrenal glands and nerves. It is a great pain reliever and helps to mend bones and aligns the spinal column. This stone has a history of treating eye disorders including night vision.

MENTALLY
- Tiger's eye is wonderful for those seeking clarity of thought and for those who must deal intelligently and methodically with scattered details. It assists in brain integration, bringing awareness of perception.

EMOTIONALLY
- Tiger's eye shifts the blues to brightness and optimism.

SPIRITUALLY
- Tiger's eye encourages us to move through difficult times and allows us to stay connected and trust God's process.

Rose Quartz

Rose quartz contributes love to all the essences and holds the vibration of all the information components. Rose quartz has a soft and silky vibration, bringing a wonderful, powerful, loving energy. Rose quartz bestows a calming, cooling energy, which supports all of the chakras to remove negativity and to reinstate the loving gentle forces of self love. It brings us patience and the knowing there is no need for haste, bringing calmness and clarity to the emotions and restoring harmony to the mind. It has been known as the " stone of gentle love".

PHYSICALLY
- Rose quartz stimulates blood circulation in the tissues. This stone fortifies the heart and sexual organs, helps with sexual problems and encourages fertility.

MENTALLY
- Rose quartz is used to help us make decisions and frees us from worry.

EMOTIONALLY
- Rose quartz helps us with empathy, and sensitivity. It encourages self love, a strong heart, romance and the ability to love.

SPIRITUALLY
- Rose quartz supports all the chakras and holds the vibration it is given.

AFFIRMATIONS

1. I accept and value myself exactly as I am.
2. I treat myself with honor and respect.
3. My personal power is becoming stronger each day.
4. I deserve all the love, respect, joy and prosperity that comes my way.
5. I am open to receiving all life's good things.
6. I know I am worth all of the love and kindness the world has to offer me.
7. I know that my presence here on earth is of great importance.
8. I honor my boundaries and I respect other's boundaries.
9. I know I am capable.
10. I know that knowledge is power.
11. I know and understand the world around me.
12. I know I am the best that I can be.
13. I know I am a beautiful person.
14. I know I can do anything I put my mind to.
15. I know I can achieve great things.
16. I know that my work is a labor of love.
17. I know that I take pride in all that I do.
18. I deeply love and approve of who I am.
19. I am worthy of my own self-love.
20. I love and respect myself at all times.
21. I trust my worthiness.
22. I know that everything is for my highest good and greatest joy.
23. I love life.
24. I listen to and trust my deepest insights.
25. I am worthy of the very best in life.
26. I release judgment and let my life flow.
27. I honor the power within me.
28. I accomplish tasks easily and effortlessly.

SACRED GEOMETRY & ANCIENT SYMBOLOGY

Sacred Geometry

Our world revolves around the realms of geometry. Geometry holds information that supports the vibration of our energy body. Some of it has been kept sacred because it exposes the essence of our being and the meaning of life.

Understanding the concepts of sacred geometry begins with the circle. According to the ancients, the circle is said to be the symbol of perfection and three-dimensional perfection is the sphere.

Six spheres compiled concentrically around a center sphere is fundamental in the development of sacred geometry. The number seven is significant in the development of the universe. The foundation for colour, music, the calendar and our being were built from the number seven. There are seven colours of the rainbow, seven whole notes of the chromatic scale, seven days of the week and seven chakras of the body.

Expanding upon the arrangement of seven spheres and adding another six spheres creates a three-dimensional model. In this configuration the new spheres actually touch the edges of the middle sphere like seven pennies would touch if making a circle. The cluster of thirteen spheres at this stage is what the ancients called the "Egg of Life". The ancients believed that everything about our physical existence stems from the "Egg of Life" structure. It is in this cluster of thirteen spheres that the geometry for the pattern of our body is exposed.

Adding another ring of six spheres around the "Egg of Life" creates the beginning of the "Flower of Life". When this arrangement of spheres is encircled completely by two parallel concentric circles, it is considered the "Flower of Life". The ancients believed that this geometric pattern has an extremely important relationship to the creation of our reality. You may recognize this symbol as it is seen all over the world and penetrates into the churches, temples, shrines and synagogues of many religions.

SEVEN CIRCLES OF CREATION

EGG OF LIFE

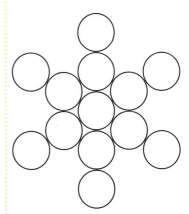

FRUIT OF LIFE

FLOWER OF LIFE

The secret to life according to ancient theory is exposed by the next phase of this pattern. The next phase is to complete all the incomplete circles in the flower of life, which will take four more rings of six equating to another twenty-four circles. By focusing solely on the thirteen circles touching each other we get what is known as the "Fruit of Life".

Energy is broken down into two basic types of energy: female and male. Circles are considered to be female energy and lines are considered to be male energy. The egg of life, the flower of life and the fruit of life are all expressions of female energy. Adding lines or male energy to the fruit of life creates the geometric shape known as the Metatron's Cube. This symbol created by basic geometry is one of the basic patterns that yield the geometric patterns of everything in existence. The Metatron's Cube has different meaning for different geometrical explorations. Metatron's Cube is said to be the basis of thirteen informational systems of the universe. The five platonic shapes are one of these informational systems exposed in the Metatron's Cube.

The five platonic shapes derived from the Metatron's Cube are fundamental of all geometry including sacred geometry. Everything we create is built from the foundation of these five platonic solids. The platonic shapes serve as the beginning of mathematics, construction and health.

What makes these shapes unique is that they are the only shapes that follow these four basic rules:

1. All faces of the shape are the same size.
2. All the edges of the shape are the same length.
3. There is only one size of interior angle between faces.

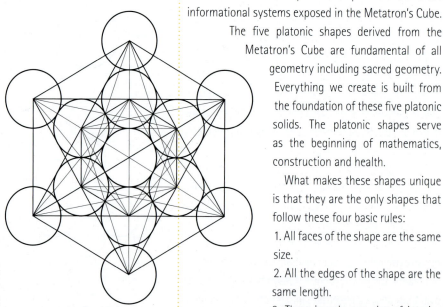

METATRON

4. All the outside points of the shape when placed inside of a sphere touch the ring of the sphere.

Engineers, architects, or anyone in construction has an understanding of these shapes because they are the basis of all structure.

These shapes, with the inclusion of the sphere, were also used to express the elements of the universe, Fire, Earth, Air, Water, Ether, and the sphere represents Voidness. The elements helped the ancients grasp an understanding of the universe and the fundamentals of universal laws. The idea of a macrocosm, the universe, and microcosm, the human body, is evident as the ancients began to understand the human body and health in terms of elements.

The Tetrahedron (4 faces) - inside angles of 60 degrees, representing the Fire element is responsible for the warmth in the body of man. Regulating temperature is vital to the health of all living matter.

The Hexahedron (6 faces) - inside angles of 90 degrees, representing the Earth element with all of its crystals and minerals provides structure to the skeleton and harder tissue matter.

The Octahedron (8 faces)- inside angles of 60 degrees representing the Air element supports the breathing system of the entire living environment.

The Icosahedron (20 faces)- inside angles of 60 degrees representing the Water element is connected with all fluid matter in the world around us.

The Pentagon dodecahedron (12 faces) – inside angles of 108 degrees represents the Universe and is the life-conducting energy sometimes referred to as ether or prana. This is connected with the pineal and pituitary gland.

The energy body surrounding the physical is also known as the etheric body. The dodecahedron is the shape that represents the ether both in terms of the human body and the universe. Because prana or ether were considered sacred by the ancients, the dodecahedron was considered a very sacred shape. What also made the dodecahedron

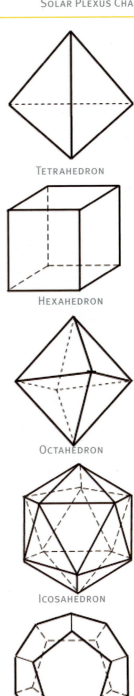

Tetrahedron

Hexahedron

Octahedron

Icosahedron

Pentagonal Dodecahedron

different from the other platonic shapes was that the five-sided shape could not be truncated to Pythagoras's right angle triangle. This shape was held to be the most sacred of all. According to Drunvalo Melchizadek in his book *The Ancient Secret of the Flower of Life*, the outer edge of our energy field, which is enclosed in a circle, is the highest form of consciousness and is shaped as the dodecahedron. So with this understanding of the five platonic shapes and their correlation to the elements we could hypothesize that the dodecahedron holds higher vibrational patterns than the tetrahedron or what is known as the pyramid.

All the water for the Sound Essence products is signatured with the vibrational imprint of the dodecahedron. In addition to the dodecahedron-imprinted water, the Chakra Sound Essences also carry to vibration of the five platonic shapes to support the energy field. The platonic shapes on a vibrational level interface the higher and lower realms.

Geometry is the foundation for many principles of the universe. Pythagoras represents creation as a progression of numbers. The progression of numbers also became the basis of a system of harmony that is the core of music. Therefore understanding geometry also leads to an understanding of music. Pythagoras describes geometry as visual music. Using the laws of mathematics and geometry creates angles and shapes, which create visual harmony known as art. Applying laws of frequency and sound creates auditory harmony, which creates music.

When you look at a yantra from the Ayurvedic tradition of symbology you get an understanding of what Pythagoras meant. Mantras are sacred sounds and the yantra is the visual aspect made of symbols expressing sacred sound.

ANCIENT SYMBOLOGY

Mandalas translate complex mathematical expressions into simple shapes and forms. They show how the basic patterns governing the evolution of life workout the most beautiful results. Mandala means sacred circle. The circle symbolizes the womb of creation and the shape of the universe. Mandalas are geometric designs that are made through uniform divisions of the circle. The shapes that are formed from these divisions are symbols that embody the mathematical principles found throughout creation. They reveal the inner workings of nature and the inherent order of the universe.

Mandalas could be considered a bridge, linking human consciousness to the higher realms. Mandalas bring the principles of nature into our field of awareness allowing us to engage with the rhythm and harmony of nature. For thousands of years, mandala imagery has served as a means to an expanded way of thinking. Mandalas bring about certain wisdom of universal knowledge that our energy bodies are able to understand and use for keeping our bodies balanced.

The symbology offered by way of the yantras and mandalas carry information that helps heal the human body. The yantras are part of the mandala imagery that visually represents harmonic tones of the sacred sounds known as mantras. By directing our thoughts to these sacred shapes, we are attuning ourselves with the harmony of universal consciousness. Symbols have been used for healing in cultural and religious teachings for thousands of years. The images transcend language and the rational mind. They bring about certain wisdom of universal knowledge and a deeper understanding of human consciousness.

An example of symbology reaching our consciousness is the yin/yang symbol. The Chinese have founded the yin/yang symbol, which offers balance but in a deeper connotation represents their entire comprehension of the universe. It gives us an understanding of the dynamics of universal movement undulating from one aspect to

YIN/YANG SYMBOL

Root Chakra Symbol

Sacral Chakra Symbol

Solar Plexus Chakra Symbol

Heart Chakra Symbol

Throat Chakra Symbol

Brow Chakra Symbol

Crown Chakra Symbol

another. The yin/yang symbol expresses the ebb and flow of everything.

The Ayurvedic system has symbols for the chakras, which describe the meaning of each of the chakras. These symbols resonate with our energy field, giving us understanding of universal energies at a subconscious level.

The Root Chakra has the symbol of a square, which symbolizes, form, foundation, instinct, touch and survival.

The Sacral Chakra is a crescent inside of a circle, which represents flow and movement, the crescent, is connected with the element of water.

The Solar Plexus Chakra is connected with the triangle; me, myself and I.

The Heart Chakra is related to the symbol of the "Star of David", which is two triangles with one inverted on the other. Joining the outside points, of the "Star of David", creates the hexagon. This symbol is the seat of vital breath and associated with the air element, with touch, and with feeling and the phenomenon of thought.

The Throat Chakra is connected with the spiral symbol of movement and expression.

The Brow Chakra symbol is associated with the mind.

The Crown Chakra is symbolized with many flower petals in a repeating pattern. This symbolizes exponential powers and eternity. Apparently this chakra increases in size as the intellect expands.

Heart Chakra
Balance/Love/Self-Control

*I am an open channel for divine love.
I open my heart and share it with others.*

LOVE IS DIVINE POWER

The Heart Chakra is the center powerhouse of the entire chakra system. It mediates between the body and the spirit and helps to determine strength and health. It mediates between the lower earthly energies and higher spiritual energies.

The reason that the Heart Chakra is so important is that an open heart is integral to an individual's ability to express love. It teaches us how to act out of love and compassion and recognize that the most powerful energy we have is love. This includes both self-love and the expression of love towards others.

The Heart Chakra is all about unity, peace, unconditional love, hope, forgiveness, compassion and generosity. As the Heart Chakra opens, so does your ability to connect with your higher self. When the fourth chakra center opens, it radiates love and forgiveness.

The Heart Chakra is representative of the element air, which relates to the heart and lungs of the body. This chakra allows us to be in touch with all things. In the fourth chakra; images, words, sounds and smells are transformed into feelings.

If we learn to love and fully accept all parts of our personality and body from the depths of our heart, we can be potentially transformed or healed.

Characteristics of a strong Heart Chakra is someone who radiates natural warmth, sincerity and happiness You put your heart in all that you do and create, you love everyone unconditionally and see everyone through God's eyes. You are living in the now.

COLOUR
Green

COMPLIMENTARY COLOUR
Red

SOUND
Note F and F#

SENSE
Touch

LOCATION
Chest

BASIC PRINCIPLE
To love and be loved

ASSOCIATED GLANDS
Thymus

ASSOCIATED MERIDIANS
Heart

EMOTIONAL COMPONENT
Grief

PHYSICAL COMPONENT
Heart, blood, circulation, lower lungs, rib cage, skin and upper back

INSUFFICIENT HEART CHAKRA ENERGY:
Anti-social and withdrawn
Intolerant
Critical and judgmental
Loneliness
Fear of rejection
Lack of empathy

EXCESS HEART CHAKRA ENERGY:
Co-dependency
Demanding
Jealousy
Clinging
Over-sacrificing

HARMONIOUS FUNCTION OF THE HEART CHAKRA:
Warmth, sincerity and happiness
Strong connection to all of life
Compassion and willingness to help
Unity
Peaceful and balanced
Loving

PHYSICAL IMBALANCES:
Chest pain
Lung congestion
Pasty complexion
Upper back tension
Blood pressure imbalance
Heartburn
Cold sweats
Cold extremities
Tight muscles
Aches, pinches
Cramps and numbing

EMOTIONAL IMBALANCES:
Needing recognition and confirmation from others
Self-doubting and always blaming others
Wanting to possess love
Financially and emotional insecure
Mistrustful of life

ISSUES

Love

The Heart Chakra is considered the rainbow bridge. This is where the physical chakras are bridged (through emotion) to the spiritual chakras. We are grounded to the earth by the lower three chakras and rise to the heavens through the higher three chakras.

The basic issues of the Heart Chakra are balance, love and relationship. Through balance we are secure enough to love, through love we form relationships, and through relationships we have the opportunity to work on ourselves, through the mirror image, and therefore move into working with self-awareness and into spirituality.

When in love, we view the world with rose-coloured glasses. The colours are brighter, places have new meaning and all experiences are larger than life.

Being loved by someone gives us more experiences to explore, as we are reflected in the eyes, words, and behavior of our lover. When we understand that we are special, we begin in a new way to truly care for ourselves and feel a sense of pride and purpose. We take better care of our bodies, keep our houses cleaner, and dare to reach further than we might otherwise if we were still by ourselves. Love brings a spiritual awakening. Intimacy in the Heart Chakra is the foundation for self-expression for the fifth chakra where we have the courage to express our truth.

Balance

The Heart Chakra sits in the middle of the seven chakras. The essential principle of the Heart Chakra is balance, both on the inside of ourselves and on the outside of ourselves.

- Love
- Balance
- Self love
- Relationship
- Intimacy
- Devotion
- Reaching out and taking in

Intimacy/Self-Love

"To love oneself is the beginning of a lifelong romance." Oscar Wilde

We have to love ourselves to be able to offer it openly to someone else. To love ourself, is to act respectfully and responsibly toward ourselves, to enjoy our own company when in solitude, to honor our limits and speak our truths. In general, self-love is an act of treating ourselves the way we would treat anyone else that we love; respectfully, honestly, compassionately, with feelings and understanding, pride and patience. This self-love is then projected to others and can be mirrored back.

Our relationships with others reflects our relationship with ourselves. We will find others who treat us the way we expect to be treated.

Relationship

Personal relationships need balance to be successful. All nature in relationship seeks balance. Lack of balance is expressed as pressure, stress and withdrawing. It is through balance that relationships enjoy success.

Reaching Out/Taking In

It is in the Heart Chakra where balance is exhibited and balance is important with giving and taking whether it be from someone else or simply from the universe. For someone to give, someone else must receive. This can be difficult for many and is an integral lesson of the Heart Chakra. At times we can reach out but we must then also take in.

Devotion

Devotion is the condition of unconditional love, where the love is greater than the self.

COLOUR

Green

With the colour green, we feel empathy and experience inner peace, serenity and are receptive to reconciliation.

Green is the middle of the colour spectrum and is the most harmonizing and balancing colour. Green is the master colour that regulates the etheric body.

Green is the colour of life, harmony and health.

Physically

- Green is related to the heart and has a direct association to the function of the heart and lungs. It dissolves blood clots in any part of the body or head.
- Green is excellent for chest complaints such as asthma, chronic bronchitis and angina. This colour has the properties to influence basic cell structure and it is used to treat tumors, cysts and growths.
- Green alleviates fear in traumatic situations and is effective in treating shock.

Emotionally

- Green is the peace restorer and promotes sharing, adaptability, generosity and cooperation. This colour balances emotions and invites good judgment, conscientiousness and understanding. Space, freedom, harmony and equilibrium all originate from green's natural sense of justice.
- Green is the renewal of life and its highest vibration reflects the spirit of evolution.

Spiritually

- To triumph over the drive to possess and to secure ourselves is to trust the universe so that we may actually become one with it.

Food
Avocados
Beans
Broccoli
Cucumber
Green Salads
Peas

Herbs
Aloe Vera
Angelica
Chamomile
Calendula
Fenugreek
Juniper Berries
Saw Palmetto

Bach Flower Essences
Beech
Centaury
Gentian
Heather
Holly
Impatiens
Larch
Mimulus
Pine
Red Chestnut
Rock Water
Star of Bethlehem
Vervain
Vine
Water Violet
Willow

Pacific Essences
Alum Root
Barnacle
Death Camas
Diatoms
Dolphins
Douglas Aster
Easter Lily
Fireweed
Grass Widow
Hooker's Onion
Nootka Rose
Salal
Sea Palm
Sea Turtle
Silver Birch
Snowberry
Surfgrass
Twin Flower
Windflower

SOUND

Note F

Physical Aspects
The note F is influential in the function of the thymus gland and the entire immune system. It is tied to the functions of the heart and the circulatory system of the body. It is physically related to the lungs, the heart, and the chest muscles. The note F is useful on a physical level for women dealing with breast cancer. Getting more connected to the heart centre allows us to give and receive freely, it is believed that breast cancer starts as an inability to receive. Using the vibration of note F bolsters the resonance of the Heart Chakra creating the capacity to overcome any kind of physical difficulties.

Emotional Aspects
Emotionally, this is the place of release, of expansiveness, joy and endurance. The vibration of the F note supports any person who is in pain, physically or emotionally. The note F will bolster their capacity to endure what they need to bear; it makes bearable the unbearable.

Spiritual Aspects
This is the mediating center of the chakras. It is the center that awakens compassion and its expression in our lives. It is our center for expressing higher love and healing energies. On a spiritual level this is the point of the cause where we sense our purpose in life. The arms reach out and receive the divine, which gives us our sense of connection to life, nature and brotherhood.

Note F♯
Transition into adulthood; finding one's calling

PHYSICAL ASPECTS
The location of the F♯ semitone on the body is where the thoracic spine meets the cervical spine. This location is at the base of the throat.

EMOTIONAL ASPECTS
F♯ is the bridge between the Heart Chakra and the Throat Chakra; taking information from the heart and moving it into the throat for expression is the primary purpose of the F♯ vibration. This vibration helps us to go after what we want. We will have a positive attitude about our accomplishments. With the support of this vibration we are supported by others and are supported by the universe. Things then happen, as they should in perfect timing without the individual pushing to get things accomplished. F♯ allows us to be in the place of community when our work is seen as an integral part of the whole. Simply said, we are in the zone. Our will is aligned with that of the universe.

SPIRITUAL ASPECTS
F♯ is significant to finding our calling in life or for those finding their path or establishing themselves in the world. This vibration is fabulous for our transition into adulthood. F♯ is crucial for the establishment of maturity, therefore it is tied to the thymus and the thyroid.

Chapter 8

Essential Oils
Cedarwood
Champa
Cypress
Eucalyptus
Fir
Lime
Oregano
Peppermint
Pine
Rose
Rosewood
Spearmint

PLANT FORM – ESSENTIAL OILS

Eucalyptus

Eucalyptus oil comes from the oil of leaves and twigs from the beautiful Australian evergreen eucalyptus tree; home of the koala bears. Eucalyptus is often noted as a medicinal essential oil because many people associate its clean camphorous fragrance with that childhood favorite Vick's VapoRub. This essential oil is probably best known for its effectiveness in combating respiratory ailments.

PHYSICALLY
- Eucalyptus improves circulation, promotes sweating and thereby relieves fever. This oil soothes the chest and respiratory tract, helps clear airways, sinus congestion, asthma, infectious coughs, colds, and flu symptoms. Other areas eucalyptus has been noted to assist in are urinary infection, fluid retention, skin infections, rheumatoid arthritic and muscular aches and pains.

MENTALLY
- Eucalyptus lifts depression, clears the head and strengthens the nerves. This oil deepens concentration and increases alertness of memory. Eucalyptus is a wonderfully energizing essential oil that can give a fresh start to any day.

EMOTIONALLY
- Eucalyptus cools and comforts. It dissolves bitterness and resentment. It helps rid addictions, guilt and self-blame.

SPIRITUALLY
- Eucalyptus acts as a regenerative remedy by opening the heart to Universal Love.

Peppermint

Peppermint is the flower of refreshment. It has a fresh cooling mint scent that stimulates the body and mind.

PHYSICALLY
- Peppermint is one of nature's finest digestives. It stimulates bile and digestive juices therefore assists indigestion, colic, diarrhea, nausea, flatulence and cramping. Peppermint has a cooling action on the skin and helps with acne, dermatitis, tooth abscess and muscular pains. This oil supports the respiratory, immune, nervous and musculoskeletal systems.

MENTALLY
- Peppermint's invigorating aroma enhances alertness and soothes headaches, vertigo and fainting, helps relieve mental exhaustion and fatigue. Peppermint stimulates the brain and increases the capacity to retain facts and to hold the memory.

EMOTIONALLY
- Peppermint is uplifting, and gently warms you up. It helps with self-acceptance and offers space to be oneself.

SPIRITUALLY
- Peppermint is invigorating, allowing us to see life from a different point of view.

Rosewood

Rosewood oil is derived from the heartwood of an evergreen tree found in the tropical rainforests of Brazil. Its fragrance is floral, warm, slightly rose with spicy woody and sweet undertones.

Physically
- Rosewood is a popular remedy for chronic complaints, especially where the immune system has been impaired, such as old wounds, oral infections and candida.

Mentally
- Rosewood is an excellent tonic for the nervous system, offering calm and vitality. It has been said that it stabilizes the central nervous system and could therefore have an overall balancing effect.

Emotionally
- Rosewood helps when one is feeling low, weary and over-burdened with problems. It gives an uplifting, enlivened feeling.

Spiritually
- Rosewood creates a feeling of peace and gentleness.

MINERAL FORM – CRYSTALS AND GEMSTONES

Aventurine

Aventurine is mostly known as a stone for the Heart Chakra which activates and clears energy. It protects and shields the heart from unwanted energy. It seems to augment the pioneering spirit. Green aventurine soothes and harmonizes allowing the serenity of nature to enter the heart center helping to release the constrictions that bind the heart and keep it from staying healthy.

PHYSICALLY
- Aventurine encourages the regeneration of the heart. It stimulates the fat metabolism and lowers cholesterol levels, which helps prevent the deterioration of the heart. Aventurine also assists the lungs, adrenal glands and muscular systems.

MENTALLY
- Aventurine encourages tolerance for other's suggestions. It promotes thinking by enhancing creativity and enthusiasm.

EMOTIONALLY
- Aventurine helps us tolerate annoyance and anger. It enhances relaxation and regeneration and recuperation.

SPIRITUALLY
- Aventurine discloses what makes us happy and allows us to see ourselves and encourages us to be true unto ourselves. It helps to make dreams come true.

GEMSTONES
Amethyst
Aventurine
Azurite
Emerald
Green Agate
Green Calcite
Jade
Malachite
Moonstone
Peridot
Rose Quartz
Tourmaline
Turquoise
Watermelon Tourmaline

Turquoise

Turquoise has been used since the time of Tibetan shamans for spiritual qualities and protective qualities. It is also one of the favorite healing stones of the Native American Indians. According to legend it has been used in ceremonies to initiate rain. It helps one to develop natural powers and enhances the art of communication.

Physically
- Turquoise is a master healer and strengthens the entire anatomy. It aids in the absorption of nutrients, stimulates the regeneration of tissue and helps to increase circulation to the muscles.

Mentally
- Turquoise can be used to balance the male and female aspects of one's character, which helps to balance mental and spiritual energies and bring clarity to both. Turquoise promotes inner calm yet allowing the mind to be alert and ready to take charge.

Emotionally
- Turquoise strengthens and aligns all the chakras, meridians and subtle bodies. It brings loving communication to personal emotional issues.

Spiritually
- Turquoise is excellent for spiritual attunement. It helps to improve meditation and is valuable for grounding during deep meditations. It is used for those participating in astral travel and vision quest.

Rose Quartz

Rose quartz contributes love to all the essences and holds the vibration of all the information components. Rose quartz has a soft and silky vibration, bringing a wonderful powerful loving energy. Rose quartz bestows a calming, cooling energy, which supports all of the chakras to remove negativity and to reinstate the loving gentle forces of self-love. It brings us patience and the knowing there is no need for haste, bringing calmness and clarity to the emotions and restoring harmony to the mind. It has been known as the " stone of gentle love".

Physically
- Rose quartz stimulate blood circulation in the tissues. This stone fortifies the heart and sexual organs, helps with sexual problems and encourages fertility.

Mentally
- Rose quartz is used to help us make decisions and frees us from worry.

Emotionally
- Rose quartz helps us with empathy, and sensitivity. It encourages self-love, a strong heart, romance and the ability to love.

Spiritually
- Rose quartz supports all the chakras and holds the vibration it is given.

AFFIRMATIONS

1. I send love to everyone I know; all hearts are open to receive my love.
2. I love myself for who I am.
3. I am grateful for all the love that I have in my life.
4. The love that I feel for others and myself is unconditional.
5. I love the peace I feel when I am in nature.
6. I love the peace and sanctity of my home.
7. I love the peace I feel when I stop controlling others.
8. I love unconditionally.
9. I love helping others.
10. I love myself enough to forgive myself.
11. I love myself enough to forgive others.
12. I love being accepted by others.
13. I love giving to others.
14. I love being generous in my everyday emotions, thoughts, and actions.
15. I deeply and truly love and approve of myself.
16. I am willing to love everything about myself.
17. I trust in love.
18. I open my heart to love.
19. I forgive myself.
20. I forgive those who need forgiving for not being what I wanted them to be.
21. I am pure, good and innocent.
22. Love is the purpose of my life.
23. Love is everywhere.
24. I open myself to the healing powers of love.
25. I follow the path of the heart.
26. I am confident that the healing power of God's love will heal my mind, heart and body.

TOUCH, CRYSTALS AND GEMS

Touch

Loving touch has always been considered healing. There are two kinds of touch; one is directly on the body like body massage and the other is what we call etheric touch or laying on of hands, in where the partner never touches the skin but makes an effect on the energy body. Our hands are natural tools for healing whether applied on the body or slightly above it. Everyone has the ability to use etheric touch but it takes practice and the belief that it works. Etheric touch is an invaluable tool and works effectively in restoring balance to the body. It works most effectively when we are in a relaxed state or in a meditative state. When we are in a relaxed state we experience all outside influences more acutely. Sounds are louder, smells are stronger, lights and colours are brighter, and touch, even etheric touch, becomes more sensitive. Remaining relaxed helps us to perceive and direct energies with the hands more effectively. The healing from the hands comes from the projection of intention and directing loving energies to the meridians or the chakras and their physiological systems. This healing energy is then taken right into the organs and glands and affects the body on a cellular level. Touch is most effective when it is used as a channel of the divine source.

One of the most effective ways of developing and testing your hand sensitivity is through using colour swatches and sensing the temperature of the colour and later holding crystals and gems and assessing their healing qualities and attributes.

Crystals & Gems

Crystals and gems are the blossoms of the inner planet. These crystalline expressions of flowers come from deep within the earth and are no less colourful and spectacular than flowers. Flowers wilt and decay, but crystals are eternal and hold universal energies and their glory over time. Crystals and gems possess the vibrations and powers of the earth, they are living and conscious. Crystal and gem therapy is a form of vibrational therapy similar to colour therapy; in fact it has been considered that colour may be the most important single characteristic of the stone's curative properties. The ability of the crystal to absorb and refract light is what gives the stone its colour; the healing comes from how we are able to absorb and refract the light available in the crystal. Gem therapy utilizes the mineral kingdom's ability to hold magnetic force fields and express a definite vibrational pattern that resonates with our bodies.

Healing also comes from the information of the geometric pattern of the crystals. It also needs to be mentioned that gem therapy, like herbology, follows the relationship known as the doctrine of signature. This doctrine suggests that the shape, colour, odor, make-up, taste and nutrient qualities of many minerals associated with the human body gives us the clues in how the gem could affect us most efficiently. An example is the red dots of bloodstone gave this stone its name and suggests that we use it for blood related issues.

Crystals and gems have been esteemed for their healing qualities since the beginning of civilization. The Christian bible refers to crystals over 200 times. Crystalline structures have been found in the ruins of Babylonia and in the ancient tombs of Egyptian and Chinese rulers. The ancient people were in wonder of the crystal energy and they believed it had a magical effect. Crystals are used for many things, they are used to treat food, water, plants and animals and are used in our computers and can help a car be more fuel efficient.

Crystals have the ability to focus energy which means they can be used as tools for etheric touch such as directing energy to a specific point, meridian, chakra or a pain point on the body. Crystal healing has wide parameters; for as many crystals as there are, there are disorders in the human body. However, there are only a few fundamental energy blocks that create these diseases. By releasing energy blocks, which create the hormone imbalance, we can embrace our full potential. By focusing on the qualities such as the colour of these earth flowers we can release the emotional blockages and move beyond dis-ease. We can also place the stone directly on the body and allow the energy of the gemstone to resonate with us, thus offering the body healing on a very physical level.

A crystal has been defined as "a substance solidified in a definite geometric form". Crystals were formed when the earth was pushing its molten interior to the surface of the earth and as the substances cooled they formed orderly patterns causing the crystalline formation.

The formation the minerals took and the type of crystal or gemstone formed is determined by the amount of pressure and temperature that the minerals were exposed to.

There are at least a hundred thousand different types of crystals. New ones are discovered every year. Just as flower families are categorized, gemstones and crystals are organized into six categories for use in identification. The six categories are: isometric, tetrahedral, hexagonal, orthorhombic, monoclinic, and triclinic.

The truncation for all these shapes is the platonic shape of the cube. It all depends on which angle you view the cube from, the square, hexagonal, or rectangular view.

There are crystals to correct all and any energetic disturbances. They deal with the causes and not the symptoms. Crystals and gemstones work on all levels of the body. They support the body on a physical, emotional, mental and spiritual level and truly fit into the realms of holistic healing and vibrational medicine.

Healing with crystals is just like homeopathy, flower and sound essences or aromatherapy; it belongs to the category of information therapies. It is not the chemical substance that is effective but the information emitted by the transference of vibration. All gemstones can be made into elixirs or essences.

Stones and minerals also possess a radiating property; this is why we can feel heat from a stone. This radiation results from the transformation of absorbed light, which our bodies pick up as a positive vibration. That's why it feels so great to discover a stone, to pick it up and to put it your pocket to play with all day.

On a vibrational level, gem therapy straddles homeopathy and flower essence therapy. Gems offer information to the body in support of the aura, chakras, meridians and five-element theory. To summarize, gem therapy offers the body healing information through colour, sacred geometry and healing radiation.

The different shapes of the crystals, depict how it transmits energy and how this affects its surroundings. For example:

- A long pointed crystal focuses the energy in a straight line. It transmits energy or draws it off, depending which way it is pointed.
- Geodes, rounded cave-like stones, diffuse and contain the energy of the crystal.
- Balls emit energy in all directions equally, used as a window they can transport energy from another time and place; past or future.
- A double terminated crystal radiates or absorbs energy at its extremities. Double terminators break old patterns and are useful in treating addictions. They can also help to develop telepathy.
- Crystal clusters radiate the energy of the crystal to the surrounding environment. They are particularly useful for cleansing energy in a room, or cleaning other crystals.
- Egg shaped crystals can be used over the body to detect and re-balance blockages. The pointed end can be used as a tool for therapies such as acupressure or reflexology.
- Square crystals consolidate energy.
- Pyramid shaped crystals tightly focus energy through the apex.

Throat Chakra

Knowledge Health Communication

*I express myself freely and easily.
I communicate my thoughts clearly
and effectively.*

SURRENDER PERSONAL WILL TO DIVINE WILL
If love is the key word for the Heart Chakra then expression is the keyword for the Throat Chakra. The Throat Chakra has been referred to as the "Holy Grail" of the chakras because it holds precious information from all the chakras.

The Throat Chakra is about communication, personal expression, speaking your truth, creativity, knowledge and harmony with others, accountability, and following your dreams. The fifth chakra is the center of the human capacity of expression, communication and inspiration. It serves as a link between the lower chakras and the crown center. Through the fifth energy center we express everything that is alive within us, such as our laughing and crying, our feelings of love and happiness, anxiety and aggressiveness, our intentions and desires as well as our ideas, knowledge and perceptions of inner worlds.

The element associated with the Throat Chakra is ether, which is a medium of sound and of the spoken word.

Our fifth chakra shows us that personal power lies in our thoughts and attitudes. It is also the center of choice and consequence. Every choice we make and every thought and feeling we have, is an act of power that has personal, social, environmental, and global consequences.

Characteristics of a strong Throat Chakra are strong communication and listening skills. People with these characteristics will tell you the truth even if you would rather not hear it. These people make excellent healers, speakers and therapists. They are very reliable and once they make a commitment they will keep their word and follow through with the promise. Someone with a strong throat chakra has independence, freedom and self-determination and will trust their inner guidance.

Colour
Blue

Complimentary Colour
Orange

Sound
Note G and G♯

Sense
Hearing

Location
Throat

Basic Principle
To speak and hear the truth

Associated glands
Thyroid

Associated meridians
Lung

Emotional Component
Lying

Physical component
Jaw, neck, throat, voice, and airways

INSUFFICIENT THROAT CHAKRA ENERGY:
Fear of Speaking
Difficulty putting feelings into words
Shy, quiet, and withdrawn
Out of touch with own desires
Not trusting intuitive powers

EXCESS THROAT CHAKRA ENERGY:
Too much talking
Talking as a defense
Dominating voice
Inability to listen
Appear strong at all cost
Language is coarse and blatant

HARMONIOUS FUNCTION OF THE THROAT CHAKRA:
Openly able to express feelings and thoughts
Living creatively
Good sense of timing and rhythm
Imaginative
Colourful and clear speech
Trusting your inner guidance
Openly passing knowledge

PHYSICAL IMBALANCES:
Cold symptoms
Coughing
Tickle and phlegm in throat
Stress
Hyperactivity
Allergies
Goiter
Depression
Fatigue
Asthma
Emphysema
Stuffed, runny nose

EMOTIONAL IMBALANCES:
Surrendering to superiors constantly
Clinging to tradition
Resisting change
Rigidity and stubbornness
Trapped by fixed ideas
Being slow to respond

ISSUES

Resonance

All life is rhythmic from the rising and setting of the sun to the in and out of our breath, from the beating of our hearts to the infinite vibrations of atomic particles within ourselves, we are a mass of vibrations that miraculously resonate together as a single system.

Resonance is a state of synchronization of vibrational patterns. All vibrations can be thought of as wave-like movements through space and time. Each waveform has a characteristic rhythm known as frequency that describes how frequently the waves rise and fall. In music, the pitch of a note can be expressed as a certain frequency – high notes vibrate more rapidly, while lower notes vibrate slower.

When two or more sounds from different sources vibrate at the same frequency, they are said to resonate together. Oscillating waveforms tend to stabilize when they enter into resonance because they are on the same wavelength. It is easier, for example to sing the same note as another than to sing a different one, as we quickly discover when we try to sing harmony. Thus resonate frequencies tend to bond together.

We experience resonating waveforms in many common ways. When we listen to a chorus of voices or a troupe of drummers, we are immersed in a field of resonance that vibrates every cell in our body. Such a field influences the subtler vibrations of consciousness and we feel pleasure, expansiveness, and rhythmic connection with the pulse of life itself. We enter even deeper resonance when we dance or move rhythmically to music. The rhythmic movements of the body stay in phase with the music and it actually becomes difficult to move out of phase.

The rhythmic entrainment of various frequencies within our body and consciousness forms a coherent, central vibration that we experience as a kind of resonant "hum" when we are having a good day. On those days, it seems we are in harmony with everything, as if we

Resonance
Communication
Creativity
Listening
Finding one's own voice

cannot miss a beat. We are in sync with the rhythm of the universe.

Understanding the principles of vibration and resonance helps to increase the coherence of our basic vibrational experience and realign our basic rhythm thus keeping our body in balance.

Resonance requires a certain balance of flexibility and tension. A string needs to be both taut and flexible in order to sound a note. In our bodies, we need to have enough flexibility to resonate with different frequencies, yet maintain enough tension to create a repeating pattern.

The state of resonance with the body/mind is a statement of our health and vitality. When we cannot resonate with the world around us, we cannot link with it. We are unable to expand, respond or receive. We become isolated and ill. Opening to resonance requires both grounding for the physical connection to earth and an openness for breath that yields softness and flexibility for spiritual enlightenment. This balance of allowing and willing allows us both to listen and respond at the same time.

Communication

Communication is the exchange of information and energy. While resonance gives the underlying principle for the fifth chakra, communication is truly its essence and function.

In the Sacral Chakra, we grasp the world through our senses; taking it all in. With the Throat Chakra, we reach out into the world, expressing ourselves because of our senses. These two chakras are often linked, such that problems in one will often be reflected in the other. Only when mind and body are connected do we have true communication.

Creativity

To fully live our truth as individuated beings is to live life as a creative act. Communication is the creative expression of all that is within us. When we create we make something that has not existed before. Creativity in the fifth chakra is a consciously willed process. We are literally creating our world each and every moment through our actions, expression and communication.

Creativity is a pure expression of the spirit within us, the natural process of self as it individuates.

Voice/ Listening

The voice is an expression of vibration. The fifth chakra's sense is sound and is located at the throat, the voice is the healthy expression of the fifth chakra. If the chakra is inhibited, the voice will also be inhibited, sounding whiny, whispered, or mumbled. If the chakra is expansive, the voice too may be expansive, it may be loud, shrill or the person may habitually interrupt or dominate conversation. A healthy fifth chakra has a rhythmic and resonate voice that speaks truthfully, clearly and concisely. Communication by conversation is balanced between listening and responding. It is integral for our health that we have the freedom to express ourselves fully.

Truth

Expressing our truth allows us to express our individuality. For us to fully and truthfully express ourselves we need the healthy development of all the chakras before the throat chakra can be balanced and operating optimally. To express ourselves, we need the self-acceptance gained from the fourth chakra (heart) and the ego and will of the third chakra (solar plexus) we need the creative expression of the second chakra (sacral) and the trust we built in the first chakra (root). We need to express our truth to keep our etheric field balanced and healthy. When we are out of our truth we are out of sync with others and our universe. Our resonance becomes interrupted and we experience disharmony. We become completely uncoordinated and our health becomes compromised.

Chapter 8

Food
Asparagus
Bramble Berries
Blueberries
Fish
Kale
Plums
Potatoes

Herbs
Blessed Thistle
Buckthorn
Cascara Sagrada
Catnip
Comfrey
Elderberry
Fennel
Feverfew
Irish Moss
Kelp
Lobelia
Milk Thistle
Motherwort
Oatstraw
Peppermint
Slippery Elm

Colour

Blue

The colour blue creates calmness and expansiveness and allows spiritual inspiration. Blue is a peaceful and relaxing colour.

Physically
- Blue increases metabolism and builds vitality and has a calm, relaxing effect.
- Blue is successfully used to treat feverish conditions, fast pulse rate and high blood pressure.
- Blue symbolizes cool and soothing and can help reduce heat and inflammation from the body like sunburn or sunstroke.
- Blue is centered in the throat, and helps to release tension stress and headache and naturally relieves all throat and vocal imbalances such as sore throats, coughs, hoarseness, and laryngitis. Women with menstrual imbalance can use the healing quality of blue to help period pain, backache and balance blood flow.

Emotionally
- Blue is part of the cool colour spectrum and in its stillness and faith; this colour promotes devotion and trust. This colour is associated with duty, beauty and fact.
- Blue relaxes the mind and controls the throat chakra, which is the creative power center.
- Blue is pure serenity bringing with it peace, faith, and lovely relaxing, healing feelings.
- Blue is the auric field of all healers.
- Blue is the colour for meditation and marks the entry into deeper realms of the spirit.

Spiritually
- Blue promotes devotion which transcends thoughts, concepts and assumptions.

THROAT CHAKRA

SOUND

Note G

PHYSICAL ASPECTS
The Throat Chakra is tied to the functions of the throat, the esophagus, the mouth and teeth, the thyroid and the parathyroid glands. The note G is the controlling center for the glands and the hormones. It is the interface between the higher mental functions and the organ level functions. If one is in physical need of gland balancing, use the note G.

EMOTIONAL ASPECTS
On an emotional level the G note is useful for those who have integrated with their family, with their community and are now experiencing the challenge of expressing not just their personal truth but the truth of their community. The Throat Chakra is about communication, expressing your emotions, beliefs and ideas. The G note supports this expression on a deeper level allowing the integrated wisdom of community thinking and collective consciousness to be expressed.

SPIRITUAL ASPECTS
On a spiritual level the keyword for this note is community. The note G supports the transition of the physical being towards spiritual consciousness. It supports those that are moving towards the service of one's highest ideals and into the concept of spiritual community. So this essence is very useful for those at the beginning of their spiritual journey moving towards conscious awareness.

BACH FLOWER ESSENCES
Agrimony
Centaury
Cerato
Chestnut Bud
Clematis
Gentian
Impatiens
Larch
Mimulus
Pine
Rock Water
Walnut
White Chestnut
Wild Oat
Wild Rose

PACIFIC ESSENCES
Bluebell
Blue Camas
Candystick
Chickweed
Chiton
Coral
Dolphin
Hermit Crab
Hooker's Onion
Jellyfish
Lily of the Valley
Nootka Rose
Pipsissewa
Poplar
Purple Crocus
Sand Dollar
Weigela
Windflower
Yellow Pond Lily

Note G#

Awakening Spiritual Consciousness

Physical Aspects

The location of the G# semitone on the body is where the cervical spine meets the skull. This location is the bridge between the Throat Chakra and the Brow Chakra.

Emotional Aspects

This vibration has a tremendous impact on the logical conscious brain and is what separates us from animals. This is where the animal instincts meet the higher brain function of humans; we call this our logical conscious brain. Humans have two brains, our back brain, which is primal and instinctive like that of animals and our forebrain which has logic and decision making capabilities. The note G# supports the logical, conscious thinking brain, especially in times of stress.

Spiritual Aspects

The Throat Chakra is about communication and expressing ourselves and the Brow Chakra is all about intuition and how we express ourselves in accordance to our life's journey. The issues related to the G# vibration is to awaken spiritual consciousness. G# is in balance when an individual is successful and well suited to their work and fulfilling their task in life. G# will support one on their life's path. It offers the trust to take a chance to go after your heart's desire.

PLANT FORM – ESSENTIAL OILS

Birch

Birch oil is a powerful oil that has a fresh, crisp, intense, woody aroma that is reminiscent of wintergreen. This oil comes from the bark of the large Birch tree native to Southern Canada.

PHYSICALLY
- Birch supports the lymphatic system, helps to eliminate uric acid in the joints, dissolves kidney and bladder stones and assists with gout. Birch helps with arthritis, rheumatism, osteoporosis, tendonitis, muscular and bone pain.

MENTALLY
- Birch invigorates and energizes the mind.

EMOTIONALLY
- Birch helps to regain dignity and self-value.

SPIRITUALLY
- Birch is said to protect the aura by raising the rate of vibration. It brings wisdom through linking with the higher mind and raising the level of consciousness.

ESSENTIAL OILS
Arnica
Birch
Black Pepper
Chamomile
Germanium
Lemon
Marjoram
Peppermint
Yarrow

Black Pepper

Black Pepper is an ancient and highly prized spice, first used in India over 4000 years ago. Black pepper has a very sharp and spicy fragrance.

Physically
- Black Pepper fortifies the digestive system by increasing the flow of saliva and stimulates appetite. It expels wind, quells vomiting and encourages peristalsis. It stimulates circulation and kidney function. It gives tone to the skeletal muscles and soothes muscle aches and pains and helps with rheumatoid arthritis and temporary limb paralysis. Black Pepper helps with lethargy and anemia in that it aids the formation of new blood cells. Black Pepper serves the immune system and helps to relieve coughs, colds, influenza and fevers.

Mentally
- Black Pepper stimulates and strengthens the nerves and mind.

Emotionally
- Black Pepper gives stamina where there is frustration and warms the heart where there is indifference.

Spiritually
- Black Pepper helps to keep us grounded and is often associated with the Root Chakra.

Geranium

Geranium is the "flower of constancy" which delivers a cozy-sweet minty scent. This oil is extracted from the leaves of the geranium plant, which offers romantic, relaxing and clarifying effects.

PHYSICALLY
- Geranium supports the digestive, liver, urinary, circulatory and nervous systems. Geranium assists the body in balancing the liver and gallbladder. It is useful for digestion, gastric ulcers, kidney and urinary stones, water retention. Geranium is an excellent hormonal balancer and helps with premenstrual symptoms and menopause.

MENTALLY
- It helps to relieve tension and anxiety or over excitement. It lifts the spirits dispelling melancholy and depression.

EMOTIONALLY
- This balancing effect on the emotions reduces mood swings and can be put to good effect when treating premenstrual symptoms and menopausal issues. Geranium is perfect to put you in a good mood, induce sleep, relax or energize.

SPIRITUALLY
- Geranium helps to release creative blocks, opening the flow of universal love.

Lemon

Lemon oil has a citrus fragrance, which is fresh and sharp. It has invigorating, enhancing and warming qualities. Lemon oil comes from the lemon fruit, grown in trees in Southern Europe, Florida and California. The lemon tree gives the impression of fresh, optimistic and fearless power.

Physically

- Lemon supports the digestive system, especially the gallbladder and the pancreas. It is a superb tonic to the circulatory system, supporting the heart and helping with high blood pressure. Lemon invigorates the immune system, helps to relieve sore throats, coughs, colds, influenza and fevers.

Mentally

- Lemon aids the mind in clear thinking and concentration.

Emotionally

- Lemon allows the mind to feel refreshed and cooled when it is feeling bothered, which helps develop a more positive outlook.

Spiritually

- Lemon gives you a love of life.

MINERAL FORM – CRYSTALS AND GEMSTONES

Blue Lace Agate

Blue Lace Agate has the reputation as a protective and good luck stone. The energy of the blue lace agate is most helpful in the Throat Chakra. Blue Lace Agate soothes and balances the throat center assisting us in the creative process of manifesting our needs. It helps us to trust in the process.

GEMSTONES
Aquamarine
Blue Lace Agate
Kyanite
Lapis Lazuli
Sapphire
Sodalite
Turquoise

PHYSICALLY
- Agate is said to help with gastritis and stomach ulcers, bladder and intestinal inflammation. Agate stimulates digestion and elimination, strengthens blood vessels, helps with uterine and skin diseases. Agate helps arthritis and bone deformity, strengthen skeletal systems including bone fractures.

MENTALLY
- This stone strengthens concentration, logical and rational thought that helps us to solve any problem in an orderly fashion. It also helps us to put our plan into action in a timely fashion.

EMOTIONALLY
- Agate offers security and safety by calming, cooling and lifting our thoughts.

SPIRITUALLY
- Agate takes spiritual inspiration to a higher vibration. It encourages a calm and contemplative perspective of life. Agate really supports the throat chakra leading us to spiritual maturity and growth, inner stability and a sense of reality.

Kyanite

Kyanite naturally aligns the chakras without initiation or deliberation. Kyanite is especially useful to help balance the Throat and Brow Chakras. Kyanite never needs clearing or cleaning. It will not accumulate negative energy and has many applications in healing making it one of the best attunement stones.

Physically
- Kyanite supports the urogenital system and the endocrine system including the thyroid, parathyroid, and adrenals. It helps support brain function.

Mentally
- Kyanite is useful in dispelling confusion arising from emotional, spiritual and intellectual issues. It disperses anger and frustration, which helps to bring clarity to mental awareness and linear reasoning.

Emotionally
- Kyanite brings tranquility and a calmness to the whole being.

Spiritually
- Kyanite facilitates meditation by slowing down the mind and promotes dream recall, dream solving, connecting with higher self and astral guides.

Sodalite

Sodalite is a great stone to use with groups as it helps to provide fellowship and the working towards a common goal and purpose for the group.

PHYSICALLY
- Sodalite supports the throat area and helps with complaints of the throat, larynx and the vocal chords. It has helped to dispel insomnia. Sodalite has also been used for the endocrine system in the treatment of gland metabolism.

MENTALLY
- Sodalite supports the freedom of expression. It pulls our thinking away from confining rules and laws. It allows us to freely express our own ideas and beliefs.

EMOTIONALLY
- Sodalite can be used to allow someone to recognize and label their true emotions and to verbalize their true feelings. Sodalite allows a clear feeling of whom we are and makes it possible for us to stand up for our own feelings, to own them and to live them out.

SPIRITUALLY
- Sodalite helps us to get in touch with the sacred laws of the universe, giving us the "knowing".

Rose Quartz

Rose quartz contributes love to all the essences and holds the vibration of all the information components. Rose quartz has a soft and silky vibration, bringing a wonderful powerful, loving energy. Rose quartz bestows a calming, cooling energy, which supports all of the chakras to remove negativity and to reinstate the loving gentle forces of self love. It brings us patience and the knowing there is no need for haste, bringing calmness and clarity to the emotions and restoring harmony to the mind. It has been known as the " stone of gentle love".

PHYSICALLY
- Rose quartz stimulates blood circulation in the tissues. This stone fortifies the heart and sexual organs, helps with sexual problems and encourages fertility.

MENTALLY
- Rose quartz is used to help us make decisions and frees us from worry.

EMOTIONALLY
- Rose quartz helps us with empathy, and sensitivity. It encourages self love, a strong heart, romance and the ability to love.

SPIRITUALLY
- Rose quartz supports all the chakras and holds the vibration it is given.

Affirmations

1. I express myself freely and easily.
2. I can communicate my thoughts.
3. I hear and speak the truth.
4. I am speaking up for myself.
5. What I have to say is worthy of being listened to.
6. I always speak from the heart.
7. I express myself without fear.
8. I express myself with clear intent.
9. It is now right for me to express the best of who I am.
10. I listen and acknowledge the needs and wants of others.
11. Everything I do is an expression of love.
12. It is now safe for me to express my feelings.
13. I love and trust my creative gifts.
14. I express sincerity towards others.
15. I express sincerity no matter what the situation is.
16. I express my creativity everyday.
17. I express my creativity by writing down my ideas.
18. I express my creativity by doing things with my hands.
19. I express my creativity in charity and love.
20. I express will power in all relationships.
21. I express will power in order to maintain my clarity.
22. I express willpower in order to set my intentions in motion.
23. I express myself verbally.
24. I express my opinions, no matter what.
25. Creativity flows in and through me.
26. Everything I do is an expression of love.
27. I love and trust my creative gifts.

SOUND

The most effective and simple means of balancing the body is through the use of sound. Life is sound and sound brings life to the earth. Sound maintains the existence of all beings. Sound is the key to the miracle of life.

Sound has a powerful effect on us. Sound can enliven us or depress us. Music or positive encouraging words can lift our mood while noise or degrading conversation can draw our energy. Sound has been used as tool to heal, support, center, empower and to expand consciousness. If our perception of sound was unrestricted, we would be able to hear the music of the flowers, grasses, trees and mountains; the singing of the skies and stars and the rhythm of all of nature and the symphony of our own being. Every being has its own melody.

If our sound spectrum were to be enhanced, we could understand how all the particles in nature and the universe are made up of musical structures, frequencies and patterns which our bodies recognize as information and etheric nourishment. This information from sound may or may not resonate with our bodies. It is due to the law of resonance that we can use sound to balance and heal the body, mind and spirit.

For example, each flower and blade of grass sings its own tune; together they create harmony. If there was no harmony, the vegetation would not be attracted to grow in the same field. Co-creative gardening is a fine example of how production is improved by planting compatible plants together. In fact, the correct combination in co-creative gardening can exponentially enhance the growth of both types of vegetation. The plants are simply in tune with their environment.

Dorothy Rettalack was curious about the effects of sound on plant life. She subjected her plants to a local radio station playing rock and the plants leaned away from the music source; the root structures were shallow and also growing away from the sound; and the petunias never flowered. She then subjected her plants to classical and religious music and the plants wrapped themselves around the music source, grew wonderfully and the flowers bloomed prolifically.

Dorothy Rettalack states, "I just can't help thinking that there is some combination of harmonic sounds that would improve human growth and heal illness."

Noticing how plants react to sound really makes one wonder how we are affected by our 21st century noisy way of living. Consciously bringing harmonious sounds into our energy field, counterbalances the discordant sounds and frequencies such as traffic, cell phones, computers and all the electrical magnetic frequencies.

Other experiments have proven that by using certain types of music like jazz, instrumental or classic, enhances egg and milk production.

Sound is a source of energy. Sound can be used to interact with other energies to enhance or amplify them. Sound alters the electro-magnetic fields and impulses of living beings. Sound by itself or combined with other forms of vibration can help restore balance, alleviate pain and accelerate healing in the body.

Sound as an energy can also support the mind and spirit by facilitating concentration, relaxation, learning, and increased awareness. Sound helps us to raise our vibration to a higher energy level in which we can open ourselves to higher consciousness and a higher degree of health.

Our bodies can detect the vibration of sound even though our ears cannot hear it. People are amazed at how simple and yet how effective sound healing can be. The most wonderful part about sound therapy and other vibrational therapies is that we do not need to fully understand them to enjoy the impact they have on the state of our existence just as we do need to have an understanding of electricity to enjoy the impact of electricity and electrical appliances on our lifestyle.

All sounds can be described as waveforms, vibrating at a particular frequency. Sound can be described through these characteristics:

- **Frequency** is a vibrating waveform. Every organ, gland, tissue and bone puts out a frequency and has its own vibration. Sickness and disease also put out a frequency and have their own vibrations.
- **Amplitude** is the distance a wave travels from crest to trough. With sound increased amplitude means increased energy therefore increased volume of the sound.
- **Timbre** is the distinctive characteristic of the sound. It has been described as the colour tone of music. It helps us to distinguish one voice or one instrument from another even when they are playing the same note. Every person and every instrument has its own distinguishable sound characteristic.
- **Resonance** is when two waveforms of similar frequency lock into phase with each other creating harmony. A great example of resonance is a wall of clocks, when first set up they are all ticking at different rates but with time they will all conform to the same resonance and tick in unison.
- **Pitch** is the speed at which the sound vibrates. The faster the vibration of sound, the higher the pitch and the slower of vibration of sound, the lower the pitch. Raising our energies and keeping our vibrations higher than sickness and disease enables us to keep and raise our level of health.
- **Rhythm** is the pulse of life. Steady rhythm restores the body's natural rhythms.

Sound and colour have a lot in common in that they resonate close to one another. Steven Halpern provides a fabulous image of the relationship of colour and sound. Light and colour are expressed as vibrations. "If we put colours in musical language, the harmonies of colour are about 40 octaves higher than audible sound." He uses the example of a piano keyboard with its seven octaves of the musical scale imaginably extended to the full range of 40-50 octaves and suggests that the keyboard would produce colours rather than sounds when played.

As we mirror the three primary colours with the complimentary colours, and then blend in six more colours, we then develop the chromatic scale of 12 colours. This colour scale divides the single octave of visible light into twelve equally spaced colours starting with red, orange, yellow, green, blue, indigo and then finally into red-violet. This colour wheel is directly linked to the chromatic scale of the piano. With this relationship of colour and sound, it makes it possible to paint the keys of music.

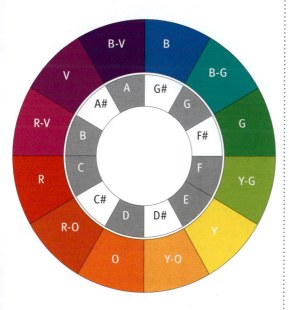

The relationship of colour and sound moves into an energy relationship with the seven spiritual energy centres; seven colours of the rainbow, seven whole notes on the musical scale, and the seven main chakras of the body. It seems more than a coincidence that there is a one-to-one relationship with these different octaves of reality. Each note has a designated colour and both relate to a chakra. The colour red associated with the Root Chakra correlates to the note C. Note C according to Pythagoras is the first audible sound to emerge from the process of vibration. In India the note C is considered the primal tone from which all sound derives. It is most fitting then that note C is related to the primal instinct chakra known as the Root Chakra and is the foundation of the chakra energy system.

The vibration of sound is recognized by the chakras of the body. The chakras are the receivers and transmitters of vibrational information to and from the body. They mediate the electro-magnetic impulses of our energy system. Specific tones, rhythms, instruments, music and notes affect the flow of the electro-magnetic energies of the chakras. Since the chakras relate also to our physical bodies we can use the power and energy of sound to balance the body itself. The tones of our musical scale resonate with the seven chakras. Each whole note resonates with a specific chakra.

All the chakras, meridian lines, acupuncture points, tissues and organs have their own individual musical note.

Crown — *ohm*
Brow — *eeee*
Throat — *eh*
Heart — *ah*
Solar Plexus — *o*
Sacral — *oo*
Root — *u*

Brow Chakra

Intuition / Mysticism / Understanding

*I am perfectly attuned to my vision.
I move towards my vision with clarity
and insight.*

SEEK ONLY THE TRUTH

The sixth chakra, located in the middle of the forehead, and sometimes referred to as the third eye, activates the lessons that lead us to wisdom. The Brow Chakra is about intuition, imagination, wisdom, understanding and enlightenment. This chakra is the centre of our higher mental powers, our intellectual capacity to distinguish intuition from will. It is considered the highest center of command for the central nervous system.

It is known that every realization in our lives is preceded by thoughts and projected images, which in turn can be nurtured by the knowledge of reality, therefore by way of this mental power we are connected with the process of manifestation via the third eye. We are then able to create new realities at the physical level and dissolve old ones.

The Brow Chakra enables us to connect with the energy of the world beyond our five senses and teaches us to go beyond superficial appearances, find deeper truths and then cultivate our resources of creativity and wisdom. Through the sixth chakra we are able to open ourselves to universal creative energy, which allows us to direct ourselves towards fulfilling our life's purpose.

Someone with strong Brow Chakra characteristics uses their intuitive abilities and is open to new information about their life's purpose. Their ego and soul spirit are balanced. They are able to create their life and manifest their dreams to the highest good.

COLOUR
Indigo

COMPLIMENTARY COLOUR
Yellow

SOUND
Note A and B♭

SENSE
Light/Colour

LOCATION
Forehead

BASIC PRINCIPLE
The right to see

ASSOCIATED GLANDS
Pineal/Pituitary

ASSOCIATED MERIDIANS
Triple Warmer

EMOTIONAL COMPONENT
Illusion

PHYSICAL COMPONENT
Face, ears, eyes, nose, sinus, and nervous system

Insufficient Brow Chakra Energy:
Lack of imagination
Difficulty in seeing the future
Easily lose your head under stress
Poor vision and poor memory

Excess Brow Chakra Energy:
Difficulty concentrating
Obsessed
Delusions
Hallucinations
Nightmares

Harmonious Function of the Brow Chakra:
Intuitive and perceptive
Imaginative
Insight about the world we live in
Integrate information on many different levels
Live and think holistically with nature
Advanced intellectual skills

Physical Imbalances:
Sleeping disturbances
Concentration difficulties
Sinus and nose congestion
Pain in the eyes and head
Hard to make decisions
Slow thinking
Headaches
Depression
Hormonal difficulties

Emotional Imbalances:
Worrying
Fear of the future
Forgetfulness
Over-sensitivity to impressions of others
Undisciplined

ISSUES

IMAGE AS SYMBOL

We enter into the realm of symbols as we move above the Heart Chakra. Language used to communicate emotion, thought and ideas is made of sound symbols. Spoken words are the audible symbol of sound while written words are the visual symbol of sound.

Symbols come to us in our dreams and fantasies, devising ideas and action plans. Symbols are a way of communicating etheric information and integrating these concepts into the physical realm of manifestation.

Image
Intuition
Imagination
Visualization
Insight
Dreams
Vision

DREAMS

Dreams link the unconscious mind with the conscious mind. Dreams present alternatives to ordinary reality. In order to have vision, imagination, clairvoyance, and insight, we need to be able to think in new creative ways. Dreams open the way for us to see things in a new light, revealing hidden feelings and understandings, desires and needs, rejected selves, unused talents and missing pieces of our wholeness. They are often profoundly irrational images that uproot the conscious mind and open it to something larger.

Dreams often bring us answers to problems that our conscious mind could not solve and so become powerful spiritual teachers. In order to understand dreams we need to use our intuition to find their meaning.

INTUITION

Intuition is the primary function of the sixth chakra. Our culture tends to favor logic over intuition. As children we use our intuition freely but as we get older we are trained to dismiss this knowing and turn to logic and reasoning. It is paramount that we develop our intuition to keep ourselves balanced and to keep the sixth chakra healthy.

Vision/Clairvoyance

Clairvoyance means clear seeing. Clairvoyance opens inner sight to non-physical planes, allowing us to see auras and chakras. Clairvoyance, like intuition is developed by surrendering the logic of conscious mind to the universal knowing of the unconscious mind.

COLOUR

Indigo

The colour indigo provides the mind with inner calmness, clarity and depth; it strengthens and heals the senses as well as opening them to subtle levels of perception. Indigo is used to obtain peace, quiet and freedom to stretch boundaries. It brings beauty, justice, and love. It offers a better understanding of life. It allows one to learn to accept, and to let go and trust. It inspires and strengthens intuition.

PHYSICALLY

- Indigo supports the entire skeletal structure.
- Indigo helps to reduce or even stop bleeding, from hemorrhages, nosebleeds and internal bleeding into tissues and organs.
- Indigo purifies the blood and supports the function of the spleen. It is fantastic for tightening, firming and toning the flesh, skin, nerves and muscles.
- Indigo reduces the pain from swelling.
- Indigo has been used as an antibiotic.
- Indigo helps to balance eye and ear dysfunction.

EMOTIONALLY

- Indigo helps to balance fear and frustrations, and strengthens and inspires intuition. Indigo governs the chakra in the center of the forehead controlling the pineal gland, which affects vision, hearing and smell on the physical, emotional, and spiritual planes.
- Indigo is excellent for healing the etheric body and is related to spiritual understanding. It is said to be the ray of Aquarian Age, the soul colour. It represents self-mastery, inspiration, understanding, and integration. It has the status of the most powerful ray in the whole spectrum, and is a bridge between the metaphysical and the spiritual planes.

SPIRITUALLY

- To have a vision of the future that is so powerful that it becomes reality.

FOOD
Broccoli
Eggplant
Grapes
Kale

HERBS
Cascara Sagrada
Pippssisewa
Red Clover
St. John's Wort
Stevia
Usnea
Wild Yam

Bach Flower Essences
Agrimony
Centaury
Cerato
Clematis
Scleranthus
Vervain
Walnut
White Chestnut
Willow

Pacific Essences
Dolphin
Easter Lily
Fairy bell
Goatsbeard
Grape Hyacinth
Hooker's Onion
Nootka Rose
Ox-Eye Daisy
Pearly Everlasting
Rainbow Kelp
Salmonberry
Vanilla Leaf
Viburnum
Weigela
Whale

SOUND

Note A

Physical Aspects
The Brow Chakra influences the functions of the pituitary gland and the entire endocrine system. Physically, note A has to do with the base of the skull, the jaw and all the organs and the parts of the body associated with the first breath. It is a balancing center for the functions of the hemispheres of the brain. It is linked to the sinuses, eyes, ears, and the face.

Emotional Aspects
Grief, deep grief that comes from lack of recognition, lack of love, lack of hope, use Note A to affirm the unique values of the individuals. This supports everyone to express their individual value, for each person needs to feel that their unique combination of their physical being is useful. This is not a sense of purpose, as purpose has to do with doing, value has to do with being.

Spiritual Aspects
This is the realm of worship. This is where all the gifts and abilities that one embodies come together as the offering. This is the offering of self to service for higher good.

Note B♭

Transition To The Spiritual World

Physical Aspects

The location of the B♭ semitone is where the physical meets the energetic, slightly above the head. This location is the bridge between the Brow Chakra and Crown Chakra.

Emotional Aspects

B♭ is the transition between the attachment to physical identity and to the identification of the self as a divine spark, a divine entity, a piece of God. This transition point cannot be activated until the other vibrational frequencies are aligned. B♭ will be less than effective if the other vibrational frequencies are not aligned. But when B♭ is used at that crucial time, that time when all the other vibrations are in line, this vibration is absolutely necessary to complete the transition to the next level of manifestation. The next level of manifestation of death and those approaching death and those who are approaching enlightenment and those who are sitting on the fence.

Spiritual Aspects

The importance of this semitone is to prepare us for the next transition and that is into the spiritual realm, which completes the cycle of life.

Essential Oils
Frankincense
Lavender
Myrrh
Patchouli
Sage
Ylang Ylang

PLANT FORM – ESSENTIAL OILS

Lavender

Lavender is a favorite essential oil with its floral, light herbal scent derived from the flowering spike of this herbaceous plant. Lavender is probably the most useful, versatile and popular healing essential oil. It calms, refreshes, invigorates and lifts the spirits.

PHYSICALLY
- Lavender is an extremely versatile oil that has traditionally been known to balance the body to work wherever there is a need. It supports the nervous, digestive, respiratory, lymphatic, urinary and cardiac systems. It soothes head, muscles, stomachaches, cramps, itching and burns.

MENTALLY
- Lavender naturally reduces stress, anxiety and exhaustion. It is good for irritability, dementia, depression, phobia and insomnia.

EMOTIONALLY
- Lavender resolves conflicts of the mind and is emotionally comforting. Lavender calms and balances.

SPIRITUALLY
- Lavender helps to enhance the meditative state therefore supporting spiritual growth. Lavender helps stabilize the auric field.

Magnolia

This native American evergreen tree grows best near swamps in Florida and North Carolina. Southern Magnolia has large showy white flowers that permeate the room with an intensely sweet and heavenly fragrance; pull up a seat on the porch and inhale the romance.

PHYSICALLY
- Because Magnolia is a fragrance oil, its physical attributes have yet to be discovered and described.

MENTALLY
- Magnolia has a calming effect on the nervous system and supports clear thinking.

EMOTIONALLY
- Magnolia gives a feeling of relaxation. It promotes the feeling of love and is said to bring peace and harmony.

SPIRITUALLY
- Magnolia enhances meditation and physic awareness.

Ylang-Ylang

Ylang Ylang is wonderfully exotic, an intensely sweet and enticing flowery fragrance derived from the blossoms of the Ylang Ylang tree. In Malayan, Ylang Ylang means the flower of flowers. In Indonesia, people spread these delicate and sweet smelling flower petals on the bed of a newly married couple.

PHYSICALLY
- Ylang Ylang helps to balance blood pressure and breathing. It relaxes muscles and relieves heart palpitations and hyperventilation. It is useful in helping with premenstrual tension and depression.

MENTALLY
- Ylang Ylang has been known to aid in stress reduction. Known for its unique calming abilities, it is especially useful when there is nervous tension, restlessness, irritability, anxiety, fear, or anger. As an essential oil it has been considered an aphrodisiac and aids in the treatment of frigidity and impotence.

EMOTIONALLY
- Ylang Ylang is often considered to have anti-depressant qualities. It helps one to reach out to others and share oneself without losing personal power. Ylang Ylang helps develop self-love and to be in touch with one's body.

SPIRITUALLY
- Ylang Ylang has warm and intoxicating effects useful for strengthening the inner being.

MINERAL FORM – CRYSTALS AND GEMSTONES

Lapis Lazuli

Lapis is renowned as the "stone of protection and enlightenment". Lapis, with its deep indigo colour is best suited for the Brow Chakra while aiding the development of insight. Some say it is the stone of friendship.

PHYSICALLY

- Lapis Lazuli is helpful with problems associated with the neck and throat, thymus and immune system. Lapis supports the larynx and throat. It helps to relieve symptoms of insomnia, vertigo and dizziness.

MENTALLY

- Lapis Lazuli quickly relieves stress, bringing a sense of peace. Lapis is known to stimulate the higher faculties of the mind, promoting clear thinking.

EMOTIONALLY

- Lapis Lazuli helps to overcome depression and bestows serenity and self-acceptance. Lapis brings us cheer and allows us to enjoy time with others and helps us to express feelings and emotions.

SPIRITUALLY

- Lapis Lazuli offers wisdom and honesty and reveals our own inner truth. Lapis promotes creativity and attunement with source.

GEMSTONES
Amethyst
Azurite
Diamond
Lapis Lazuli
Moonstone
Quartz Crystal
Silver
Tanzanite

Moonstone

Moonstone is a stone for hoping and wishing. It allows us to understand life's ups and downs and to recognize the changing cycles. The energy of the moonstone relates to new beginnings and with new beginnings we must release the old and initiate each ending. Moonstone helps us get out of our own way and onto our spiritual path. It assists one in the total fulfillment of one's destiny.

PHYSICALLY
- Moonstone stimulates pineal gland function and helps to balance the hormonal cycles with the rhythms of nature; a good example of this is women menstruating in rhythm with the moon cycle.

MENTALLY
- Moonstone brings calmness with awareness. It stimulates confidence and composure, which allows one to move through life knowing that everything will be fine.

EMOTIONALLY
- Moonstone enhances our intuition allowing us to tap into the flashes of insight rather than exploring reasoning with the rational mind.

SPIRITUALLY:
- Moonstone cleanses negativity from the chakras and provides spiritual nourishment and sustenance.

Silver

Silver brings advantage throughout life. Silver is used extensively with gemstones because it enhances the properties of the gemstone.

PHYSICALLY
- Silver helps to eliminate toxins from the body on a cellular level. Silver helps the body to absorb vitamins A and E and helps vision.

MENTALLY
- Silver has been used to improve one's quality of speech.

EMOTIONALLY
- Silver offers the body balance by pulling out negativity.

SPIRITUALLY
- Silver strengthens the "silver cord" connecting the astral body with the physical body, which allows the assurance of one coming home. It is also used as a mirror for the soul, offering insight into our self-journey.

Rose Quartz

Rose quartz contributes love to all the essences and holds the vibration of all the information components. Rose quartz has a soft and silky vibration, bringing a wonderful powerful loving energy. Rose quartz bestows a calming, cooling energy, which supports all of the chakras to remove negativity and to reinstate the loving gentle forces of self love. It brings us patience and the knowing there is no need for haste, bringing calmness and clarity to the emotions and restoring harmony to the mind. It has been known as the "stone of gentle love".

Physically
- Rose quartz stimulates blood circulation in the tissues. This stone fortifies the heart and sexual organs, helps with sexual problems and encourages fertility.

Mentally
- Rose quartz is used to help us make decisions and frees us from worry.

Emotionally
- Rose quartz helps us with empathy, and sensitivity. It encourages self love, a strong heart, romance and the ability to love.

Spiritually
- Rose quartz supports all the chakras and holds the vibration it is given.

Affirmations

1. I see solutions to all situations.
2. I see energy in all things.
3. I see intuition as my God-given gift.
4. I see each day as an opportunity to do good things for the sake of humanity.
5. I see beauty in all things and in all people.
6. I recognize the need for silence and stillness in my life.
7. The answers to all my questions lie within me.
8. I trust my feelings.
9. I am the Divine Plan manifesting itself.
10. I trust that my imagination will create a world of happiness and security for me.
11. I choose to accept others and myself exactly as we are.
12. I open myself to my intuition and deepest knowing.
13. I acknowledge that I am the source in creating my life the way I would like it to be.
14. I accept that I am an unlimited being and that I can create anything I want.
15. I focus on what I love and draw it to me.
16. I am open to new ideas, people and situations that will enhance my joy and happiness.
17. I am responsible for the quality of love and happiness in my life.
18. I create clarity and unlimited vision for myself about my life.
19. I trust that whatever comes to me is for my greatest joy and highest good.

LIGHT AND COLOUR

Exposure to sunlight is essential for our health and colour is as necessary to the soul as air is to the body. In our society, we are spending more and more of our time indoors and covered up. We drive from our garages to our offices and work under fluorescent lighting.

Educated in the hazards of the diminishing ozone layer we cover ourselves either with sunscreen or clothes for protection. We are rarely exposing ourselves to the full spectrum light that actually nourishes us. Jacob Liberman states that we not only suffer from malnutrition but also from mal-illumination.

Our brain can detect light without using the eyes and this is called "eidetic ability". This means that looking and seeing take place exclusively in the brain, which create strong mental images without the eyes and without the sense of the optic nerves. The fact that the body has two ways to detect light demonstrates the importance of light on the body and in our lives. Even if we were to be blinded, we would be able to detect light.

The spectrum of light extends far beyond what is visible for human beings. We use invisible light for many daily uses: radio waves, radiant heat, laser beams, x-rays, gamma rays and microwaves. Visible light and colour is only a fraction of light in the electromagnetic spectrum.

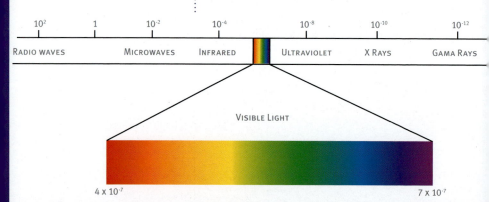

The light spectrum is the paintbrush of the creator. All life on earth depends on light from the sun, which is the ultimate source of life and energy. We receive all knowledge of the universe through this electromagnetic radiation that we call the sun. White light contains the energies of all elements and chemicals found in the sun. This white light of the sun is absorbed from the atmosphere by the physical body and is split into component colour energies, which in turn flow to different parts of the body to vitalize them. Light is a force that stimulates growth: every living thing depends upon it to build and maintain its form. Light brings about chemical changes in nature; by changing the qualities of light we can also bring about chemical changes in the body. Therefore, light whose source is solar energy is one of nature's greatest healing forces.

It is when light and darkness meet that our eyes perceive colour. Total light would blind us and total darkness would render us unconsciousness hence, colour is the healing force. The vibration of colour is the bridge between light and dark. Life is colour. All minerals, plants and animals have colour.

Our bodies are an intricate mix of physical, emotional and spiritual realms. The bridge between the spiritual and the physical is colour; this is how we get colour in the aura. It is through this colour in the aura that the emotions are realized. The aura is the bridge between our physical bodies and our spiritual bodies. Consider that our physical body is the densest therefore the darkest of the three realms and our spiritual body is the least dense therefore the lightest of the three realms. The bridge between these two realms is the rainbow of the chakra colours in the auric field.

Colour influences the way we think. Our emotions and actions affect the electromagnetic field, which surrounds us and is reflected in our aura. The colour

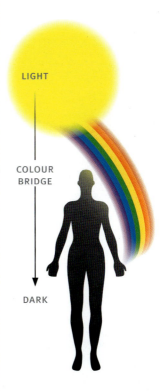

of our subtle bodies and chakras can change by how we react to life. Colour can restore the balance when a blockage or imbalance of this energy has resulted in disease. The use of colour can help restore vitality to the etheric body through the projection of specific colour rays, which are then absorbed by the chakra centres.

Each chakra has its own colour, each energy band in the aura has its own colour and each organ has a specific colour. Each colour has intelligence and polarity, knows its functional role and works selectively. Colour is a vibratory energy that can activate a particular organ, gland and system in the body. The application of the correct frequency of the electromagnetic force field will change the altered function of the body and help return it to its original patterns. It is this energy, which is the result of applying colour, which is important in the healing process. Colour therapy is the science of the use of different colours to change or maintain vibrations of the body to that frequency which signifies good health and harmony. Healing by means of colour was the first type of therapy used by humans. It's nature's own method for keeping the body in balance with the rhythms of nature. Colour therapy will create harmony and balance in the mind and in the body.

Light and colour (which are variant wavelengths of light) enter the body through the eyes, which send signals directly to the autonomic nervous system and the endocrine system, which are both directly related to the chakra system. The Brow Chakra related to the pineal gland is especially light sensitive. The pineal produces melatonin, which regulates sleep cycles and our reactions with the environment. People who are subjected to long periods of darkness during which their body cannot absorb light, suffer from vitamin deficiencies, hormonal disorders, depression, chronic fatigue, stress, sleep impairment, and disturbances of the normal body cycles. The importance of light and colour in keeping our bodies healthy can not be over emphasized.

In 1665 Isaac Newton beamed sunlight through a prism and found the presence of the seven basic colours. Sunlight was simply broken down into the spectrum which ranged from red to orange to yellow to green to blue to purple and then to violet. Nature represents this as a rainbow. Red, orange and yellow are considered the "warm" colours and green, blue, purple, and violet are considered the "cool" colours.

There is a special magic about colours: the three primary colours red, yellow and blue cannot exist without one another. When we look at red for a length of time and glance over to a white spot we see green. Green is the complimentary colour of red but it is also the combination of the other two primary colours, yellow and blue. This is a colour example of trinity. The same holds true for the colour yellow. Its complimentary colour is purple, the combination of red and blue. Lastly, the complimentary colour of blue is orange which is the combination of red and yellow. When utilizing the healing of therapy of colour, complimentary colours are vital for balance.

We intuitively use colour daily by what we choose to wear. Our taste in colours change month by month and day by day. An article of clothing that we absolutely have to wear today can appear to be impossible on another day. A different colour would throw us off completely today, even though it appeared harmonious and calming a few days ago. We go through stages in regards to our emotions and our outlook for the day. The sensitivity to colours not only comes from our eyes but from our skin, as our skin absorbs the colour of what we are wearing. Have you ever noticed that at the end of the day, you simply have to change your clothes and usually into a completely different colour?

Einstein writes that all forms of matter are light waves. All colours represent the energy of light waves in motion, vibrating at distinct and measurable rates. Colour is just variant wavelengths of light. Even though we have ancient teachings of chakras and auras having colours; Valerie Hunt has only scientifically proven this in the last twenty years. She has recorded wave shape patterns from the energy field spectrograms relating to the auric field colours of the body.

Valerie Hunt has proven what the mystics have known for centuries: colours relate to certain frequencies.

Each of the colours has its own waveband clearly denoting the specific colour. The findings first focused on the primary colours. Red had a waveform of 640 – 800 hertz, had irregular groupings of short spikes, sounded like a siren, and was found at the Root Chakra. Yellow had a waveform of 400 –600 hertz, resembled a smooth sine wave, sounded like a musical note, and was found in the Solar Plexus Chakra. Blue had a waveform of 100-240 hertz, exhibited larger peaks and troughs with small deflections riding upon them, sounded like a rumble, and was found in the Throat Chakra. The complimentary colours seemed to be a combination of the sine waves of the primary colours. Green would show the characteristics of blue and yellow, orange has the sine waves of yellow with plateaus of red, and violet resembles a faster version of blue and red.

The aura readers would determine the colour and Valerie would record the wavelength and as the experiments continue, Valerie could predetermine from the wavelength as to what the aura readers were about to see. This work gave us empirical data supporting the idea that the bridge between our physical self (our dense black body) and our spiritual self (our white light) is the auric band, which carries the colour of the rainbow and our emotional self (the colours).

Rueben Amber, author of *Colour Therapy: Healing with Colour*, theorizes how colour evolves as a spiral. The spiral can be seen everywhere in nature, leaves are coiled before they open, vines coil around trees, shells have spiral energy just as the umbilical cord is spiral. Spiral energy seems to have a quality all of its own. When we place direct light through a crystal it conforms to spiral energy, which healers have come to recognize as a more potent energy. Using the crystal light wand, which shines direct light through a crystal and then through a coloured gel, is a very effective colour-energy healing tool.

How Colour affects our physical well being

Colour represents potencies in higher octaves of vibration.

Red — 500hz
Orange — 600 hz
Yellow — 400 hz
Green — 300 hz
Low blue — 200 hz
High blue — 700 hz
Violet — 800 hz
White Light — over 1000hz

Each organ system in the body is stimulated by a particular colour. By knowing the action of the different colours upon the different organ systems the application of the correct colour will help to balance the actions of any system that has become out of balance in its function or condition.

Red
Red is an energizer and supports the nerves and the blood systems. It stimulates the cerebral spinal nerves, sympathetic nervous system and the adrenal gland for the release of adrenaline. It helps with low red blood cell count, lung congestion, paralysis and blood poisoning.

Orange
Orange aids in the uptake of calcium offering a anti-spasmodic properties. It Increases lymphatic movement and raises the pulse rate without raising blood pressure. Orange is known to enlivens emotions and creates a general feeling of well-being. It helps with muscle cramps and spasms, under-active thyroid, colds, gallstones, lung conditions and overall metabolism.

Yellow
Yellow supports digestion and activates the motor nerves and generates energy in the muscles. It loosens calcium deposits and stimulates the flow of bile. It helps with joint inflammation, indigestion, skin conditions, blood issues, constipation and nervous disorders.

Green
Green relieves tension of all sorts. It dilates the capillaries and produces a sensation of warmth. Green is the master healing colour that regulates the etheric body. It helps with heart conditions, hay fever, breathing and stomach problems.

Blue
Blue has cooling and antiseptic qualities. It helps reduce fever symptoms and can assist the quick healing of burns. It promotes growth, and increases metabolism. Emotionally, blue is a good vibration for impatience and over-activity. It helps with itching, hysteria, burns, overweight, fever, vomiting and throat problems.

Indigo
Indigo has astringent properties and can reduce or even stop bleeding. It offers relief from swelling and is good for muscle toning. Indigo positively affects the emotional and spiritual attitudes. It helps with convulsions, tremors, insanity, nasal problems, inflammation of the appendix, eye and ear dysfunctions and improves the sense of smell.

Violet
Violet has diuretic properties helping to purify the blood and suppressing the growth of tumors. It helps maintain the potassium-sodium balance in the body and promotes bone growth. Violet supports the mind by improving thought form and intuition. It helps with bladder problems, skin conditions, mental disorders, sciatic nerve pain, tumors and cramps.

Using colour as thought power:

Red — Highest expression is to reach our fullest potential.

Orange — To share ourselves and to be able to relate to others.

Yellow — To discover the self-sense that includes all other self-senses as well as dissolving the separation between ourselves and others.

Green — To triumph over the drive to possess and to secure ourselves to trust the universe so that we may actually become one with it.

Blue — When devotion transcends thoughts, concepts and assumptions.

Indigo — To have a vision of the future that is so powerful that it becomes reality.

Violet — To become masters of our imaginations and attains control over our thoughts.

Crown Chakra

Beauty / Creativity / Inspiration

*I am one with all creation.
I am consciously living my divine purpose.*

LIVE IN THE PRESENT MOMENT

The Crown Chakra is considered one of the highest vibration centers and is associated with "spiritual quest". This chakra is most open when people are in prayer or searching for the meaning of life. The opening of the Crown Chakra allows one to enter the higher states of consciousness. It is the chakra of prayer.

The Crown Chakra is about oneness with God, beauty, creativity, divine inspiration, faith and spirituality.

This chakra is located on the top of the head. Through the seventh chakra we get our divine inspiration and our divine creativity. This is the chakra where everything comes together and we get the big picture. This is where all the information from all the chakras, merge. When this chakra is open there is a sense of peace, serenity, knowing and a connection with the universe.

Being dedicated to one's life path is characteristic of a strong Crown Chakra. These people have a soul connection with God and are able to access knowledge from this higher intelligence.

When your Crown Chakra is balanced, your life is working in all areas and you feel totally at peace with yourself, God and life itself.

COLOUR
Violet

COMPLIMENTARY COLOUR
Yellow

SOUND
Note B

SENSE
Thought

LOCATION
Cerebral Cortex

BASIC PRINCIPLE
The right to know and learn

ASSOCIATED GLANDS
Pineal/Pituitary

ASSOCIATED MERIDIANS
Central and Governing

EMOTIONAL COMPONENT
Attachment

PHYSICAL COMPONENT
Brain and the central nervous system.

INSUFFICIENT BROW CHAKRA ENERGY:
Spiritual cynicism
Learning difficulties
Feeling separated from abundance and wholeness
Fear of death
Uncertainty and lack of purpose

EXCESS BROW CHAKRA ENERGY:
Over intellectualism
Confusion
Spiritual addiction
Disassociation from body

HARMONIOUS FUNCTION OF THE BROW CHAKRA:
Intelligent, thoughtful and aware
Sense of spiritual connection
Open minded
Wisdom
Ability to perceive and analyze
Assimilate information
Mastery

PHYSICAL IMBALANCES:
Nervous system imbalances
Poor short term memory
Poor co-ordination
Tired
Hallucinations
Ringing in the ears
Dimming of vision

EMOTIONAL IMBALANCES:
Feeling misunderstood
Needing sympathy
Shame, self-denial and self-abasement
Negative self-image
Not understanding need for tenderness

CROWN CHAKRA

ISSUES

HIGHER POWER

The Crown Chakra is the connection between our physical and our etheric body. This is the place where we connect to higher power. Sometimes the higher power is our higher-self, sometimes it is universal power, and sometimes it is the power of our spiritual guides. Nevertheless, the concept is that there is a power larger than ourselves that we can tap into to receive guidance and clarity. It is through the Crown Chakra that we can connect with this level of knowing.

- Transcendence
- Immanence
- Belief systems
- Higher Power
- Divinity
- Union
- Vision

BELIEF SYSTEM

The main purpose of the Crown Chakra is to derive meaning from thought and feelings. Meaning gives us our position in the world. It gives us the knowledge of how to interpret something, how to react, how to compute, and how to register and organize our experiences.

Our beliefs are made of interpretations based on our experience. They help us to create our experiences and to shape our reality.

TRANSCENDENCE AND IMMANENCE

"Transcendence is the path of liberation. Imminence is the path of manifestation. To embrace them both is to see the divine within and without as an inseparable unity."

(from *Western Body Eastern Mind*, by Anodea Judith)

Transcendence is detaching ourselves from the shoulds, coulds, and need-tos of our material world. It is finding oneself in a place of bliss wherever we are in the physical plane. Once we have this bliss it is easy to shine it outward as an expression of immanence. When we have achieved this state of bliss we view everything with a wholistic perspective. Everything is part of everything: The "we are all one" approach to living.

DIVINITY AND UNITY

Divinity and unity is seeing "I" as part of "We". This is where all boundaries have dissolved and we all accept that we are part of the universal whole and "I" is "We".

FOOD
Broccoli
Eggplant
Grapes
Kale
Plums

HERBS
Echinacea
Ephedra
Ginkgo Biloba
Golden Seal
Horehound
Oregon Grape
Uva Ursi
Wood Betany

COLOUR

Violet

The colour violet brings about transformation of mind and soul and opens both to the spiritual understanding of cosmic unity. This colour has the shortest wavelength of the visible colours. It is a colour of both royalty and spirituality assisting in the creative expression of authors, healers and artists.

PHYSICALLY

- Violet supports the chakra system and the central nervous system. It normalizes all glandular and hormonal activity, regulating water balance in the body and normalizes heart rhythms.
- Violets work well for cerebral-spinal meningitis, concussion, epilepsy and any other mental or nervous disorders such as obsessive-compulsive disorders and personality imbalances.
- Violet relieves general nervous disorders, sciatica, neuralgia and problems associated with the eyes, ears and nose.

EMOTIONALLY

- Violet reflects dignity, nobility and self-respect. This colour implies royalty and vibrates with the power of integration and oneness.
- Violet is soothing and contains a calming power.
- Violet evokes artistry, consideration and tolerance.
- Violet, the ray of creativity, brings us to our own level of self-realization and helps with spiritual transformation.

SPIRITUALLY

- Violet allows us to become masters of our imaginations and attain control over our thoughts.

CROWN CHAKRA

SOUND

Note 'B'

PHYSICAL ASPECTS

The note B on the body is located at the top of the skull, the anterior fontanel, the baby's soft spot on the top of the head. This note supports the function of the nervous system and the entire skeletal system of the body. It influences the pineal gland, all nerve pathways and electrical synapses within the body. It is also linked to the balanced functioning of the hemispheres of the brain.

EMOTIONAL ASPECTS

At this point there is little to distinguish the physical, the emotional and the spiritual because they come together. The note B brings us to spiritual source and a place of emotional completion and integration, physical peace, a jumping off point to the next level.

SPIRITUAL ASPECTS

The Crown Chakra is the link to our spiritual essence. The note B accentuates this spiritual essence. It aligns us with the higher forces of the universe. The Crown Chakra is about physical departure. Either leaving one's physical body through astral journey or by death. Note B supports us gently on the journey of choice.

BACH FLOWER ESSENCES

Aspen
Beech
Gentian
Gorse
Mustard
Rock Water
Sweet Chestnut
Water Violet
Wild Oat

PACIFIC ESSENCES

Arbutus
Brown Kelp
Dolphin
Easter Lily
Forsythia
Harvest Lily
Hooker's Onion
Nootka Rose
Periwinkle
Plantain
Poison Hemlock
Purple Magnolia
Snowberry
Snowdrop
Sponge
Starfish
Urchin
Vanilla Leaf
Whale

Essential Oils

Camphor
Frankincense
Gardenia
Hyssop
Jasmin
Lavender

PLANT FORM – ESSENTIAL OILS

Frankincense

Frankincense is derived from the gum resin of a small, bushy Bosudia Carterii tree. It has a warm rich smell with a hint of lemon and woody camphor. Historically it has been attributed with spirituality. It was a prized possession in the ancient world, rivaling the value of many precious gems and metals. Its centering aroma slows the nervous system and promotes the feeling of calm and introspection.

PHYSICALLY
- Frankincense helps with asthma, bronchial congestion, sinus congestion and laryngitis. It heals wounds, scars and burns and replenishes the skin.

MENTALLY
- Frankincense has an elevating and soothing effect on the mind. It helps to relieve nervous tension, lessens stress, lowers anxiety, eases nightmare and dissipates obsessive thinking.

EMOTIONALLY
- Frankincense is excellent for tiredness, grumpiness, negative moods, gloomy thoughts and emotional turmoil. It brings a feeling of calmness, complete acceptance and understanding.

SPIRITUALLY
- The holy oil of frankincense helps one to connect to the higher mind through meditation and facilitates the opening of the Crown Chakra.

Gardenia

Gardenia is found in Southern China, Taiwan, and Japan and nearby regions of the subtropical eastern hemisphere. It is an evergreen shrub widely cultivated for its large fragrant waxy, creamy-white flowers and glossy leaves. The flowers of Gardenia are very fragrant with powerful, sweet smell. The affect of the smell can be described as floating in and out of a dream.

PHYSICALLY
- Because Gardenia is fragrance oil, its physical attributes have yet to be discovered.

MENTALLY
- Gardenia uplifts the spirits. It is stabilizing to those who work with emotionally disturbed people.

EMOTIONALLY
- Gardenia promotes the feeling of peace and love. It is recommended for healers, counselors, etc. as it helps prevent becoming emotionally tied into other people's problems. It helps repel negativity so that it does not have a chance to manifest physically in the body.

SPIRITUALLY
- Gardenia strengthens the aura and is useful for people that need to be propelled into higher levels of vibration. It has a high spiritual vibration and helps people connect with nature spirits and telepathy.

CHAPTER 8

GEMSTONES
Amethyst
Diamond
Ruby

MINERAL FORM – CRYSTALS AND GEMSTONES

Amethyst

Amethyst is a powerful healer and protector. It enhances spiritual awareness and is considered the "stone of spirituality and contentment". It is also considered the stone of meditation and provides a bridge between the earth plane and other worlds. As it conducts calming energy it is able to assist the entering and maintaining phases of meditation. Amethyst with its incredible violet colour opens and activates the Crown Chakra.

PHYSICALLY

- Amethyst helps to release pain and tension especially from headaches and injuries. It helps with nervous complaints, aids insomnia, boosts the production of hormones and supports the endocrine system. Amethyst regulates intestinal flora and stimulates the digestive tract, it supports the respiratory tract and helps lung imbalances.

MENTALLY

- Amethyst calms the mind and enhances meditation and visualization. Amethyst promotes awareness and clear thinking. It helps us with our perception and clears addictive behavior.

EMOTIONALLY

- Amethyst helps us alleviate emotions such as anger, rage, fear and resentment. This stone promotes selflessness and consoles us in times of grief, sadness and loss.

SPIRITUALLY

- Amethyst, the stone of meditation assists us in finding inner peace and truth and encourages spiritual awareness and wisdom.

Rose Quartz

Rose quartz contributes love to all the essences and holds the vibration of all the information components. Rose quartz has a soft and silky vibration, bringing a wonderful, powerful, loving energy. Rose quartz bestows a calming, cooling energy, which supports all of the chakras to remove negativity and to reinstate the loving gentle forces of self love. It brings us patience and the knowing there is no need for haste, bringing calmness and clarity to the emotions and restoring harmony to the mind. It has been known as the " stone of gentle love".

PHYSICALLY
- Rose quartz stimulates blood circulation in the tissues. This stone fortifies the heart and sexual organs, helps with sexual problems and encourages fertility.

MENTALLY
- Rose quartz is used to help us make decisions and frees us from worry.

EMOTIONALLY
- Rose quartz helps us with empathy and sensitivity. It encourages self-love, a strong heart, romance and the ability to love.

SPIRITUALLY
- Rose quartz supports all the chakras and holds the vibration it is given.

AFFIRMATIONS

1. I am in tune with my Higher Self.
2. I accept myself as I am, with love and gratitude.
3. I choose to live my life from a place of love and contentment.
4. I am open and receptive to all of life.
5. I am willing to go beyond my limitations to express and experience greater love and joy.
6. I am always willing to take the next step on my path.
7. I am divinely guided and protected.
8. I am one with God.
9. I am open to the goodness and abundance of the Universe.
10. I trust the will of God.
11. I trust and surrender to love.
12. I trust that all things happen for a reason.
13. I trust that God is always working through me.
14. I trust that there is always a gift attached to any painful event; therefore I thank God for all events in my life.
15. I trust in the grace of God.
16. I trust that to live in grace is to live in peace.
17. I trust in myself.
18. I trust that everything is perfect in my life.
19. I open myself to the Divine.
20. I live in love and joy each and every day.
21. I trust in the guidance that I receive from God and the angels.
22. I believe in the power of prayer.
23. I express gratitude each and every day for my life.
24. I take time to meditate on a daily basis.

THE POWER OF THOUGHTS

The sense of the Crown Chakra is that of "thought". The power of thought- we are what we think. The symbol of the crown chakra is the lotus with its many petals opening into infinity. This truly symbolizes the power of our mind working, like an antennae picking up information from all sources. It is through the Crown Chakra that we channel incoming information through the senses for interpretation. Thought is abstract and etheric and once it moves through the chakras it becomes denser and changes into feelings and then moves into the physical as action or speech.

Thought — Spiritual
Feelings — Emotional
Action — Physical

Once we understand the information, we process it, then screen and sort it according to our own beliefs and experiences. We get the feeling of the message and bring it into the physical realm through the chakra filtering system and then the information is manifested. Thought is revealed by the use of words. Words have meaning that our bodies understand and it does not matter which language we think in. Some words make us feel fantastic and others make us feel lousy. The way in which words are spoken to us also have meaning and the tone in which they are spoken can change the context. Sometimes from our reference point a person can say something with their own meaning and we can take it completely differently from what they meant. This is because of differing experiences. This happens inside of the sifting and sorting process and organizing of information in regards to our experiences and self-talk. If our mind is in a positive state then all the information we gather gets processed in the positive framework. However, if we are into our negative self-talk, the information gathered gets filtered from a less positive framework and the meaning of this information changes. Our feeling towards this information is filtered differently, this then creates less than a positive action.

All names and words have their own meaning and their own magic, if we learn how to hear them. In fact the most powerful word in the universe, when spoken, is a person's own name. The vibration of the vocalized name totally nourishes and balances the person.

It has been known since ancient times that words and language have power. The ancient teachers knew that certain words attracted blessings, gave power, strength and courage. Other words brought comfort and relief of pain and suffering and some words brought release from illness. The power of words can be exponentiated by the voices of many people repeating certain phrases, a practice used in religious ceremonies such as with prayer, the singing of hymns, and the use of mantras. The use of words in these ways are considered another form of energy medicine.

Music is played and the sound is heard outside of ourselves but the meaning is realized deep within us. This holds true for all words and their sounds. The sounds of words vibrate to different parts of our bodies. Words vibrate to different chakras, different organs of the body. Words vibrate us into different emotional and mental states and to different states of consciousness.

All energy follows thought. Vocalizing our thoughts creates momentum towards physical manifestation.

Thought is a magical force and language is its vehicle. It is through language that we manifest our thoughts. This is extremely valuable when following "the law of attraction" which suggests that we are what we think and we are masters of our reality. The subconscious mind controls about 90% of our body's activities and functions. The subconscious mind responds literally to every thought and word within our lives. When we wake up reluctantly and think about having a horrible day, we have subconsciously programmed this into our physical body and will manifest a less than perfect experience. Once we understand this basic concept we can use the energy of thought and vocalization to manifest and create the world which brings us joy, peace and contentment. Our words and thoughts then become self-fulfilling prophecies. The more we think about something, the more we say something in conjunction with our thoughts, the stronger and quicker the energy will manifest into our physical lives. We are multi-dimensional and words are energy medicine which supports our bodies on all levels.

TONING THE CREATIVE POWER OF THE VOICE
by Laurel Elizabeth Keyes DeVross & Company, Santa Monica, California, 1973 (p. 18-19)

"The Egyptians taught that the Father Spirit was the generative power; the Mother, (or form) was the conceptive power; the issue or product of this union was the child.

In other words, everything that is, results from a union of positive and negative units of energy. The negative force, or mother is that which is acted upon. In the human, it becomes the feelings, which give form to the idea. But, whether the substance, which takes the idea, is for a statue, a garment, or is steel and concrete giving form to a picture in the architect's mind, or is used for healing the body, the manifestation is from surrender of negative force to positive. The negative aspect must yield and permit itself to be used, and then molds its properties into the form of the positive pattern.

There can be no harvest without seed in the soil, no child without the union of man and woman, no anything without this combination of positive and negative forces. And, it must be remembered that it is the mother, who gives birth, not the father. Feelings must be fecundated by idea or image, to bring about results.

This may explain why many prayers, affirmations and positive thinking seem to fail. They remain bachelors. The idea has no mate to give birth to the desired offspring – mental pictures which have not stirred feelings into productivity."

So it's not only the words but the image and the feeling of what we affirm.

The Power of Mantras

Mantras are chants used in spiritual practices. Mantras work on four different levels.
1. They work because we believe that they will.
2. They work because we associate definite ideas with sounds.
3. They work because of what they mean.
4. They work because of their sound.

The Power of Prayer

Prayers are simply a technique for imprinting positive thoughts into our conscious and subconscious mind. Prayer works in two stages.
1. First they initiate a positive thought form.
2. After the thought form; a strong will and visualization are implemented

Prayer is not wishing for something. It is concentrated visualization and proper vocalization and often done with groups of people, which intensifies the healing energy. The use of prayer unites our meditative state of consciousness with the power and magic of word, will and visualization.

The Power of Affirmations

Affirmations are stating our desires in a positive framework to allow our subconscious to create the energy of manifesting positive outcomes in the physical realm. Affirmations when repeated and expressed with passion can shift our thinking towards manifestation of the new state. The energy body shifts first and then the physical body shifts towards this new reality.

Chapter 9

Auric Field

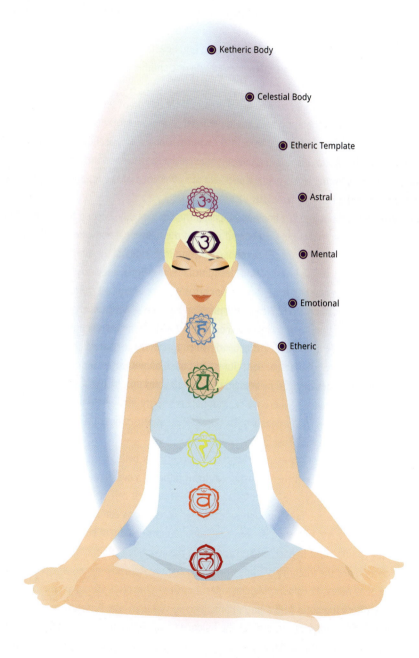

INTRODUCTION

Aura is life. It is the energy that operates our physical body. The auric field exists in different layers sometimes referred to as harmonics because of the colour fields they emit. Each layer of the auric field is a body just as real and alive as the physical body. Each layer is a mini world with its own sense of purpose. The magic of the auric field is in how these mini worlds intertwine and dance with one another. These layers interconnect with one another determining our experience with our physical reality.

The physical body is surrounded by an ovoid emanation made up of seven layers of the auric field. The seven bands of the auric field can be divided into two planes; the physical and the spiritual. The physical plane of the auric field is composed of the Physical, Etheric, Emotional, and Mental level. The Astral plane is the bridge between the spiritual and the physical levels of the auric field. The spiritual levels of the auric field are composed of the Etheric Template, the Celestial level, and the Ketheric Template.

The innermost band outlines the body and is called the Etheric body. Beyond this is a band of finer substance, which reflects our desires and is called the Emotional body. Beyond this lies a level of emanation often in a bright yellow colour, which reflects rational thinking, which is called the Mental body. Bridging the physical and the spiritual is the Astral body, rose hued with the light of love. It is at this plane that we explore our heart's desire and move from physical desire to soul desire. The next band is a replica of the physical body on a higher level and is the home of the Etheric Template that holds a higher will connected with divine will of consciousness. The next glow of light comes from the Celestial band, which is referred to as the light body because its matrix patterns are spun of actual light fibres. This band allows us to tap into higher truths and helps us create images that can be actualized in physical reality. The final band holds iridescence of the Ketheric Template, where we explore timeless space and where the appearance of being separate disappears. This connects us to the spiritual aspect of absolutely everything and everyone, to leave us with the sense of oneness.

Creation or manifestation takes place when a concept or a belief is transmitted from its source in the higher levels and then transduced down into the more dense levels of the auric field creating our own reality.

When checking the auric field through Kinesiology, we check to see if the aura is ovately surrounding the body and mirroring the physical body proportionately. We check the three dimensions: side to side, front to back, and up and down the centre line. Checking the auric field's alignment determines the integrity of auric balance. Using the Aura Joy mister, which contains the vibration of 12 notes, 12 colours, 16 gemstones, 7 ancient symbols, 5 sacred geometries, and aromatherapy offers the auric field a potential balancing vibration. The Aura Joy mister works like an energetic finishing spray to protect the balanced body holding its new vibration. Aura Joy is a full spectrum vibrational remedy that restores the healthy vibration to the etheric body, allowing the physical body to re-balance itself.

Etheric Body

The Etheric Body is the energy body that directly interfaces with the Physical Body and is in association with the acupuncture meridian system. The meridian system transduces the electromagnetic energy from the Etheric to the Physical Body. We understand this to be Chi. The Etheric Body is the primary interface between the electromagnetic flow of the Physical Body and the auric field. The Etheric Body supports us physically by holding space, reflecting our feelings and allowing us to express our spirit into the physical world.

The following is the writing from Phillip Rafferty's Kinergetics Manual:

The Etheric Body is composed of tiny energy lines "like a sparkling web of light beams" which is in constant motion. It is an energy matrix from which the Physical Body exists. The cells of the body grow along the lines of energy of the etheric matrix. It varies from this fine network of pale blue light to thicker, darker blue-grey lines.

It integrates the individual into the Earth's energy field, and the physical with the emotional, mental and spiritual. It is a filter of all things coming to the body, as a protector, as an immune field, and an explainer for the body. It represents the survival level of the psyche, the ego. Am I safe? Am I comfortable? Am I free of pain? It represents the base survival level of our being and is demonstrated by the Root/Base Chakra.

When there is perceived threat, the Etheric Body increases in size to protect, accommodate the fear, and create added space for safety. In doing this it can overpower the Emotional and Mental Bodies, imitating their functions to assume complete control over the Physical Body.

It is the connection between the Physical Body and the Light Bodies, "ether" - the state between energy and matter. It vitalizes and energizes the Physical Body,

COLOUR
White, outlining the body

SOUND
Note C

LOCATION
Skin and ¼ – 1 inch away from skin

ASSOCIATED CHAKRA
First chakra – Base chakra

EXPRESSION OF CONSCIOUSNESS
Physical sensation

STATEMENT OF CONSCIOUSNESS
I feel physically

PROPERTIES
Physical
State between energy and matter. It has the same structure as the physical body including all the anatomical parts and all the organs.

PURPOSE
Bridges the connection of material bodies to higher spiritual bodies.

ASSOCIATED
with physical aspects and awareness of the material body.

ISSUES
Roots
Grounding
Nourishment
Trust
Health
Shelter
Family
Prosperity
Appropriate boundaries

PHYSICAL ATTRIBUTES
Skin and skin disorders
Acne
Psoriasis
Shingles

MENTAL ATTRIBUTES
Deservedness
Safety
Sexuality

EMOTIONAL ATTRIBUTES
Thin skinned
Anger
Hurt
Rage
Terror
Joy
Pain
Guilt
Shame

SPIRITUAL ATTRIBUTES
It draws forth our hidden or learned beliefs about the divine source and our relationship to it.

HEALING APPLICATIONS
Our basic programming
Family of origin belief system
Childhood abuse

providing good health, vitality, and connectedness with the flow of life.

The Physical Body is held in place by the Etheric Body's network of light lines, which exactly replicate the form of the Physical Body. People who see auras mostly see the Etheric Body.

It contains the aspect of judgment, which is needed in its position as our watcher for potential danger. It holds the keys to flight and fight. It is also presents a position of armored defense, and justifies any means to stimulate the physical into action and defense. It will even present false images, symbols, memories and emotions to justify and maintain its protective posture and stand.

The acupuncture meridians, which regulate the flow of bioenergy (also known as Chi, Orgone or Prana), lie between the Physical and Etheric Bodies. Points along the acupuncture meridians relate to stresses in both the physical and etheric levels.

The Etheric Body relates to the sense of touch, and it is affected by any physical pain or pleasure. It also influences and is influenced by the body's physiological and autonomic functions. Any injury to the Physical Body will have a corresponding disturbance in the Etheric Body.

The Etheric Body also protects the Physical Body against karmic influences and from disturbances in the other Light Bodies, as they could lead to disease if they accumulate in the Physical Body. So it is important to maintain the Etheric Body's integrity by physically nurturing our bodies through regular exercise, appropriate nourishment, rest, sleep, relaxation, cleansing, hygiene, and the pleasurable sensations of massage, baths, or other tactile therapies.

Emotional Body

The Emotional Body helps us to creatively and emotionally express ourselves in a manner that exhibits our true nature. Emotions exist as a vibration pattern that then interface with the Physical Body, which transpires into feelings. Feelings are then experienced on the physical level, which drive us into action. The purpose of the Emotional Body is to both protect us from external energies that could harm our feelings and to register realities by awakening or deadening certain feelings.

The following is the writing from Phillip Rafferty's Kinergetics Manual:
"The Emotional Body is fluid-like and appears as clouds of constantly moving multi-coloured light of all the colours of the rainbow including white. Clear and highly energized feelings such as love, excitement, joy or anger produce bright, clear vibrations; those feelings that are confused produce dark, muddy vibrations.

It extends from the body, out past the Etheric Body. This colourful body contains the potential for being-ness in the physical dimension.

The Emotional Body is a responsive body; it interprets, without judgment, the symbols of the Mental Body, into emotions for physical experience, which are filtered by the Etheric Body before passing into the Physical Body. The Etheric Body places judgment on the Emotions as it responds to its perceived survival function- good/bad, right/wrong, etc., giving us the experience of opposites and separation.

It brings into physical experience, the mind of the Mental Body. Its nature is energy in motion, and it is highly energetic and fluid, constantly changing from emotion to emotion, full of the potential for new creation. It is a swirling field of different sounds like a symphony tuning up with tones of all types and intensities, with colours corresponding to each changing tone which can often be quite brilliant.

COLOUR
Fluid, watery, shimmering

SOUND
Note D

LOCATION
3 inches away from skin

ASSOCIATED CHAKRA
Second chakra – Sacral chakra

EXPRESSION OF CONSCIOUSNESS
Personal Emotions

STATEMENT OF CONSCIOUSNESS
I feel emotionally

PROPERTIES
Emotions
The feeling layer. Its structure is more fluid than the etheric body.

PURPOSE
Expresses the full spectrum of our emotions.

ASSOCIATED
with the vibrational level of inner feelings.

ISSUES
Movement
Sensation
Emotions
Sexuality
Desire
Pleasure

PHYSICAL ATTRIBUTES
Links us to the energies that create passion. Helps us to stay in the flow and be energized.
Co-dependency
Stress- related illnesses
Poor relationships
Creativity issues

MENTAL ATTRIBUTES
Affirming feeling in others and ourselves. Keeps the 2nd auric field in shape and operational.

EMOTIONAL ATTRIBUTES
Connects us to earth and every feeling that we have ever had or every feeling that lies dormant within us. It feeds and heals our feeling bodies and protects us from feelings that are not ours.

SPIRITUAL ATTRIBUTES
It keeps us alive and connected to our honest reactions.

HEALING APPLICATIONS
Recognize the link between feeling and illness. Helps clients to label and understand their feeling, clear blocked emotions and release feelings that are not theirs. The Emotional Body renews and lightens the second chakra.

It is related to the Sacred Chakra, our creative Chakra. It is our emotional experience that motivates our being to live.

When the Mental and Emotional Bodies come into alignment with joy, love, and total trust, the Etheric Body will shed its protective, judgmental role and take on wholeness (holiness) and total freedom, producing bright, clear colours in the Emotional Body, enabling acceptance, clarity and creative being-ness in our physical day to day existence. We can acknowledge our emotions non-judgementally and can honor our feelings, seeing all emotions as the very beautiful and very personal landscape of our life that we are meant to discover and explore.

When our Etheric Body tries to suppress our feelings and judge them, the energy becomes stagnate, causing dark, murky clouds of energy in the Emotional Body. This stagnation can then be transferred to the Etheric and Mental Bodies, resulting in distorted mental activity, justifications, replaying scenarios over and over in the mind (real or imagined), projecting doom and gloom into future events, exacerbating fears out of proportion, etc. The constantly changing energies within this body can result in disease. When you have a good relationship with yourself, love and honor all of yourself, you will have a strong, healthy Emotional Body. Affirmations can help with this process, particularly affirmations about loving and accepting Self.

Our judgments upon our emotions affect our thoughts, which affects our moment by moment creativity, which affects our other Light Bodies e.g.,. The Astral Body and the way we relate to others, and the Ketheric Template influencing the Collective Consciousness."

Mental Body

The Mental Body generates thoughts as vibrational patterns that can be called thought form. Thought form is the way in which the Mental Body can transmit ideas to the brain for screening, manifestation, expression and possibly action. The Mental Body gives the body the ability to discern abstract thoughts and make decisions. This auric body allows our mind fields to interconnect with other mind fields creating a wholism of thought and learning that moves beyond our time and space continuum. When enough people start doing or thinking similar patterns we are able to shift consciousness. We sometimes call this the 100th monkey theory. Scientists have found that when monkeys in laboratories are taught to do certain things that somehow monkeys in the wild can inherently do the same task without training. Through the Mental Body, we can tap into a cross-dimensional pool of wisdom that supports our body, mind and soul with ideas that support us in health and wealth.

The following is the writing from Phillip Rafferty's Kinergetics Manual:
The Mental Body is composed of still finer substances radiating out in light lemon, bright yellow and gold hues, like rays of light. It is inherently structured in its nature. Yellow is the colour of the intellect and of mental activity. The Mental Body extends from the Physical Body, out past the Emotional Body. It is related to the Solar Plexus Chakra.

It is a mental field and provides reasoning and directives to the body, through its language of symbols. It also is non-judgemental, and its service is to take the metaphoric symbols of our life experience and interpret them, to provide a stable, logical framework, with names of things, functions of things and the nature of things, in which life can be experienced and lived. It is associated with both our physical bodies and our spiritual dimension. Physically it is associated with the logic brain,

COLOUR
Yellowish

SOUND
Note E

LOCATION
3-8 inches away from skin

ASSOCIATED CHAKRA
Third Chakra – Solar Plexus Chakra

EXPRESSION OF CONSCIOUSNESS
Thinking

STATEMENT OF CONSCIOUSNESS
I think

PROPERTIES
Mind and rational thinking
Thought form can be seen in this layer.
Matrix lines are quite apparent.

PURPOSE
It contains the structure of our ideas.

ASSOCIATED
with the vibrational level of thoughts and mental processes of ego.

ISSUES
Energy
Activity
Autonomy
Individualism
Will
Self-esteem
Proactivity
Power

Chapter 9

PHYSICAL ATTRIBUTES
Assists in opening us to energy, ideas, concepts and notions that affect us physically with metabolism and digestion

MENTAL ATTRIBUTES
Potentially links us to infinite storage and processes of data, information, and concepts.

EMOTIONAL ATTRIBUTES
Connects the thought with the feeling, which creates momentum called emotion.

SPIRITUAL ATTRIBUTES
Helps us open ourselves to structures, ideas, explanations and assistance for achieving our soul purpose.

HEALING APPLICATIONS
By working with the third auric layer, we can isolate thought processes and beliefs that are harming us. After diagnosing them, we can change them. This auric layer can also change them. This auric layer can be used to diagnose and work with intellectual problems or learning difficulties.

our thoughts, mental processes and our states of mind. It enables people to think in a clear and rational fashion. It can be influenced by the Etheric Body perceiving danger or a threat, and taking control by expanding into the Mental Body. It can produce symbols from the past that are inappropriate, to produce thoughts and then actions, that seem logical, to support and justify its need to fight for survival.

These seemingly logical thoughts can become habitual and then difficult to change. So the pulsating energy lines in the Mental Body can darken, distort and slow down.

When the Etheric Body is still and takes on its proper function without fear for survival the Emotional and Mental Bodies maintain their proper functions. The Mental Body is thus able to, like a loving father; interpret our experiences with enlightenment, expansive awareness and knowing, opening a merging with the Universal Mind. When this occurs all the higher Bodies are also clear and open and expanded and energized.

We use our thought-energy to create the realities about us. Therefore, when we focus more emotional and thought-energy into an idea, it empowers the manifestation of a thought-form onto the physical. The Emotional Body and Etheric Body influence the Mental Body as it overlaps with them. This connects emotions to most of our thoughts.

A weak and under active Mental Body produces low mental agility and clarity of thought. When strong and charged, it produces a clear mind, an active mental life and an interest in learning. When overcharged it leads to being too rational, and being out of touch with both feelings and intuition. Barbara Ann Brennan in her book "Hands of Light" states that when the intuitive and rational mind coexists harmoniously, then the Mental Body is balanced. When all of the first three Light Bodies are balanced, then an individual feels the strength of self-acceptance and inner sense of power.

Astral Body

The Astral Body is the bridge between the physical manifestation of sensation, emotion and thought to the etheric expression of divine will, universal love and divinity.

Our Astral Body links us to the astral plane, which is a dimension that our spiritual guides and teachers dwell. We will travel "home" to this astral plane in times of need when we require help beyond the physical. Via a silver cord we visit this astral plane when we are children and even when we as adults become students of the universe at night. It is in this astral layer where we store our cords and contractual agreements.

The following is the writing from Phillip Rafferty's Kinergetics Manual:

The Astral Body is shapeless in form and is composed of clouds of colour more beautiful than the Emotional Body, which are infused with the rose pink light of love. It is associated with the Heart Chakra and it extends from the physical body out past the Mental Body. On this level a great deal of interaction takes place between people. Cords exist here between people in close relationship, and these tear when the relationship ends. The Astral Body is based on relationship.

The first type of relationship it encompasses is the marriage and the joining together of masculine and feminine energies as the one energy. It sees the need for this relationship and marriage due to its strong functional desire to create balance. This helps to move Yin and Yang, linear and expansive, logical and intuitive, into the one divine balanced energy.

The Astral Body also has orders, and keeps records by a system of relationships, all our life experiences and memories. It relates all our experiences, one to another, chaining events and experiences into a system or order for record retrieval. In this aspect it organizes all our experiences by their relationship to each other, and

COLOUR
Rose glow

SOUND
Note F

LOCATION
6-12 inches away from skin

ASSOCIATED CHAKRA
Fourth Chakra – Heart Chakra

EXPRESSION OF CONSCIOUSNESS
I and Thou Emotions

STATEMENT OF CONSCIOUSNESS
I love humanity

PROPERTIES
Higher expression of the physical, emotional and mental levels.
It is the layer that all energy must pass through when going from one world to another.

PURPOSE
Connects us with the higher dimensions of reality. Higher expression on the physical, mental and emotional level. It is the bridge between the denser or lower vibrations of the physical plane and the finer or higher vibrations of the spiritual plane.

ASSOCIATED
with areas of expression on a physical, emotional and mental level.

ISSUES
Love
Balance
Self-love
Relationship
Intimacy
Devotion
Reaching out and taking in

Physical Attributes
Provides information on general physical issues

Mental Attributes
Clues us into our ideas about relationships and our beliefs regarding deservedness.

Emotional Attributes
Melds physically oriented feelings and awareness with spiritually adept feelings and awareness. The astral level provides us with the opportunity to experience and manifest all we dream about.

Spiritual Attributes
Working through life's lessons with others from the astral plane. We allow divine source energy to support us.

Healing Applications
Detect physical heart imbalance
We can explore our heart's desire.

it can retrieve these records at anytime for us. It can access from its records the total accumulation of the personality, traumatic memories, DNA patterns, and spiritual patterns.

It also assists the whole system to experience itself in relationship. It can do this because it creates a systems management program. It relates all of life to points of reference for us. It thus gives us the experience of relationship to all things and the Universe as a whole. It is the first of the Light Bodies to understand and appreciate separateness.

In the relationship of separateness, the Astral Body can function separately from, yet to connect to, the physical body through astral projection, usually at night or during near death experiences. The Astral Body experiences this level as unlimited by three-dimensional time and space. It exists as a timeless, spaceless continuum. The clearer the Astral Body's energy, the more these relationships are based on unconditional love.

Underactivity or weakness of this field usually denotes problems with intimacy and human relationships which may seem unimportant or too difficult, feelings can be masked, and hermit consciousness or feeling overpowered by others may be present. A strong, healthy Astral Body leads to many fulfilling relationships, where love plays a strong role. An overcharged Astral Body can lead to relationship addiction and over-sensitivity. It is the energy on this level that can reach out across a room to touch other people. It is how some people can communicate and relate without talking. The Astral Body encompasses the Physical, Etheric, Emotional and Mental, to form the seat of man's mental and emotional nature. An astral being works with his consciousness and feelings from unconditional love. The astral spheres are visible to the sixth sense of intuition and telepathy. The Astral Body desires clear vibrations in all aspects, and to work with all objects and experiences as forms of light.

Etheric Template Body

The Etheric layer searches for the truth hidden behind the illusion of appearances. It is in the Etheric Template where we get the will that provides us with the power to create our divine purpose in this world. Our lives seem to flow effortlessly when we are aligned with our sole purpose and trusting the universe.

The following is the writing from Phillip Rafferty's Kinergetics Manual:
The Etheric Template is the Light Body, which contains all the forms that exist on the physical plane in a blueprint. It is the template for the Etheric Body, which is in turn the template for the Physical Body. It looks like the negative of a photograph. It forms exist in negative space, creating an empty space in which the etheric grid structure grows and upon which all physical manifestation exists. It extends out from the body past the Astral Body.

It contains in symbol form, all the archives for the physical experience of life. It's a library, where records of all our experiences and memories, which relate to our Mental and Emotional Bodies, are placed, put in order and retrieved by the Etheric Body. It holds the laws of physicality, for the emotional being and for the mental being.

The Etheric Template is related to the Throat Chakra because it is a dynamic and expressive Body that presents and receives its content freely.

A lot of interplay occurs and energy flows between these Light Bodies. The symbols and records of this Body are retrieved and ordered by the Astral Body, interpreted by the Mental Body, presented as emotion for physical experience by the Emotional Body to the Etheric Body, which then filters the images and feelings and presents them to the Physical Body to elicit defensive actions or thought. The Physical Body finally chooses to respond to those filtered images providing "real" experiences. This process works the other way when records are to be placed in the Etheric Template.

COLOUR
Blue

SOUND
Note G

LOCATION
18-24 inches away from skin

ASSOCIATED CHAKRA
Fifth Chakra – Throat Chakra

EXPRESSION OF CONSCIOUSNESS
Higher will

STATEMENT OF CONSCIOUSNESS
I will

PROPERTIES
Template
Contains all the forms that exist on the physical plane in a blueprint or template form. It is the grid structure upon which the physical body grows.

PURPOSE
is to provide support to the Etheric Body. It is the level at which sound creates matter: It is at this level that sounding in healing is the most effective.

ASSOCIATED
with aspects of the physical body. It is the blue print of the lower etheric body where matter is shaped into the physical aspect.

ISSUES
Communication
Creativity
Listening
Resonance
Finding one's own voice

PHYSICAL ATTRIBUTES

The Etheric spiritual body is the place where the soul connects to the body. By working with the parallel auric layer, we gain access to the data and the energies available to acknowledge or speak the truths and wishes of our being. This is a very important step in manifesting the physical.

Mental Attributes
Connects us to the realms of possibilities so that we can select which beliefs, truths, and realities most authentically reflect us.

Emotional Attributes
We can receive new insights in ways to feel and express ourselves more.

Spiritual Attributes
Allows the soul to explore its options.

Healing Applications
Becoming conscious of this auric layer specifically of its two-fold nature, can help us become conscious of our decisions and their potential outcomes. Through this layer we can also gain access to the words or actions that created our current conditions. The opportunities for change and transformation are limitless.

The Etheric Template form represents the Divine laws for physical, mental and emotional existence. Through this body we can be very dynamic, expressive, purposeful, have strength of will, experience life as being a plan of perfect order, and realize our power of co-creation. Such individuals can surrender to whom they really are and are not shaped according to societal norms.

In disease, when the Etheric Body becomes disfigured, the Etheric Template must be repaired, as the Etheric Template is the origin of the Etheric Body.

Distortions on this level can be expressed as a lack of a sense of purpose or a feeling of being unconnected to life, out of sync with life, not truly belonging on Earth. An imbalance in the Etheric Template may lead to feeling intimidated by others who strive for precision or who exhibit a strong, clear will. Such individuals may rebel against clarity and order, seeing it as a hindrance to freedom, and a block to creativity.

Distortions on this level of the aura can also lead to difficulties in speaking and following one's own truth. Such individuals may feel inhibited to stand up for what they know, or if they do express themselves, they may have trouble maintaining and expressing truth in a positive way.

However, if the Etheric Template is over-active, individuals may be denying their creative freedom with a rigid dictatorial point of view of order. They may feel as if everything must go according to plan, resisting any flexibility. They will likely be lacking a stimulating emotional life.

It is on this level where sound healing is most effective; as it is at this level that sound not only changes matter, but also creates matter.

Celestial Body

The Celestial Body is called the Light Body because its matrix patterns are spun of actual light fibres.

This auric layer amalgamates the more structured fifth auric field and the less formed seventh auric field. It combines the necessities of choices and consequences with the truth of universal love and support. When working with the Celestial Body, we are tapping into higher truths for creating images that can be actualized in physical reality.

This energy layer disposes all veils and allows the truth to be seen.

The following is the writing from Phillip Rafferty's Kinergetics Manual:

The Celestial Body is known as the Celestial or Buddhic vehicle. It extends out from the physical body, past the Etheric Template. Its form is less defined than the Etheric Template, and it appears like the glow around a candle as it radiates from the body. It has a gold/silver shine with an opalescent pearl quality and pastel colours of beautiful shimmering light.

The Celestial Body works with the intuition of the body. It also interprets the law within the functions and actions of each body and system, and for the whole system. It is our learned ethical sense, our conscience. It is related to the Brow Chakra intuiting the knowing that is the universal field, providing ethical judgment and conscious thought to our experience. Through accessing our intuition, through connecting with the silence and space between thought, spiritual ecstasy of peace, unconditional love and joy can be experienced within our physical being and mind. Divine perfection can be witnessed within all earthly matters. Inner knowing, intuition and wisdom are anchored in the mind and physical being. Divine love for humanity is experienced with the feelings of expansion due to communion with others. One can identify beauty everywhere and all things are truly appreciated.

COLOUR
Glow of light

SOUND
Note B

LOCATION
24-32 inches away from skin

ASSOCIATED CHAKRA
Sixth Chakra – Brow Chakra

EXPRESSION OF CONSCIOUSNESS
Higher feeling

STATEMENT OF CONSCIOUSNESS
I love universally

PROPERTIES
Enlightenment and intuition
Composed of light. This intuitive level gives us access to higher qualities of feelings thoughts and manifestations.

PURPOSE
It is the level through which we experience unconditional love and spiritual ecstasy.

ASSOCIATED
with the process of enlightenment.

ISSUES
Image
Intuition
Imagination
Visualization
Insight
Dreams
Vision

Physical Attributes
Enables physical manifesting and healing

Mental Attributes
Reflects thoughts and thought patterns that we hold about ourselves. They reflect the achieved level of self-acceptance.

Emotional Attributes
Attaches us to higher order of feelings

Spiritual Attributes
Gives us access to the higher qualities of feelings and thoughts and manifesting possibilities that feed our soul.

Healing Applications
Working on the whole body.

If the Celestial Body is under-active, the field is dark and thin in places. The individual may not be able to relay their intuitive, spiritual aspects and have little experience of it. They may not even know the full joy of being inspired, or believe in God, believing you would be too gullible if you did. They can feel lost due to the lack of connection with their spiritual and intuitive aspects, not knowing exactly what they are missing. Also there is a lack of commitment to their own decision making processes, their own conscience, and own ethical sense, causing them to take on the laws and principles of others.

If the Celestial Body is over-active, individuals may be too much in their own intuition and not remain present to the physicality of their being. They may have very strong opinions and judgments that they do not re-evaluate. They may live by principles they have put in place from their own life experiences, but they do not live by the universal SPIRITUAL LAWS THAT GOVERN ALL EXISTENCE. They may judge themselves and others very harshly, and not see the perfection in all aspects of being, using judgement only to see where changes can be made and not using it for causing separation and withdrawal of love. They may see themselves as special because they can experience the mystical, and may also constantly attempt to prove that they are better than others because of it. This is of course, a defense, due to feelings of inadequacy on the physical level and due to poor grounding. The higher bodies out from the Astral Body are known as the Causal Bodies. They include the Etheric Template, Celestial Body and the Ketheric Template. They enable beings to bring Universal Consciousness into manifestation, and materialize thought, and bathe in the White Light of Love.

Ketheric Body

The Ketheric Body gives us the connection with our spiritual purpose. This layer allows us to witness our inner gifts and gives us the insight in how to use these gifts for the betterment of the universe and ourselves.

The Ketheric Body connects us to the spiritual aspect of everything and everyone. All sense of separation disappears leaving us with a sense of oneness with the universe.

The following is the writing from Phillip Rafferty's Kinergetics Manual:

The Ketheric Template is composed of tiny threads of gold-silver light that look like a beautiful golden shimmering light which is pulsating very quickly. It is most connected to the Physical Body through the medulla oblongata. It extends out from the Physical Body past the Celestial Body. It is related to the Crown Chakra.

The Ketheric Template co-ordinates, choreographs, and regulates the functions and activities of all the energy fields. In so doing it provides powerful guidance and direction for the energy system as a whole. Like a conductor of a symphony orchestra, the Ketheric Template directs the efforts of the Light Bodies to produce a meaningful experience.

The Ketheric Template also co-ordinates the connection and unification of the information and records from the higher Spiritual Bodies, the Unification Bodies, with the records and information of the physical body from the lower Light Bodies.

As the Etheric Template is the template for the physical body, the Ketheric Template is the template for the spiritual concepts of the higher Light Bodies within the physical dimension, thus coordinates the assimilation of spiritual laws with physical laws. Its template form holds the physical template and creates the empty space which allows the spiritual grid structure to develop, and upon which all spiritually aware physical manifestation exists.

COLOUR
Iridescence

SOUND
Note B

LOCATION
24-42 inches away from skin

ASSOCIATED CHAKRA
Sevens Chakra – Crown Chakra

EXPRESSION OF CONSCIOUSNESS
Higher concepts

STATEMENT OF CONSCIOUSNESS
I know I am

PROPERTIES
I know I am one with God
Contains the life plan or soul purpose.
Contains all the auric bodies associated with the present. It contains a golden grid structure of the physical body and all of the chakras.

PURPOSE
Purest form and a link to God within each of us.

ASSOCIATED
with the divine.

ISSUES
Transcendence
Immanence
Belief Systems
Higher Power
Divinity
Union
Vision

PHYSICAL ATTRIBUTES
Affects our entire existence. It is tied to both the brain and the spine.

MENTAL ATTRIBUTES
Enables us to tie into correct thought processes and seek advise for spiritual matters guiding us towards the divine.

EMOTIONAL ATTRIBUTES
Feeling held together. Resulting in total bliss.

SPIRITUAL ATTRIBUTES
Where all is spirit.

HEALING APPLICATIONS
Connects physical self to all of life. It has immeasurable potential for drawing healing and abundance towards us.

It is also like a doorway to higher states of consciousness and it facilitates attunement with astrological influences.

The seventh level gives access to the divine mind, to a connection with the great pattern of life, the universal knowing, and a deep knowing of our perfection within our imperfections. If this body is active, individuals have the capacity to generate spiritual inspirational ideas, and they understand broad, general concepts about the world and existence.

If this body is under energy, individuals may find it difficult to understand the Universal Plan and hope they fit in. They may experience life as chaotic and random and their personalities will reflect this. They most likely will not understand the paradoxical concept of perfection and they may go into denial about their shadow side. Such individuals may feel disempowered about their destiny and feel isolated.

If this level is too strong, individuals will probably have problems making their ideas practical or be decisive about commitments.

Chapter 10

Figure Eight Energy

The Figure eight energy is a universal energy seen both in and out of our body. Figure eight energy not only integrates each individual energy system but integrates all energy systems to work interrelated. It can be found on a cellular level in the pattern of the DNA molecule, in the meridian system, as the central and governing meridian intertwine, in the chakra system weaving the charkas front and back, and in the auric field connecting the physical body with the energy body.

The figure eight energy system weaves all our force fields into resonance. It holds our energetic patterns and structures together. The figure eight weaves the dense body with the light body, it intertwines the flow of energy between your ego self and your I AM presence.

In the figure eight pattern where the loops cross over is a point of intersection. This intersection point is a gateway for healing energies to interject. The loops define the area needing the healing, and the intersection point is where the healing energy is directed.

The Tibetans believe that there is figure eight energy everywhere in the body in all different sizes, directions and dimensions. According to their belief, if there is pain in the body then the figure eight energy for that area is depleted and by tracing the invisible eight in the healing direction, pain can be alleviated. Using figure eight energy tracing is a successful tool used by many health practitioners.

It can be used for bumps and bruises, sprains, muscle and bone pain. It can also be used to integrate right and left-brain function. Just trace an imaginary eight over the painful or non-integrated area and allow the pain relief or integration to take place.

FIGURE EIGHT ENERGY IN THE MERIDIANS

Figure eight energy in the meridians is observed in the central and governing meridian flow. The energy flows from the perineum up the outside front (central meridian) of the body to the bottom of the lip and then flows deep inside downwards to the perineum to pick up the outside back upwards (governing meridian) flow over the top of the head, ending at the top of the lip and returns deep inside downwards to the perineum where it connects to the central meridian flow and the pattern repeats itself. The figure eight pattern encompasses the energy of the top and bottom of the body and draws it to the intersection point, which is the core and energy source for the body, where the healing can take place. The central and governing meridians together in this figure eight pattern unify and stabilize the entire meridian system.

Figure Eight Energy in the Chakras

Figure eight energy is realized in the chakra system as one half of the life-force energy emerges from the right side of the base chakra and travels up the body winding in and out of the charkas all the way up to the brow chakra. The second half of the life force energy emerges from the left side of the base chakra and travels up the body winding in and out of the charkas from the other direction connecting to the first half of the life force energy at the brow chakra creating figure eights all the way up. As the figure eight energy circulates in this pattern it is linking the emotions and attitudinal hues through the entire charkas system. It links the feelings of the root chakra through the filters of every chakra right up to the brow chakra where insight about the situation is realized and the idea which may induce action is then sent back down through the filters of each chakra creating a new reality.

Figure Eight Energy in the Auric Field

Figure eight energy in the auric field connects our divine nature with our human experience. Soul is not a constant identity; it is forever changing and evolving. As we integrate our human experience with our divine nature, our soul grows with every choice we make. The exact moment we are mature enough to make a moral choice, the divine spark joins with our moral consciousness and begins the process of soul growth. Soul growth is essential in supporting our potential of what we are capable of becoming. Using figure eight energy in the auric field supports the interaction of the divine nature with the human experience for positive enlightening soul growth.

Chapter 11

Kinesiology

Imbalance shows up first in the body's energy anatomy. It could be an imbalance in the figure eight pattern, the auric field, chakra system, or an imbalance in the meridian system. All systems are fluid in that they are constantly self-adjusting to keep our body healthy and balanced. The meridians balance us through our daily cycle; the chakras and the auric field are more stable and balance us through our stages in life.

The meridians, chakras and auric field are the body's protection layers and indicators of health. An imbalance will first show in the energy field and will then manifest as sickness in the body. There is a significant time delay in the process. When we learn to read and detect imbalance in the energy field is when we will gain the insight to prevent disease. This is the job of health practitioners who follow the energy model of healing such as Energy Kinesiologists. The key component to keeping our health is to listen to our body and to work with a health care practitioner who believes in the preventative approach to health.

Kinesiology is the study of movement of muscle. Energy Kinesiology is using muscles of the physical body to assess the integrity of the energy body. Energy Kinesiologists have organized muscles in relation to meridians. By isolating the muscle and assessing its integrity, the Energy Kinesiologist assesses the integrity of the meridian. With this assessment, the Energy Kinesiologist then explores the potential possibilities ranging in all dimensions and vibrations to find the key corrective technique or tool that will support the meridian flow allowing the body to re-balance itself. The healing knowledge of the Energy Kinesiologist includes herbs, food and supplements. The Energy Kinesiologist also understands the anatomy of the physical body and the energy body and often uses vibrational remedies such as light, colour, sound, crystals, flower essences, homeopathy etc.

Everybody is different and everyone gets stressed or out of balance for different reasons. The success of the Energy Kinesiologist is directly related to addressing the emotional dimension of the body. The emotional body and the energy body are one and the same. The emotional body is the bridge between the physical body and the spiritual body. The energy system which includes the meridians, chakras, auras, and figure eight pattern are all emotionally charged.

When the Energy Kinesiologist detects the system needing fortification, the body responds positively when the right match is found. This is called resonance; finding the key to fit the keyhole.

Raising the body's vibration is the key to keeping the body healthy. We start by consuming vibrant food and water that is alive and surrounding ourselves with people that bring out the best in us. As we raise our vibration, we naturally become aware and in tune with nature and get a different sense about our reality. By becoming more in tune with nature, we become more in tune with ourselves. It becomes natural to listen to our body. By listening to our body and offering it what it needs- rest, proper nutrition from food, herbs and homeopathy and emotional support from various essences- we can restore vitality and delay degeneration. As we become more and more in alignment and can keep balance in our life, we can receive our power and energy from crystals, sound, colour, thought and light. Our bodies are multi-dimensional and to stay healthy we need to explore the possibility of raising our vibration with various vibrational remedies. These are the gifts nature intended for us.

There are many types of Kinesiology and the profession of Energy Kinesiology is growing substantially as more and more people understand the benefits of biofeedback and muscle monitoring. Energy Kinesiology grew out of Applied Kinesiology which began inside the chiropractic profession when Dr. George Goodheart, D.C. discovered the co-relation between muscles and meridians. This information was taught to chiropractors throughout the world. Dr. John F. Thie, D.C. recognized the incredible importance of this information and how it could affect the health of people if they were to be empowered with this information. Dr. John F. Thie D.C. created a workshop that stood outside of the chiropractic profession and called it Touch for Health. Kinesiologist Dr. Bruce Dewe MD, a medical doctor who was a Touch for Health student of Dr. Thie recognized the value of this system and began developing research in support of Dr. Thie's work and made many other discoveries and published this work as Professional Kinesiology Practice. The work of Dr. Thie and Dr. Dewe is the foundation for most of the Kinesiology systems that we are practicing to date. Others like Richard Utt, Phillip Rafferty, Sheldon Deal, Charles Krebs, Hugo Tobar, Alan Sales, Jimmy Scott, Paul Dennison, Gordon Stokes, Daniel Whiteside, John Varun Mcguire, Wayne Topping, Donna Eden have developed other types of Kinesiology from the foundation of Touch for Health (TFH) and Professional Kinesiology Practice (PKP). This type of work has become known as Energy Kinesiology and what makes it so different from its roots of Applied Kinesiology is that Energy Kinesiologists access both the physical and the energy bodies rather than just the physical body looking for the reason of pain or sickness.

Conclusion

Having an understanding of the way in which our energy systems operate and knowing that these systems too need nourishment, we can make healing choices in support of our overall health which includes the physical, emotional and spiritual aspects of ourselves. Historically, we have not been educated on how emotions and attitudes effect our health, or that we even have and energy field which stores these feelings and beliefs. It is only when we examine "life-force" and understand that life is blood and force is our energy field, that we can fathom the wholistic approach to health. This approach allows us an opportunity to take charge of our total health and vitality.

With this wholistic approach and new understanding that everything vibrates we can take the opportunity to implement our knowing and participate in our own health and vitality. We now understand the importance of offering our "force" or more commonly known as our energy fields, the vitalization necessary by using vibrational therapy. Having explored the value of various vibrations in this manual such as sound, herbs, light, colour, aroma, gems, crystal, thoughts and symbols, we get a better understanding of the importance of implementing a variety of these vibrations into our daily life.

Our physical body gets nourished from the earth sources such as water, food and herbs and the energy body gets nourished from the cosmos sources such as thought, light, colour, and sound. Historical healers believed that our bodies are bridges between earth and heaven. Our physical body is denser than our energy body and needs food and herb sources of nourishment that the earth can provide to stay balanced. Then, as we achieve physical health, we automatically shift our frequency and raise our vibration. We become less dense. Once we raise our vibration and become less dense, we can then receive the benefit of the healing energies that the universe has to offer. These energies have a lighter and higher vibration and come from thought, symbols, light, colour and sound.

Vibrational Remedies normally never contain any chemical constituents, just the information that is carried in the vibration associated with our senses. Since we now have a better understanding from quantum physics that everything is vibration, we only need to match the vibration of the energy out of balance in the energy system to what is needed for balance. We, therefore never treat the ailment, only the complaint or emotion surrounding it.

Everything has a balance; we need strong physical health and strong energy health to gather our optimum vitality. The more effective we become at conducting and transforming energy, the more effect vibrational remedies have on optimizing our health. Everything one does affects the energy field for better or worse. Disease is simply a vibrational imbalance of the energy field and to correct this imbalance is to offer the energy field the balancing vibration, may that be positive word affirmations, colour, sound, touch, ancient symbology, sacred geometry, crystal and gems or aroma. The language of vibrational therapy is that which arouses the senses. These vibrations are as vital to our energy systems as air, water, and food are to our physical being.

Healing with vibration is one of the safest methods of remedy because if we do not choose the correct modality, nothing happens. We simply do not resonate with this vibration and it does not affect us. There is nothing to lose but the effort and thought put into the healing process and this is never a waste.

The Sound Essence products were designed to support the energy systems of the body by embracing various vibrations. These essences carry with them a profound effect on our aura, chakras, meridians, and figure eight patterns, and we get the sensations and healing attributes at the core of our being.

The Sound Essences on their own are multidimensional as they carry the varied frequencies of vibrations and are well suited for the challenges offered to them.

Multi dimensional implies that there are many angles and as we are physical, emotional, mental, and spiritual there are many angles and approaches to our health. I like to think of the body as a giant puzzle and if there is a piece missing, we don't get the whole picture. The missing piece has its own identity and the picture will only become complete if the piece fits into the empty hole. The essences offer the body the different healing vibration and the body will accept the vibration that can fill the hole. This is what gives you the marvelous wholesome sensation after using them. Unlike other remedies, there is little knowledge or study required to use the Sound Essences. Our intuition is the best tool for choosing the most suitable essence and until our ego gets in the way, our intuition is 100% correct. The Sound Essences are so fun and simple to use and well received when brought into your home. Simply step into the mist or mist our entire being, everyone in the room including animals.

Making healing vibration available, the body will wisely accept the vibration it needs to ensure balance and health.

The Sound Essences products are endorsed by the *International College of Professional Practice* (www.icpkp.com). This manual and its workshop are ICPKP approved. The PKP database includes Sound Essences in the protocol by assigning them to the finger mode *Emotional #8c*. There are PKP practitioners and instructors internationally employing the Sound Essences in their practice and classrooms. From my clinical kinesiology experience, using Sound Essences as a corrective tool in a balance, offers the indicator muscle more integrity than I have ever experienced with any other correction. The essences have cleared many modes easily, proficiently and extremely effectively. I use the Essences daily in my practice and home. Sometimes I need to rid myself of a tension headache and other times I put the essence on my fingers and temporal tap while confirming a positive affirmation for the purpose of shifting my frequency towards positive change in my life. I have used the essences on my fingers to trace meridians or figure eight energy to relieve a pain or strain in the body.

All of my reflexology clients have experienced the Sound Essences on their feet. I have found that the Sound Essences break up the crystal and assist the healing energy directed to the associated organs. The Sound Essences make my work more effective and of course the client automatically feels the difference. I often correlate Chakra Sound Essence with the chakra locations on the feet. My greatest pleasure has been watching children choose their Sound Essence and notice their joyful expressions when experimenting innocently. Children are well attuned to these healing vibrations.

I feel privileged to share this work with you. My sincere hope is that you will enjoy these as much as my family, friends, and colleagues do. May Sound Essence make your heart sing.

Appendix A

Testimonials

Dear Evelyn,
I would like to provide a few comments concerning your Sound Essence Chakra Misters. I ordered the complete set plus the Aura Joy. I was very pleased to discover that the complete Chakra Set comes in an attractive plastic display holder that looks great in my office.

I have used the Chakra Misters five times to date and every time the correction has been instantaneous. The Sound Essences are a real show stopper for my clients to say the least. Wow what a wonderful product. I am using the Aura Joy Mister to clear out my office of residual energy between clients and it is working like magic and it leaves a delightful fragrance in the air.

I love your Sound Essences and would highly recommend them to any energy worker. Thank you for providing such wonderful and useful products.
In love and inner peace,

Gary Travis, Ph.D.
Energy Psychology Practitioner
Http://innerbeingcenter.com

The Chakra Sound Essence Misters have NEVER failed to correct a chakra weakness. They make me look so professional to my clients. They work like magic... how cool!
Best regards,
Gary

Hello from a re-energised Ireland.
The misters are amazing people especially when they are used directly on the skin just over the chakra. It's amazing - many people feel intense heat others feel nothing but all acknowledge that change is taking place.
Love, light, and happiness.
Padraig

》

When I did a muscle test, I received a very strong yes. Even from just holding the bottle, I could feel its energy.

The spray certainly does create an altered state of consciousness. It is quite different from the Aura Joy. I was wondering if you could send me some information on how you use it. You are doing some remarkable work. I hope we get to meet sometime.

Love and harmony,
Sharon Carne

》

Hi Evelyn,

These essences are so powerful.

Every one of my clients benefits immediately when we use the mists, meridian sound essences. Even my sceptical clients are amazed at how quickly and easily the essences and mist remove pain, discomfort and bring such a deep sense of joyful calm.

I have shown the sound essences to some therapists and they are testing them at present. They are reporting the same amazing results with their clients.

Thank God you took the time, energy and patience to develop these incredible essences. Thanks for the wonderful products. I have my mother-in-law staying with us from a broken hip, her ankle on her good leg was swollen so I tested as to which meridian's needed attention and used the meridian sound essence oils she needed. By the next day the swelling was down by 75% and day after back to normal.

Thank you again
Sandi Boilard

》

Evelyn has brought to us a wonderful exciting tool. It smells good, looks good and best of all - feels good. I use the Chakra Sound Essences when my digestion is poor and the second and third chakras need a boost. I mist my energy field and then tension and heaviness in my abdomen eases instantly.

The other day, I noticed that my whole energy was low. I felt heavy, the energy around me felt thick and I noticed my vision was worse than usual. After using the Chakra Sound Essence mist, my head cleared, my vision cleared and then the heaviness and thickness around me was gone. I felt lighter and energized. I love how the Sound Essences clear and heal my energy field"
Beverly Hunter, TFH Instructor, Edu-K Instructor, Kelowna, B.C. Canada

» I use the chakra sprays almost daily. I love how they balance the chakras, how they smell, their colour, and their sound essence. I use them before, during or after a balance in order to support healing and activate a chakra. My whole body comes alive when I spray them on myself. My clients often ask if they need a chakra spray before they leave a session. I also use them to energetically clear or refresh a room.

Evelyn has created something wonderful and has really captured the sound vibration of the chakras in these sprays. I can't say enough good about these products.
Thanks Evelyn!

Tawni K. Lawrence L.M.T.
TFH Instructor, Brain Gym Instructor, Kinergetics Instructor
Salt Lake City, Utah, U.S.A.

» Sound Essences are wonderful, leading edge vibrational tools available to all practitioners. They raise frequencies,, release blocks and establish a general over-all well being for the client.

Giving a client Sound Essences before, during or after a treatment session enables deeper clearing as a client's body has to reach specific frequencies before it is able to release fully and begin to heal. The Sound Essence can be misted on the hands and then over a chakra to establish a higher frequency. Placing two Sound Essences , one on each hand, and then holding the corresponding chakra can re-establish the frequencies within and between the two chakras. Drawing your hands through the Auric Field with Sound Essence on them, clears the static from the field and then re-establishes a healthy, strong vibration which enhances everything we do in our life. The misters can be sprayed in a room or around your body to raise frequencies and create the healing environment you desire.

The frequencies fit in nicely as home maintenance tools to thoroughly establish a frequency in an organ, gland, or body system that might not have been completely accomplished in a single treatment session."

Karen Olsen
Vibration Therapist
Langley, B.C., Canada

I spray when I see them & they want some.

I find the Sound Essences help clear negative patterns without needing to consciously identify the problem.

They also help balance the density, rotation and projection of my client's chakras. "Before and after" muscle testing of chakra imbalances demonstrate that the essences easily and simply adjust the chakras to their correct "settings"

I also believe changes made with the auric levels can affect some of the most powerful changes and cannot wait to continue testing and using your Sound Essences in my practice much more thoroughly over the next several years!

Denise Cambiotti

Specialized Kinesiologist and Certified Body Talk Practitioner, Vancouver, B.C. Canada

Today I used F sharp Chakra Sound Essence mist with a child. I was using it to help the child pronounce "R" sound. After two or three sprays and a tiny bit of encouragement the four year old girl said Robert, Rachel and a few other "R" - words perfectly.

Then we used the B flat Chakra Sound Essence mist to help her pronounce them more clearly. That was when she really spoke with clarity and the "R" sounds rolled off her tongue.

Later we worked on the "L" sound and we used a drop from the Yin/Yang Meridian Sound Essence vial on her belly button and lower lip. She can now say Laura, long and school using the correct "L" sound.

P.K., Ireland

I used two drops of the LU-LI Meridian Sound Essence vial to free out a man's two shoulders. We put a drop on the tight muscles and they just melted to normal muscle tone. He could not comb his hair or reach across to his opposite shoulder so we used TW-CX vial to free out his Teres Minor muscle and now he has restored function. The power of these Sound Essence products is beyond belief. If you have not used them you might be skeptical but as one using them every day I witness miracles daily when we use the Chakra Sound Essence mists and the Meridian Sound Essence vials.

P.K. Ireland

> I once offered a bottle of Heart and Root Chakra Sound Essences sublingual drops to an out-of-town client. He was in the Lower Mainland of BC to receive cancer treatments, and was referred to me to include kinesiology support to help deal with the stress of his illness. One night he awoke in great pain and after doing all the old standbys to help ease his suffering without avail, his wife remembered the bottle of Meridian Sound Essence drops she had placed in her purse and the instruction to use it to help with pain. It had been determined through muscle testing during his previous session that he needed to apply the essence to his skin. Both he and his wife were amazed at the instant elimination of the pain and phoned the next day to ask if I could mail more to them to their home address in California. I recall the joy I felt for their success, and also remember the big grin on my face because the client and his wife were both doctors who had just been introduced to the power of vibrational remedies. They didn't know why it worked, but they were sold on the effectiveness. Thank you Evelyn for the opportunities I have to enjoy sharing your products, and helping make a positive difference in people's lives!
> D.C., Vancouver

Appendix B

Deciding Which Meridian Sound Essence To Use

Score the following questions to determine which Meridian Sound Essence to use. The Meridian with the lowest score is the Meridian needing the Meridian Sound Essence.

1. Never   2. Occasionally   3. Sometimes   4. Mostly   5. Always

	1	2	3	4	5
YING/YANG Central and Governing Meridian Couple					
1. Are you manifesting abundance?					
2. Can you easily make decisions?					
3. Do have the sense of knowing that you know?					
4. Do you feel connected to your source?					
5. Do you exercise your free will?					
6. Do you have clear thinking?					
7. Is your memory sharp?					
Total Score ____					
SOVEREIGN FIRE ELEMENT Heart and Small Intestine Meridian Couple					
1. Can you prioritize effectively?					
2. Can you adapt to new situations easily?					
3. Are you easily inspired?					
4. Are you following your passion?					
5. Can you take in information or ideas and assimilate it into your life?					
6. Do you have the energy to do everything that you would like?					
7. Can you sleep without disturbance?					
Total Score ____					

	1	2	3	4	5
MINISTERIAL FIRE ELEMENT Circulation/Sex and Triple Warmer Meridian Couple					
1. Do you have balance in your life?					
2. Do feel internal encouragement for you accomplishments?					
3. Are you generally happy and fulfilled?					
4. Do you feel empowered to do anything you want to do?					
5. Can you let go of a grudge?					
6. Do you sense that your hormones are balanced?					
7. Are you living in the present?					
Total Score ____					
EARTH ELEMENT Spleen and Stomach Meridian Couple					
1. Are you making choices for your highest good?					
2. Are you enthusiastic about life?					
3. Can you handle stress?					
4. Are you at your optimum weight?					
5. Are you free of worry?					
6. Do you operate your daily life at a steady pace?					
7. Would you consider yourself easy-going?					
Total Score ____					
METAL ELEMENT Lung and large Intestine Meridian Couple					
1. Are you living in the moment?					
2. Can you let go of the past?					
3. Can you easily let go of loss?					
4. Do you prefer to have things out of order?					
5. Are you receptive to new ideas?					
6. Is it okay not to be right?					
7. Would you consider yourself spontaneous?					
Total Score ____					

	1	2	3	4	5
WATER ELEMENT Kidney and Bladder Meridian Couple					
1. Do you have patience?					
2. Can you trust others?					
3. Are you uncritical?					
4. Do you live without secrets?					
5. Do you have stamina?					
6. Do you have strong healthy bones?					
7. Do you have fluidity in body movement and with your thinking?					
Total Score ____					
WOOD ELEMENT Liver and Gall Bladder Meridian Couple					
1. Can you manage your stress?					
2. Would you consider yourself gracious?					
3. Are you able to communicate effectively?					
4. Do you feel supported?					
5. Do you feel that you are in the rhythm of life?					
6. Do you feel successful?					
7. Is it okay to not always take control?					
Total Score ____					

APPENDIX B

DECIDING WHICH CHAKRA WHOLE NOTE SOUND ESSENCE TO USE

Score the following questions to determine which Sound Essence to use. The Chakra with the lowest score is the Chakra needing the Sound Essence.

1. Never   2. Occasionally   3. Sometimes   4. Mostly   5. Always

	1	2	3	4	5
ROOT CHAKRA - C NOTE					
1. Do you feel that your family supports you in the choices & changes you have made in your life?					
2. Does your work support you and provide the quality of life you deserve?					
3. Do you enjoy your home?					
4. Does the structure in your life allow you to enjoy your family, friends and the possessions in your life?					
5. Do you feel secure in yourself?					
6. Is your life & home organized?					
7. Do you feel that you have the right to have your dreams come true?					
Total Score ____					
SACRAL CHAKRA - D NOTE					
1. Do you feel that you have the right to enjoy yourself?					
2. Do you allow abundance in your life?					
3. Are you able to distinguish earning your livelihood from having a sense of abundance?					
4. Do you feel loveable without an active sexual life?					
5. Do you look after yourself well with good quality food, exercise & a clean environment, at home & at work?					
6. Do you keep your promises?					
7. Do you consider yourself a creative person?					
Total Score ____					

	1	2	3	4	5
SOLAR PLEXUS - E NOTE					
1. Do you love and value who you are?					
2. Do you give yourself the pride you deserve?					
3. Do you feel confident that you are good enough to do the things you want?					
4. Are you a respected person in a friendship, partnership or an organization?					
5. Are you able to admit when you are wrong?					
6. Do you exercise your right to choose freely without guilt or for the sake of keeping peace or for approval?					
7. Are you capable of taking good care of yourself?					
Total Score ____					
HEART CHAKRA - F NOTE					
1. Do you feel you are open to love?					
2. Are you willing to release anger & resentment so that there is more love available to you?					
3. Do you feel emotionally connected to others?					
4. Do you sense that you are loved for who you are and the joy that you have brought to other peoples lives?					
5. Have you ever experienced a deep peace that goes beyond all understanding?					
6. Do you let your heart show to your family, friends and children?					
7. Do you consider yourself passionate and generous?					
Total Score ____					
THROAT CHAKRA - G NOTE					
1. Do you focus your intent on honest and sincere communication?					
2. Do you speak up for yourself?					
3. Do you do what you say you will do?					
4. Do you believe you have the right to ask for things you want?					
5. Do you honour the truths of others?					
6. Do you take time to listen to the higher voice in yourself?					
7. Do you express yourself creatively with writing, art, dance, music, sport, cooking, gardening or a hobby?					
Total Score ____					

	1	2	3	4	5
BROW CHAKRA - A NOTE					
1. Do you validate your worth and intelligence?					
2. Do you trust your inner knowing and intuition?					
3. Do you use knowledge to enhance your life?					
4. Do you use your imagination?					
5. Are you in tune with your soul's desire?					
6. Do you listen to the messages from your body?					
7. Do you make sound decisions?					
Total Score ____					
CROWN CHAKRA - B NOTE					
1. Do you feel loved, accepted and connected with your God?					
2. Do you feel that you are divinely guided and protected each & every day?					
3. Are you living your life on purpose?					
4. Are you experiencing serenity in your everyday life right now?					
5. Do you have faith that life is good?					
6. Do you give thanks for the opportunities life gives you?					
7. Do you take time to appreciate the wonder of music, the magic of colours & the beauty in the world around you?					
Total Score ____					

Deciding Which Chakra Semi-Tone Sound Essence to Use

Score the following questions to determine which Sound Essence to use. The Semi-Tone Chakra with the lowest score is the Chakra needing the Sound Essence.

1. Never   2. Occasionally   3. Sometimes   4. Mostly   5. Always

	1	2	3	4	5
Sacral Chakra - C♯ note					
1. Do you feel that you can express your sensuality?					
2. Can you fully embrace life?					
3. Can you express your feelings with your body movements?					
4. Do you get to do the things you want to do?					
5. Do you get along easily with others?					
6. Do you get wonderful ideas and act on them?					
7. Do you dance?					
Total Score _____					
Solar Plexus Chakra - E♭ note					
1. Can you enjoy yourself without anyone else?					
2. Can you make decisions without family input?					
3. Can you easily handle life's ups and downs?					
4. Do you create sacred space for yourself?					
5. Do you ever hug yourself?					
6. Do you feel that you have the power to create your own destiny?					
7. Do you have good mid back movement?					
Total Score _____					

	1	2	3	4	5
HEART CHAKRA - F♯ NOTE					
1. Do you celebrate your accomplishments?					
2. Do you feel supported and cherished?					
3. Can you look at others without judgment or criticism?					
4. Are you doing what you love to do?					
5. Do you feel that you are in the flow of life?					
6. Are you fulfilling any passions?					
7. Do you have free movement of your upper back?					
Total Score ____					
THROAT CHAKRA - G♯ NOTE					
1. Can you think before you act?					
2. Can you make decisions easily?					
3. Can you express your beliefs easily with others?					
4. Do you sense that the people see you for all that you are?					
5. Are you following your dreams?					
6. Do you feel solid in your life's work?					
7. Does your neck turn easily?					
Total Score ____					
BROW CHAKRA - B♭ NOTE					
1. Are you ready to let go?					
2. Are you ready for a change?					
3. Are you good at getting things done?					
4. Do you feel spiritually connected?					
5. Are you good at making transitions in life, circumstances, or thought?					
6. Do you feel at one with yourself?					
7. Do you have mental clarity?					
Total Score ____					

Appendix C

MERIDIAN IDENTIFYING STATEMENTS

YIN/YANG Central and Governing Meridian Couple
- I am never going to get ahead.
- How am I supposed to know that?
- Everyone's telling me what to do.
- I just can't think.
- I couldn't' tell you what's best for me.
- I never know what to do.
- I just don't feel like I belong here.

SOVEREIGN FIRE ELEMENT Heart and Small Intestine Meridian Couple
- I never know what to start first.
- Can you give me more notice?
- I never have any good ideas.
- I just don't have it in me.
- I need to know ahead of time what we are doing.
- They all think they are so funny.
- It's hard to sort this all out.

MINISTERIAL FIRE ELEMENT Circulation/Sex and Triple Warmer Meridian Couple
- Work is just taking over my life.
- I am just not satisfied with what's going on
- I can never throw anything out.
- My co-ordination is really off.
- Who cares about what I do any way.
- I never did like him/her.
- What's the use?

EARTH ELEMENT Spleen and Stomach Meridian Couple
- How am I suppose to know what's right for me?
- I just worry about it all the time.
- Are they going to be okay?
- What happens if something goes wrong?
- I don't feel like doing anything.
- That just makes me sick to the stomach.
- We always call them, they never call us.

METAL ELEMENT Lung and Large Intestine Meridian Couple
- Those were the good ol' days!
- Things should always be in their place.
- I hate it when I'm wrong.
- I'll have to put that on my calendar.
- Where's my list, it won't get done unless it's on the list.
- Bygones are never bygones.
- Things just need to be done the way they've always been done.

WATER ELEMENT Kidney and Bladder Meridian Couple
- Why is it that everyone has an opinion of what's best for me?
- It's tough to get through the day.
- I just don't have the patience for this.
- How can I trust anyone?
- What's going to happen next, it's always something.
- Those people just don't know anything.
- I just can't wrap my head around it.
- People don't need to know everything that's going on.

WOOD ELEMENT Liver and Gall Bladder Meridian Couple
- I hate feeling like it's out of my control.
- The stress is getting to me.
- No one is listening to me.
- I just can't get my ideas across.
- I am never going to get anywhere.
- I just can't get into the flow of things.
- I always stick my foot into my mouth.

Chakra Identifying Statements

Root - C note
- What's the use?
- When will I get a break?
- I have to do everything myself.
- I hate my job, house, and life.
- I have to watch my back or I'll get ripped off.
- I don't really know where I stand.
- My parents really let me down.

Sacral - D note
- I never get to have any fun.
- Nobody likes me.
- Nothing I do fulfills me.
- I don't feel like doing (want to do) anything.
- When is it going to be my turn?
- I don't deserve it.
- I hate change.
- Pleasure seems elusive.

Solar Plexus - E note
- I have no energy.
- I hate dealing with authority.
- It's just easier to go along with the crowd.
- I'm never good enough.
- Who wants to hear my story anyway.
- I hate it when I am wrong.
- Everyone's picking on me.
- It's not my fault.

Heart - F note
- Why would anyone want to love me?
- I feel all-alone even in a crowd.
- People always want something from me.
- To forgive is not even an option.
- I find myself getting upset about the stupidest things.
- Nobody does what I tell them to do.
- I don't love what I see in the mirror.

Throat - G note
- Nobody wants to hear what I have to say.
- It's easier to go along with everyone rather than disagreeing.
- I like things just the way they are. Don't upset the apple cart.
- It's easier to make up a story than to tell the truth.
- I always get interrupted.
- That's how it has always been and that's how it will always be.
- It's hard for me to let others know what I want and how I feel.

Brow - A note
- I don't pay any attention to my dreams.
- It's hard for me to make decisions.
- How am I supposed to create my life when I don't even know what I want?
- Sleeping does not refresh me.
- I haven't got any answers.
- I can't barely get through the day let alone think about tomorrow.
- I can't hear myself think.

Crown - B note
- I can't remember names or faces.
- I have no idea what my life's purpose is.
- I have a constant voice in my head telling me I should or I could or I need to...
- I can't find inspiration in anything.
- I have no idea what I believe in anymore.
- I have tried to meditate but it doesn't work for me.
- I can't trust anyone but myself.

Chakra Identifying Statements – Semitones

Sacral - C♯ note
- I just can't get anything started.
- I wish I had the secret to feeling sexy.
- I would love to jump into life and participate.

Solar Plexus - E♭ note
- Its tough to break away from the family.
- I feel like an odd duck out.
- Changes are coming too fast, I cant keep up.

Heart - F♯ note
- I can't find my place in this world
- I know that I have a calling but don't know what it is.
- I can never get it right.

Throat - G♯ note
- The risk is too great to follow my dreams.
- I don't even know what I want.
- I hate my position.

Brow - B♭ note
- I need to move on from here.
- I would love to finish this phase.
- I am ready for the next step.

Appendix D

BACH FLOWER ESSENCES

Flower Essences are the most recognized of the healing energies thanks to the work of Dr. Bach who popularized them in England in the 1930s. He theorized that people fell into seven groups, based on their reactions to illness. The groups are fear, uncertainty, loneliness, over-sensitivity, lack of interest in present circumstances, despondency, and over-concern for others. He determined that to treat illness, one had to address patients' emotional and mental states. Following the principles of homeopathy, he devised the flower essences for that purpose. Today, essences are being made not only from flowers, but crystals, sound, herbal tinctures, environments and other energies found in nature.
www.bachremedies.com

Agrimony	Mental and physical torture, worry concealed from others; over-indulgence
Aspen	Vague fears of the unknown origin; anxiety apprehension, startles easily
Beech	Intolerance, criticism, passing judgments, lack of understanding
Centaury	Weak-willed, too easily influenced, willing servant, quiet and timid
Cerato	Distrust of self, doubt of one's ability
Cherry Plum	Desperate frame of mind, fear of losing control, fear of losing mind
Chestnut Bud	Failure to learn by experience, lack of observation in the lessons of life, hence the need of repetition
Chicory	Possessiveness, self-pity, self-love, needs attention
Clematis	Indifference, dreaminess and absentminded, inattention, unconsciousness, fainting, lack of concentration (school children)
Crab Apple	The cleansing remedy, despondency, despair in mind and body
Elm	Occasional feelings of inadequacy, despondent, exhaustion from responsibility
Gentian	Doubt, depression, discouragement from setbacks
Gorse	Hopelessness, despair (thru a condition of long endurance)

Heather	Self-centeredness, self-concern, talkative about self
Holly	Hatred, envy, jealousy, suspicion, lack of love, revengeful
Honeysuckle	Dwelling upon thoughts of the past, nostalgia, homesickness
Hornbeam	Tiredness, weariness thru mental and physical exhaustion
Impatience	Impatience, irritability, quick to anger, extreme mental tension
Larch	Lack of confidence, anticipation of failure, despondency
Mimulus	Fear of anxiety of a known origin, fear of illness, disease or height, etc.
Mustard	Deep depression, melancholia, gloom; can bring joy back into life
Oak	Despondency, despair, but never ceasing effort
Olive	Complete exhaustion, mental and physical fatigue
Pine	Self-reproach, feelings of guilt, despondency, self-blame
Red Chestnut	Excessive fear, anxiety for welfare of others
Rock Rose	Terror, panic, extreme fatigue
Rock Water	Self-repression, self-denial, self-martyrdom, rigid lifestyle
Scleranthus	Uncertainty, indecision, hesitancy, procrastination
Star of Bethlehem	After effects of mental or physical shock from accident, or bad news, etc.
Sweet Chestnut	Extreme mental anguish, hopelessness, depth of despair, lost all faith
Vervain	Strain, stress, tension, over-enthusiasm
Vine	Too dominating, inflexible, too ambitious, bossy
Walnut	Over sensitive to ideas and influences; changes that require adjustment (teething, puberty, menopause)
Water Violet	Pride, aloofness, rigidity
White Chestnut	Persistent, unwanted thought, mental arguments, and conversations with self
Wild Oat	Uncertainty, despondency, dissatisfaction, no direction in life
Wild Rose	Resignation, apathy
Willow	Resentment, bitterness, negative thoughts
Rescue Remedy	Use in the case of sorrow

Pacific Flower and Sea Essences

Pacific Essences®, est. 1983 in Victoria, Canada is founded by Sabina Pettitt, M.Ed., Dr.TCM, Dr. of Traditional Chinese Medicine & Chopra Center Instructor. Pacific Essences® is dedicated to the promotion of Flower and Sea Essences as non-invasive, gentle, and effective tools for healing. Pacific Essences® believes that an essence is the manifestation of Spirit in each physical form. It reveals itself as the unique vibration or frequency in all living things. It is the energetic imprint of the life force of a particular plant.

In 1985 Pacific Essences® developed the first Sea Essences made from indigenous plants and creatures of the Pacific Ocean. They are clearly about transformation in consciousness. They are dynamic and act quickly and help us to flow with inner strength and knowingness.

In the first kit of 12 Sea Essences there is one essence which resonates specifically with one of the 12 channels/meridians of Traditional Chinese Medicine. The second kit of Sea Essences offers a range of frequencies, primarily keyed to refine the human nervous system and upgrade the electrical system to support expanded growth of our sensory systems. It has become clear that many of these essences like Whale and Dolphin have been given to us at this time because of their ability to help humans expand into new levels of consciousness and dimensions of being.

Much of the research integrates the wisdom and knowledge of Traditional Chinese Medicine with the Flower and Sea Essences in the Pacific Essences® repertory. Acknowledged internationally as a pioneer in the field of marrying the knowledge of these two fields of healing, the founder Dr. Sabina Pettitt teaches people how essences can be used to heal physical, emotional and mental dis-ease and nourish Spirit simultaneously.

www.pacificessences.com

Pacific Flower Essences

Alum Root	The power of the small; manifestation of "god-ness"; ability to move in a pattern without having to do it "your" way; willingness to choose "to be"
Arbutus	Spiritual tonic enhances qualities of depth and integrity
Bluebell	Giving up constraints, opening the channels of communication
Blue Camas	For acceptance and objectivity; balances the intuitive and the rational; unifies the right and left brain
Blue Lupin	For clear and precise thinking
Camellia	A catalyst to opening to new attitudes, which reflect one's true inner nature
Candystick	Physical tonic: releases pelvic tension and promotes pelvic alignment

Chickweed	For acknowledging and experiencing timelessness: being fully present and able to respond
Death Camas	Spiritual rebirth: for awareness of the spiritual connection with all of life
Douglas Aster	Endless expansion while maintaining center; savouring life experience; living fully and consciously; promotes courage and adaptability
Easter Lily	Encourages free expression of self; eliminates solid masks
Fairy Bell	Lighthearted release from murky thoughts; expands willingness to follow one's guidance; eases depression
Fire Weed	Realization of the abundance of love both within and without
Forsythia	Provides motivation for the transformation of old useless patterns of behaviour; helps to break addictions
Fuchsia	Re-creation; letting go of dysfunctional patterns; being the change we wish to see in the world
Grape Hyacinth	For times of external shock, despair, stress; allows the individual to step back from the situation while harnessing inner resources to meet the challenge
Grass Widow	For releasing old beliefs and limiting patterns
Goatsbeard	For the power to visualize oneself in a state of deep relaxation
Harvest Lily	Supportive to group energy; supports the ability to see another's point of view
Hooker's Onion	For feeling light hearted and refreshed; nurtures creativity
Indian Pipe	Reconciliation with others and making peace with self; reverence for all of life
Lily of the Valley	Allows for freedom of choice by discovering the simplest mode of behavior
Narcissus	For identification and resolution of conflicts by going to the center of the problem/fear; from there the issue(s) can be faced by determining what is essential and nurturing to the self
Nootka Rose	For expressing love of life, laughter, and joy
Orange Honeysuckle	Evokes peaceful creativity
Ox-eye Daisy	Total perspective, for being centered
Pearly Everlasting	Commitment and lasting devotion; opening to the mysteries of life; transformation through service

Periwinkle	Encourages the ability to respond to depression and thereby dispel it; for clear memory
Pipsissewa	Decision maker; clears ambivalence
Polyanthus	Dissolves blocks to abundance consciousness; transforms attitudes of scarcity into ones of worthiness and willingness to receive
Plantain	Releases mental blocks and draws off negativity
Poison Hemlock	For letting go: for moving through transition periods without getting stuck
Poplar	For contacting Spirit; for ability to transmit healing energies; to improve choice making; attunes to the gentleness of nature
Purple Crocus	For resolving tension generated from grief and loss
Purple Magnolia	Promotes intimacy and non-separateness; enhances all the senses
Red Huckleberry	To experience the power of introspection; allowing ourselves to be nourished by taking time to digest; storehouse of intelligence, discretion, and spiritual wisdom; regeneration
Salal	For realizing our power to forgive others and ourselves
Salmonberry	Physical tonic, spinal alignment and structural balancing
Silver Birch	Enhances ability to receive and to conceive; softens the need to control; dispels suffering and develops humility
Snowberry	For accepting life as it is, in the moment
Snowdrop	For letting go, having fun, lightening up
Twin Flower	Non-judgment
Vanilla Leaf	Affirmation and acceptance of one's self
Viburnum	Strengthens our connection with the subconscious and our psychic abilities
Wallflower	For hopelessness, endurance, preparedness; attuning to our own inner rhythms
Weigela	Helps to integrate experiences on the physical and emotional planes
Windflower	Spiritual tonic: provides grounding and inner security
Yellow Pond Lily	Floating free of emotions and attachments; feeling strong and secure in my path; blesses relationships

Pacific Sea Essences

Anemone	For acceptance of self and others by taking responsibility for one's own reality; allowing oneself to be organized by the universe
Barnacle	For attuning with the feminine aspect of the self; for developing radical trust
Brown Kelp	For shifts in perception leading to clarity
Chiton	For gentleness, which serves to break up and to dissolve blockage and tension
Coral	For living in community; respect for self and others
Diatoms	Re-patterning cellular memory; letting in the light
Dolphin	Appreciation for "all that is"; playful, lighthearted; inter-species communication
Hermit Crab	The ability to enjoy "aloneness", contentment and sensitivity
Jellyfish	For fluidity and letting go into the experience
Moon Snail	To cleanse the mind and let in light
Mussel	For releasing the burden of anger and to enable one to stand up straight
Pink Seaweed	A grounding remedy; for patience before new beginnings; to harmonize thought before action
Rainbow Kelp	Alignment of front and back brain i.e., reactivity and sensibility; alchemical transformation
Sand Dollar	To create a disruption of the mirage; coming to your senses
Sea Horse	Energizing the spine and central nervous system; accessing the "wild one" within
Sea Lettuce	Embracing and healing the shadow; for dispersal and elimination of toxins
Sea Palm	Meetings at the edge of breakthroughs in consciousness; balances "hurry for nothing" attitude
Sea Turtle	For persistence, grace and commitment
Sponge	Everything is unfolding in perfection; nothing happens to me without my consent
Staghorn Algae	Holding ground (sense of self) amidst turbulence and confusion; accessing higher consciousness

Starfish	For willingly giving up the old and allowing the experience of being empty; a grief remedy
Surfgrass	For courage, strength and power rooted in stability and flexibility
Urchin	For irascibility and coming to the point; for safety and psychic protection
Whale	Enhances ability to communicate through vibration and sound; expansion of human consciousness; ability to contact the record keepers

Appendix E

AROMATHERAPY

ARNICA – Restores Overworked Muscles [Arnica montana]
Helps revive tired, aching muscles before and after physical activity. Use to treat severe bruises, sore muscles, swelling, sprains, fractures, joint pain and stiffness. Arnica oil draws fresh blood to the surface and breaks up congested fluid to heal bruising of the skin.

BASIL – A Tonic for Fragile Nerves [Ocimum basilicum]
A herbal oil that helps alleviate depression, sharpen the senses and encourage focus & concentration. Use to calm hysteria or to reduce motion sickness and stomach cramps. Relieves headaches, migraines, allergies, sinus congestion, asthma, flu and acne. It enhances the luster of dull looking skin as well as hair.

BENZOIN – Rejuvenating & Soothing [Styrax benzoin]
This vanilla-like scent has powerful skin & respiratory healing qualities. Use to heal dry/itchy/cracked/chapped skin/wounds/sores. Protects elasticity of the skin. Clears mucous, increases circulation, soothes arthritic & rheumatic inflammation. Helps dispel anxiety, nervous tension and general stress.

BERGAMOT – Stress Reducing, Uplifting & Refreshing [Citrus bergamia]
A perfume-like citrus oil used to reduce anxiety & fear and provides stability to the emotions. Anti-depressant action boosts physical and psychological energy. Inspires your day! Beneficial for people with eating disorders as it helps to regulate appetite. Strong antiseptic used to treat skin infections.

BIRCH, Sweet – Purifying [Betula lenta]
This intense, sweet, woody, wintergreen scent invigorates & refreshes the mind. An analgesic useful for inflamed tendons, arthritis, rheumatism & general muscle aches. Purifies the body by helping to release harmful toxins. As a diuretic, this oil can help combat obesity, cellulite & edema. Boosts the lymphatic system.

BLACK PEPPER – Stimulating & Warming [Piper nigrum]
A very spicy fragrance, highly stimulating and strengthening to the nervous system. Eases frustration and warms the heart, increases blood flow to the muscles/eases muscular aches & pains. Stimulates appetite/aids digestion, expels toxins.

CAMPHOR – Prevents Aging, Pioneering Spirit [Cinnamomum camphora]
Camphor (White) is a balancing oil and helps to relax people who are generally nervous. Warms or cools where necessary. Helpful with arthritis, rheumatism and muscular aches & pains. Camphor has a crystalline structure that gives it the ability to amplify energy and awakens you to your consciousness in life.

CARROT SEED – Tonic for the Skin [Daucus carota]
This popular skin care oil can nourish, revitalize, tone and tighten skin, resulting in a vibrant face lift while encouraging new skin cell growth. Excellent purifier, cleanses the liver. As a diuretic, it helps release toxins.

CEDARWOOD – Calming & Balancing [Cedrus atlantica/Juniperus virginiana]
A rustic, woody scented oil that is used to calm nervousness & fear, alleviate anger & aggression and provide stability. A strong antiseptic that is effective for bronchial/kidney infections. Supports breathing & clears nasal passages.

CHAMOMILE – A Traditional Remedy for Children
[Roman-Anthemis nobilis/Blue German-Matricaria recutita]
A highly respected, soothing oil that eases tension, anxiety, anger and promotes relaxation & peace. It has been applied as a calming remedy for children for decades. Aids in reducing stress and insomnia. Useful in regulating the menstrual cycle and easing pain from PMS. Known as a powerful skin tonic that decreases inflammatory conditions.

CHAMPA (Mix) – Exotic Perfume & Aphrodisiac [Michelela champaca]
This delightful, sweet, delicate, floral scent helps to relieve anxiety, depression & fatigue. Also helpful for reducing fever, swelling & pain associated with arthritis. Blood purifier.

CINNAMON LEAF – Rejuvenating & Antiseptic [Cinnamomum zeylanicum]
This familiar warm aroma is a great mind & body revitalizer, helping to alleviate exhaustion, depression and weakness. A powerful antiseptic used for respiratory ailments/resisting viral infections/colds & flu and helps ease breathing. Assists in blood circulation & purification. Soothes arthritis, diarrhea, menstrual cramps, heavy menstruation, yeast infections and digestive problems.

CITRONELLA – Insect Repellent & Antiseptic [Cymbopogon nardus]
A strong fragrance best known as an insect repellent. Used by the Chinese for headaches, migraines, and rheumatism. Can be used as an antiseptic to sanitize kitchen counters, chopping blocks & cutting boards.

CLARY SAGE – Relaxing, Hormonal Balancer [Salvia sclarea]
This acrid herbal oil is a powerful stimulant for the nerves/anxiety and panic. It is a good hormone balancer and thus a good tonic for the womb. Strengthens the defense system and aids with convalescence.

CLOVE BUD – Uplifting & Antiseptic [Syzygium aromaticum]
A strong, spicy and penetrating aroma. It has a positive and stimulating effect on the mind, helping with depression. It also helps with sinusitis, asthma and bronchitis. Can be used as a disinfectant.

CORIANDER – Mentally Uplifting & Releases Toxins [Coriandrum sativum]
This sweet, woody-spicy, musky scented oil is a stimulant used to combat fatigue and enhance memory/creativity. Helps flush out toxins/fluids that contribute to arthritis/gout/muscular pain/rheumatism/poor circulation. Also a pain reliever, anti-inflammatory, useful for neuralgia. Apply for digestive problems & appetite stimulation.

CYPRESS – Calming, Soothing & Healing [Cupressus sempervirens]
This green woody aroma has a soothing effect on anger and calms talkative or irritable people. It is used to control excessive menstrual flow/bleeding/sweating. Useful for the circulatory system and the liver, which helps the composition of the blood.

EUCALYPTUS – An Effective Respiratory Remedy [Eucalyptus globulus/radiata]
A strong medicinal fragrance that aids concentration. Used in a number of respiratory remedies. Effective antibacterial/cough suppressant/expectorant. Its anti-viral properties help fight colds, flu & ease breathing, headaches, muscular aches and pains. Apply to burns and cuts. Has been used to treat malaria.

FENNEL – A Tonic for Stomach Ailments [Foeniculum vulgare]
This licorice-type fragrance supports the nerves and gives courage during times of adversity. Rids the body of toxins. A wonderful tonic for the stomach, assists with digestion and is helpful for weight loss & to control nausea.

FIR, Balsam – Uplifting Yet Grounding [Abies balsamea]
Its overall action is considered stimulating, and can be used to bring alertness to the mind, or diluted and applied topically to the adrenal areas to help general fatigue. Fir is often included in cough and cold remedies/rubs, and has been researched for its ability to kill airborne germs and bacteria.

FRANKINCENSE – Comforting & Protecting [Boswellia carteri]
Considered a "holy" oil, this ritual oil is often used during religious ceremonies. Anoint the chakra points in meditation to help open up the psychic centres. Very effective at clearing up mucous and regulating its secretion. Supportive during labour and in cases of post-natal depression. Soothing and helps slow heavy menstruation.

GERANIUM – Heals Body & Psyche [Pelargonium odorantissimum/graveolens]
This strong flowery fragrance has a calming/balancing effect. Known as a hormonal balancer, Geranium is especially beneficial for PMS, menstrual pain, mood swings, bloating and menopause. Can also be used to repel insects.

GINGER – Warming & Cheerful [Zingiber officinale]
A spicy aroma that warms and fortifies the psyche. Stimulating/cheering when one is lonely and listless. Sharpens the brain (memory) and senses. Helps with colds/flu/sore throats/runny noses. Inhibits bacterial growth and expels phlegm and toxins. Use for digestion problems. May also help with nausea/hangovers and travel/sea sickness. May relieve arthritic/rheumatic/lower back pain.

GRAPEFRUIT – Detoxifying, Reviving & Euphoric [Citrus paradisi]
This crisp citrus oil is an anti-depressant that reduces stress with its uplifting and rejuvenating effects. Aids in weight loss and cellulite. It help with lymphatic drainage and fluid retention. Helps relieve digestion and premenstrual tension. Eases grief, resentment and envy. Relieves jet lag and migraines.

HELICHRYSUM – Immortal & Everlasting [Helichrysum stoechas]
Helichrysum oil has a powerful, rich, floral, tea-like scent that comforts, lessens the effect of shock and phobias, and improves the flow of energy through the body. Helps promote cell growth and heal scars and skin tissue. Boosts the immune system. Aids the respiratory system. Helps relieve fevers, coughs, colds and flu, aches and pains as well as headaches and migraines.

HYSSOP – Respiratory Tonic [Hyssopus officinalis]
Sweet yet spicy, Hyssop is a nerve soother as well as a stimulant to help clear the mind. Powerful oil for the entire respiratory system, especially for chronic complaints/chest infections/clears the lungs of excess mucous/eases tightness in the chest. Anti-viral, helps fight infectious diseases, such as herpes. A good tonic to the body when in a weakened condition of convalescing.

JASMINE – The King of Flowers [Jasminum grandiflorum/sambac]
This exotic fragrance calms the nerves, warms the heart & inspires the spirit. Produces positive feelings of confidence. Stimulates creativity and is deeply relaxing. Eases impotency/frigidity and soothes menstrual pain. Has a calming effect on coughs and helps deepen breathing.

JUNIPER BERRY – A Traditional & Effective Diuretic [Juniperus communis]
A sweet, fresh-woody-balsamic scent that will calm & rejuvenate the psyche. Supports the spirit in challenging situations. A remedy for skin/urinary tract/blood/nerve disorders. It is a good antiseptic. As a diuretic it has been used to cleanse/detoxify the body and relieve urine retention.

LAVENDER – A Broad Spectrum Healer [Lavandula angustifolium]
Lovely, deep floral aroma that warms the heart and steadies the emotions. It's the most useful essence for therapeutic purposes, it fights infection, and eases muscular pain & headaches. Lavender is a wonderful natural sedative for sleeping problems.

LEMON – Refreshing, Uplifting & Cleansing [Citrus Limonum]
A familiar fresh, clean fragrance used for calming the emotions. Stimulates mental activity, increasing concentration/memory. Excellent anti-bacterial/disinfectant properties that can be used to soothe throat infections. Induces firmness in muscles, while refreshing the mind & spirit.

LEMONGRASS – Enhancing & Reviving Tonic [Cymbopogon citratus]
An uplifting aroma that helps with mental exhaustion/jet lag, clearing headaches/relieving fatigue. Strong antiseptic. Effective with respiratory infections. Use on aching muscles/to stimulate circulation/to tone the skin. Helps keep insects away, a pleasant alternative to Citronella.

LIME – Invigorating & Elevating [Citrus aurantifolia]
Restores health, an overall tonic for wellness. This crisp citrus scent uplifts and refreshes the senses. Alleviates depression/anxiety and inspires a tired mind. Strengthens the immune system and helps with coughs/colds/respiratory congestion. Stimulates digestion & boosts appetite.

LITSEA CUBEBA – Prized for Perfume Blending [Litsea cubeba]
A fresh, fruity, lemon-scented oil that has an uplifting effect on the mind and body. Antiseptic/disinfectant/insecticidal/deodorizing properties. Improves appetite, relieves flatulence & indigestion. Mix with water for cleaning surfaces in the home.

MANDARIN – Safe for the Young, Old & Pregnant [Citrus retilculata]
This sweet, almost floral scented oil is calming & soothing. It relieves nervous tension/insomnia/restlessness.

MANUKA – Strong, Anti-microbial Activity [Leptospermum scoparium]
Manuka oil has a strong camphoraceous scent similar to tea tree. It possesses anti-bacterial, anti-fungal, anti-inflammatory, anti-histamine & anti-allergenic properties. Useful for skin/hair care, acne, skin irritation, body and foot odour, and oral hygiene.

MARJORAM – Comforting, Calming & Warming [Origanum marjorana]
This bold herbal fragrance promotes good health, and comforts during times of grief. Calms the nervous system/alleviates anxiety/a tonic for hyperactive people. Aids in reducing muscle pain/rheumatic aches/swollen joints by stimulating blood flow. Lowers blood pressure. Use for stomach cramps, indigestion, headaches and migraines. Helps clear the head during colds & flu.

MELISSA – Uplifting & Refreshing [Melissa officinalis]
This oil is a strong tonic to the nervous system. Can be helpful for anxiety/panic/vertigo/worry/depression/nervous tension. Soothing when experiencing grief, shock, or bereavement.
Assists in lowering high blood pressure and regulating the menstrual cycle. As an antispasmodic, helps respiratory system with asthma, bronchitis and chronic coughs. Can have a cooling effect on fevers & ease headaches.

MYRRH – Strength, Stability & Meditative [Commiphora myrrha]
An ancient spiritual oil used in purification processes that was said to deepen one's connection to the universe. Provides a sense of strength, stability & courage. This oil has a "grounding" effect on the psyche, easing fear. Facilitates meditation.

MYRTLE – Mild Respiratory Aid, Suitable for Children [Myrtus communis]
A clear, fresh, camphoraceous, sweet-herbaceous scent. Use for children's respiratory problems, asthma, bronchitis & coughs because of its mild nature. Use as an immune booster to combat colds/flus/infections/diseases. Astringent & anti-bacterial. Useful in treating acne/oily skin/large pores/hemorrhoids.

NEROLI – Aphrodisiac, Indulge Skin & Senses [Citrus aurantium-bitter orange]
This sweet orange scent stabilizes and regenerates the soul. Esteemed by the Egyptians for its great abilities to heal the body, mind & spirit. Effective remedy for depression, anxiety, emotional exhaustion.

NIAOULI – Immune System Booster [Melaleuca quinquenervia]
Related to Tea Tree. Stimulates the mind and clear thinking. Said to increase white blood cells and antibody activity. Helpful in fighting infections/colds & flus/expectorant/decongestant. Aids respiratory conditions such as asthma/bronchitis/chest infections/sinusitis. A beneficial anti-inflammatory for rheumatism.

NUTMEG – Stimulant to Body & Mind [Myristica fragrance]
This familiar smelling oil is a helpful digestive aid in breaking down fats and starchy food. For a digestive aid, add 1 drop to 5ml of carrier oil and apply to abdomen, rubbing gently in a clockwise movement. Also has a history of being used to attract money!

ORANGE, Sweet/Bitter – Zesty & Joyful [Citrus cinesis/ aurantium]
A happy oil that is known for its anti-depressant qualities. This fragrance cleans the air and has a very calming effect on the stomach. May help lower cholesterol levels. The bitter variety of Orange oil is cold pressed from the peel and is said to be an aphrodisiac. Its properties are very similar to the sweet Orange.

OREGANO – Pleasant, Friendly & Uplifting [Origanum vulgare]
A relative of marjarom, this oil is a natural infection fighter. Recent studies suggest that it has antiviral, antibacterial and anti-fungal properties. Useful for relieving children's coughs, allergies, hay fever, colds, influenza & indigestion. Soothes menstrual pain.

PALMAROSA – Clarifying & Uplifting [Cymbopogon martini]
An earthy, uplifting fragrance that calms, refreshes & clarifies the mind. Stimulates the appetite, assisting individuals with eating disorders since it has a positive influence on the emotions. Also calming for children.

PATCHOULI – Earthy & Anxiety Releaser [Pogostemon cablin]
Known as "hippy juice", this earthy fragrance may be used to balance and ground the psyche. Sedates in small doses but sharpens the wits and stimulates the mind in high doses. Relieves water retention.

PEPPERMINT – Physically and Mentally Refreshing [Mentha arvensis]
This cooling, minty fragrance is an effective stimulant, alleviating mental fatigue. Helps to relieve anger/hysteria/nervous trembling/travel sickness/nausea/stomachaches/indigestion. A powerful antiseptic. Use for respiratory disorders such as colds/coughs/asthma/bronchitis/pneumonia.

PETITGRAIN – Assuring & Sedating [Citrus aurantium]
A fresh floral scent with a woody-herbaceous, nutty undertone. Its refreshing/calming characteristics address anger, panic, insomnia and other related conditions. Petitgrain is excellent for reviving the body, mind & soul.

PINE – Balancing, Deodorizing & Disinfecting [Pinus sylvestris]
This green woody scent soothes mental stress/refreshes a tired mind/relieves anxiety. Pine is a restorative and cleansing oil to the aura. A powerful antiseptic. Useful for respiratory problems & muscle aches to stimulate the circulation and relieve pain. Repels fleas. A common household disinfectant.

RAVENSARA – Fights Infection, Safe for Children [Ravensara aromatica]
This steam-distilled oil has a scent reminiscent of Eucalyptus. It is used to treat flu symptoms and bronchitis. Useful for fighting viral infections and to rid the body of toxins produced during illness. Said to enhance libido.

ROSALINA – The 'Lavender Tea Tree' Oil [Maleluca ericifolia]
Rosalina is a gentle oil and is therefore an excellent choice for children for its softer aroma. Can be soothing for infections like herpes, fungal and bacterial infections.

ROSE – The Queen of Flowers [Rosa damascena]
Rose is unparalleled in its beauty and scent. As an age old symbol of love, it is not surprising that the oil has a substantial balancing effect on the heart. Rose oil enlivens the spirit! It comforts and refreshes, addressing heartache, sorrow and other psychological pain. A deep loving aphrodisiac.

ROSEMARY – Stimulates the Mind & Senses [Rosmarinus officinalis]
This fragrance provides mental awareness and clarity. Use when studying and problem solving. It strengthens the nervous system/stabilizes emotions/minimizes mood swings. It is an effective antiseptic.

ROSEWOOD – Calms the Nerves [Aniba Rosaeaodora]
Rosewood's warm woody fragrance reduces stress and relieves fatigue. Boosts the immune system. It is a valuable antiseptic. Also assists with reviving the libido.

SANDALWOOD – Comforting, Grounding & Aphrodisiac [Santalum album]
This warm spicy fragrance calms and slows the psyche. Sandalwood is an ideal remedy for the hectic, fast paced world we live in. Its grounding qualities encourage openness & understanding. This powerful oil is often used for yoga or meditation. Also considered an aphrodisiac, restoring sensuality in both sexes.

SPEARMINT – The Sweet Gentle Mint [Mentha spicata]
Spearmint oil is cleansing and uplifting, and the aroma sharpens the senses. It is better suited for children than peppermint essential oil, and is good for upset tummies, nausea, headaches and fever (rub a small amount into the temples or stomach). Spearmint oil has traditionally been used for stimulating the mind, supporting digestion and as a decongestant and insect repellent.

SPIKENARD – Healing Skin Tonic & Perfume [Nardostachys jatamansi]
This heavy, sweet-woody, spicy oil is said to be one of the most powerful sedatives in aromatherapy. It is a diuretic and helps the body to detoxify, which helps fight cellulite. Beneficial for the menstrual cycle.

SPRUCE, Black – A Warm & Inviting Evergreen Aroma [Picea mariana]
This aroma is both calming and elevating, making it excellent for yoga and meditation or uplifting the atmosphere of any space. Black Spruce is best for restoring depleted and overworked adrenal glands. Apply for muscular aches and pains, poor circulation and rheumatism. Spruce oil is ideal for all respiratory ailments.

TANGERINE – Soothing, Antiseptic & Aids Digestion [Citrus reticulata]
Soothing to the nervous system and may help relieve stress and tension. Aids digestion by stimulating the flow of bile, thus excellent to assist in burning fats. Helps to purify the blood and reduce inflammation and nervous afflictions.

TEA TREE – Anti-viral, Anti-bacterial & Anti-fungal [Melaleuca alternifolia]
Tea Tree is essential for any first aid kit. This powerful oil kills a number of bacteria, viruses and fungi. Use as a disinfectant/antiseptic remedy. Useful for acne, athlete's foot, blisters, burns, vaginal thrush, dandruff, herpes, insect bites, chest congestion, rashes, varicose veins, warts, wounds, infections and any viral related skin problems.

THYME – A Strong Disinfectant & Immune System Tonic [Thymus vulgaris]
The supportive & fortifying nature of Thyme is gently empowering, helping you overcome physical, emotional & mental exhaustion by improving mental clarity & memory. This very potent oil is strongly antiseptic, aids concentration and is an effective treatment for coughs/colds/sore throats. Clears the respiratory system of catarrh. Also aids digestion.

VANILLA – Warm, Pleasant & A True Aphrodisiac [Vanilla planifolia]
A popular familiar scent that can relax and soothe sexual tension. Neutralizes effects of free radicals & oxidants, repairs damage due to oxidation and enhances libido. Inhaling this oil can calm the nervous system in general and helps to reduce anger, frustration and irritability. Fights depression & uplifts mood, reduces inflammation & nervous afflictions, promotes sleep, gives relief from anxiety & stress. A mild stimulant for menstruation.

VETIVERT – The Oil of Tranquility [Vetiveria zizanioides]
This deep earthy fragrance is a panacea for stress & tension. Very grounding, calming, helps balance the central nervous system. Helps with insomnia and exhaustion. Use to clean the aura. Boosts the immune system. Increases blood flow to the muscles and therefore could help with arthritis & rheumatism. Helps with acne.

YARROW, Blue – Fortifier, Improves Health & Immunity [Achilea millefofium]
A dark blue oil that has a fresh sweet herbal scent. Boosts the immune system, calms skin disorders and eases digestive problems. Anti-inflammatory action helps with burns/cuts/wounds. Lowers blood pressure. By improving circulation it can help varicose veins/arteriosclerosis and hair growth.

YLANG YLANG – The Flower of Flowers [Cananga odorata]
In some cultures the Ylang Ylang flower is strewn across the marriage bed as a symbol of love. This calming sweet essence brings feelings of joy and sensuality, and is widely used as an aphrodisiac to help with impotency and frigidity. Ylang Ylang balances the hormones and mood swings. Lowers blood pressure and provides a sensual glow.

Appendix F

SELF-MONITORING BIOFEEDBACK
HOW TO ACCESS THE MAGIC OF BIOFEEDBACK FOR YOURSELF:

By using the body as a pendulum, we can access our bio-computer. To set the barometer for the response of "yes" and "no" stand relaxed with the knees slightly bent and shoulders relaxed and notice your breath. The "no" response is used to determine the imbalanced meridian or chakra in the Sound Essence Protocol. The "no" response is used to indicate the midline of the three dimensions; side to side, front and back, up and down, for the auric field in the Sound Essence Protocol.

EMOTIONAL CIRCUIT MONITORING:

Think about your most embarrassing moment and notice how your body responds to this thought or feeling. Did your body, as a pendulum, sway forward or back? Did it move from one side to another? Or did your body spin clockwise or counterclockwise or was it still? There is no right answer, but there must be a noticeable body stance. Remember this stance or movement as a personal "no" response.

Think about your most fulfilling experience and again notice the movement of your body as a pendulum. Remember this stance or movement as a personal "yes" response.

MENTAL CIRCUIT MONITORING:

Ask your body simply, "Give me a no response." This body stance or motion will likely match the response you had with the most embarrassing moment.

Ask your body simply, "Give me a yes response." The body stance or motion will likely match the response you had with the most fulfilling experience.

PHYSICAL CIRCUIT MONITORING:

Hold chocolate or candy against your cheek and notice your body pendulum response. This should be the same as any of your previous "no" responses.

Hold water or fresh produce against your cheek and notice your body pendulum response. This should be the same as any of your previous "yes" responses.

ELECTRICAL CIRCUIT MONITORING:
Trace the central meridian backwards (from the bottom of the lip to the pubic bone within two inches of the body). Notice your body pendulum response. This should be the same as any of your previous "no" responses.

Trace the central meridian in the correcting direction (from the pubic bone to the bottom of the lip within two inches of the body). Notice your body pendulum response. This should be the same as any of your previous "yes" responses.

Practice this until you can trust yourself noticing clear "yes" and "no" responses.

You have successfully tapped into the body's innate biofeedback system. To ensure the most accurate of responses, we will check the body for "switching". This term simply refers to bio-electrical integrity.

For optimum responses check the body for three types of bio-electric switching:
1) **Hydration** – the body needs to be hydrated in order to conduct an electrical current or charge for accurate monitoring. Touch your hair and notice your body pendulum response:

YES	body is adequately hydrated, move to the next test for switching
NO	drink water

EMPOWERMENT OF BIOFEEDBACK

2) **Central Meridian Integrity** – the body requires that the electrical circuitry be operating for accurate monitoring. Trace the central meridian in the correcting direction (from the pubic bone to the bottom of the lip within two inches of the body). Notice your body pendulum response.

YES	the body's electrical system has integrity; move to the next test for switching
NO	trace the central meridian in the correcting direction (from the pubic bone to the bottom of the lip within two inches of the body) three times

3) **Switches** – checking that the circuits are all on for accurate monitoring.

   a) Touch upper lip and bottom lip simultaneously (GV 27 and CV 24) (up and down switching).

YES	move to the next test for switching
NO	rub gently above the upper lip and below the lower lip

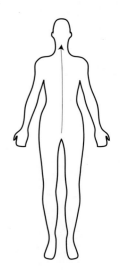

   b) Touch the junction of the clavicle and the sternum (K-27) (side to side switching).

YES	move to the next test for switching
NO	rub gently the K27's

   c) Touch the tailbone (GV 2.5) (front to back switching).

YES	move to the next test for switching
NO	rub the tailbone gently

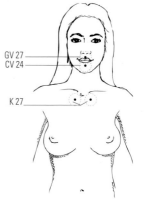

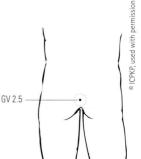

GV 27
CV 24
K 27
GV 2.5

© ICPKP, used with permission.

APPENDIX F

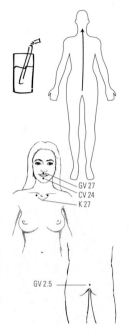

© ICPKP, used with permission.

PARTNER MONITORING BIOFEEDBACK
HOW TO MONITOR MUSCLES FOR BIOFEEDBACK

Both partners perform the **"Five Minute Set Up"**

1. **Drink water**
2. **Trace Central Meridian**
   Trace the central meridian in the correcting direction (from the pubic bone to the bottom of the lip within two inches of the body).
3. **Rub Switches**
   a) Touch and gently rub upper lip and bottom lip simultaneously (GV 27 and CV 24) (up and down switching)
   b) Touch and gently rub the junction of the clavicle and the sternum (K-27) (side to side switching)
   c) Touch and gently rub the tailbone (GV 2.5) (front to back switching)

FIND AN INDICATOR MUSCLE

Use an easily accessible indicator muscle for example the middle deltoid or the anterior deltoid.

To position the middle deltoid muscle have the partner extend their arm directly out to the side of the body, 90 degrees away from the body, and then bend the elbow 90 degrees.

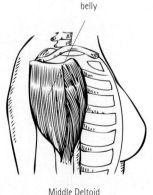

Middle Deltoid

© ICPKP, used with permission.

© ICPKP, used with permission.

To position the anterior deltoid muscle for monitoring, have the partner extend the arm straight in front of the body and raised 30 to 40 degrees out from the body.

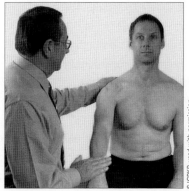

Pinch the belly of the muscle and retest the muscle; this should switch off the muscle giving a stressed response.

Spread the belly of the muscle apart; this should switch on the muscle offering a balanced response.

> Do this several times to give you a clear indicator of a "yes" and "no" response.

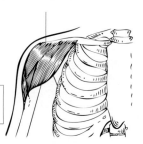

Anterior Deltoid

© ICPKP, used with permission.

SETTING UP AN INDICATOR MUSCLE:

1. Ask permission to work with each other.
2. Explain to your partner that muscle testing is about feeling the quality of their response. The muscle will either feel 'integrous," "locked", or "mushy," "unlocked".
3. Ask your partner if either arm shouldn't be tested due to an injury or strain and proceed accordingly. Ask them to relax their muscle immediately if pain is felt while being tested.
4. Demonstrate and explain the direction you are going to push.
   a. Be precise in the starting position and direction.
   b. Always stabilize with the other hand on the opposite shoulder and to make sure you both have good balance.
5. Have an unbiased attitude to get accurate results.
6. Test the muscle.
   a. Have your partner keep their body relaxed, actively contracting only the muscle your testing.
   b. Ask your partner to hold the muscle in position and keep breathing. You get the best results if both you and your partner breath during the testing. If either of you notice continual breathe holding, you can quietly say: "push-sh-sh-sh as pressure is applied.
   c. Ask your partner to meet your pressure as you are adding pressure or gently pushing on the arm.
   d. Gradually and smoothly increase your pressure on the forearm just above the wrist using the flat of the palm, or fingers- avoid gripping or squeezing.
   e. Feel for a 'lock' as you push for two seconds with about two pounds of pressure no farther that two inches of distance.
   f. Be sure your partner doesn't compensate by bringing other muscles into the test (bending the elbow, shrugging the shoulder, shifting their weight or straining).

Used by permission from Denise Cambiotti and Karen Olsen.

Appendix G

Contacts for Kinesiology:

Kinesiology College of Canada
Evelyn Mulders (Canada)
www.kinesiologycollegeofcanada.com

Canadian Association of Specialized Kinesiology
www.canask.org

Advanced Kinesiology
Dr. Sheldon Deal DC (USA)
http://www.kinesiology.nu/sheldondeal

Australian Kinesiology Association
http://www.aka-oz.org

Applied Physiology, AP
Richard D. Utt - USA
http://www.appliedphysiology.com/

Biokinesiology, BK
(John Barton - USA)
www.biokinesiology.com

Brain Gym (Educational Kinesiology)
Paul Dennison - USA
http://www.braingym.org/

Crossinology
Susan McCrossin, AP - USA
www.crossinology.com

Cyberkinetics - Cybernetic Kinesiology
Alan Sales - England, UK
http://www.cyberkinetics.co.uk/

Clinical Kinesiology, CK
Alan Beardall, D.C. - USA
http://www.clinicalkinesiology.com/

Energetic Kinesiology
(Hugo Tobar - Australia)
www.kinstitute.com

Energy Kinesiology Association - USA
www.energyk.org

Health Kinesiology, HK
Jimmy Scott, Ph.D. - Canada
http://www.subtlenergy.com/

Integrative Kinesiology, IK
(Trevor K. Savage, ND. - Australia)
www.kinesiology.nu

International Association of Specialized Kinesiology (IASK)
www.iask.org

International Kinesiology College
Australia
www.ikc-info.org

International Neurokinesiology Institute
www.kinesiology.pl

K-Power
www.k-power.com.au

Kinergetics
Philip Rafferty - Australia
http://www.kinergetics.com.au/

Kinesiology Institute
John Varun Maguire – USA
www.kinesiologyinstitute.com

LEAP - Learning Enhancement
Advanced Program
Charles T. Krebs - Australia
LEAP

Neural Organization Techniques, NOT
Carl Fererri, D.C. - USA
http://www.notint.com/

Neuroenergetic Psychology
(Richard Duree / Shanti Duree - USA)
www.neuroenergetic.com

Neural Systems Kinesiology
(Hugo Tobar - Australia)
www.kinstitute.com

One Brain (3-in-1 Concepts)
Gordon Stokes, Daniel Whiteside - USA
http://www.onebrain.com/
http://www.3in1concepts.net/
http://www.onebrain.ca (Canada)

Professional Kinesiology Practice, PKP
Bruce Dewe, M.D. / Joan Dewe
- New Zealand
http://www.icpkp.com/

Self Help for Stress & Pain
Hap & Elizabeth Barhydt (USA)
www.lovinglife.org

Touch for Health, TFH
(John F. Thie, D.C. - USA)
http://www.touch4health.com
(U.S. Association)
http://www.tfhka.org
(Australia)
www.touch4health.org.au

Transformational Kinesiology, TK
(Grethe Fremming / Rolf Hausbøl - Denmark)
www.polariscentret.dk
www.tk-us.com

Wellness Kinesiology
Wayne W. Topping, Ph.D. - USA
http://www.wellnesskinesiology.com/

Listing of many other kinesiology systems throughout the world.
http://www.kinesiology.com/

Bibliography

Amber Reuben, *Colour Therapy* (Aurora Press, Inc.,Santa Fe, N.M., U.S.A. 1983)

Andrews Ted, *Sacred Sounds: Transformation through Music and Word* (Llewellyn Worldwide St. Paul MN U.S.A. 2001)

Andrews Ted, *Music therapy for Non-Musicians* (Dragonhawk Publishing Batavia, Ohio, U.S.A. 1997)

Andrews Ted, *The Healer's Manual: A Beginner's Guide to Vibrational Therapies* (Llewellyn Publications St. Paul Minnesota, U.S.A. 1994)

Antonoff Lesley and Bedford Denise, *Crystal Light Balancing & Chromotherapy (Colour Healing) Workbook* (Renascent Nunawading, Australia)

Beinfield Harriet, L.Ac. and Korngold Efrem, L.Ac., O.M.D., *Between Heaven and Earth: A guide to Chinese medicine* (Ballantine Books, Random House, Inc. New York, N.Y., U.S.A. 1991)

Bergland Richard, M.D., *The Fabric Of Mind: A Radical New Understanding of the Brain and How it Works* (Viking Penguin Books Harmondsworth, Middlesex, England 1985)

Booth Mike and McKnight Carol, *The Aura-Soma Sourcebook: Color Therapy for the Soul* (Healing Arts Press, Rocester Vermont, USA, 2006)

Bown Deni, Cavendish *Plant Guides – Garden Herbs* (Cavendish Books Inc. Vancouver, B.C., Canada, 1998)

Brennan Barbara Ann, *Hands of Light: A Guide to Healing Through the Human Energy Field* (Bantam Books New York New York U.S.A. 1987)

Brennan Barbara Ann, *Light Emerging: The Journey of Personal Healing* (Bantam Books, New York, New York, U.S.A. 1993)

Brodie Rene, *The Healing Tones of the Crystal Bowls: Heal Yourself With Sound and Colour* (Vancouver, Canada: Aroma Art Ltd., 1996)

Bruyere Rosalyn L., *Wheels of Light: Chakras, Auras, and the Healing Energy of the Body* (Fireside, Published by Simon & Schuster, New York, U.S.A. 1994)

Burroughs Stanley, Healing for the age of Enlightenment Balanced Nutrition Vita Flex Colour Therapy (Burrough Books, Reno, Nevada, U.S.A. 1976, 1993)

Cho Hun Young, *Oriental Medicine: A Modern Interpretation* (Yuin University Press, Compton, Ca. U.S.A. 1996)

Christopher John, Dr., *The School of Natural Healing* (Provo, Utah, U.S.A. 1976)

Cousens Gabriel, M.D., *Spiritual Nutrition: Six Foundations for Spiritual Life and the Awakening of Kundalini* (North Atlantic Books, Berkeley, California, U.S.A. 1986, 2005)

Dale Cyndi, New Chakra *Healing The Revolutionary 32- Energy System* (Llewellyn Publications, St. Paul, Minnesota, U.S.A. 2003)

Dalichow Irene and Booth Mike, *Aura-Soma Healing Through Colour, Plant and Crystal Energy* (Hay House Inc. Carlsbad, Ca, U.S.A. 1996)

Dawson Adele G., *Herbs – Partners in Life: A Guide to Cooking, Gardening and Healing with Wild and Cultivated Plants* (Healing Arts Press, Rochester, Vermont, U. S. A. 1991)

Bibliography

Dewe, Dr. Bruce A.J. MD, NZRKP and Dewe, Joan, R. MA, NZRKP, *The ICPKP Database* (Bruce and Joan Dewe and the International College of Kinesiology Practice, St. Heliers, N.Z. 1999)

Eden Donna with Feinstein David, *Energy Medicine* (New York, N.Y.: Penguin Putnam Inc., 1998)

Fallon Nancy, Ph.D., *Acupressure for the Soul: Biological Spirituality and the Gifts of the Emotions* (Light Technology Publishing, Sedona, Arizona, U.S.A. 1993)

Fisher-Rizzi Susanne, *Complete Aromatherapy Handbook: Essential Oils for Radient Health* (Sterling Publishing Co. Inc. New York, N.Y. U.S.A.)

Gach Michael Reed, Ph.D, *Basic Acupressure: The Extraordinary Channels and Points* (Acupressure Institute, Berkely, CA, U.S.A. 1999)

Garudas, Flower Essences and Vibrational Healing (San Rafeal, Ca: Cassandra Press, 1983, 1989)

Geinger Michael, *Crystal Power, Crystal Healing: The Complete Handbook* (Wellington House, London, England, 1996,1997, 1998)

Gerber Richard M.D., *Vibrational Medicine: New Choices for Healing Ourselves* (Santa Fe: Bear & Company, 1988, 1996)

Gimble Theo, *Healing Through Colour* (C.W. Daniel Company Limited Saffron Waldon, Essex, Great Britain, 1980, 1983, 1985, 1987, 1988, 1989, 1991)

Gimble Theo DCE, MIACT, MLHRC,NFSH, CERT. ED., *Form, Sound, Colour and Healing* (The C.W. Daniel Company Limited Saffron Waldon, Essex, Great Britain)

Gladstar Rosemary, *The Science and Art of Herbology: Sage* (E. Barre, Vt., U.S.A.)

Author name?, *Herbal Healing for Woman: Simple Home Remedies for Women of All Ages* (Simon and Schuster Inc., New York, N.Y., U.S.A., 1993)

Goldman Jonathan, *Shifting Frequencies* (Light Technology Publishing, Flagstaff Arizona, U.S.A 1998)

Hackel Minnica, *Crystal Energy: A Practical Guide to use of Crystal Cards for rejuvenation and Health* (Element books Limited Shaftsbury, Dorset, Great Britain 1994)

Hall Judy, *The Illustrated Guide to Crystals* (Sterling Publishing Company, Inc. New York, N.Y., U.S.A. 2000)

Hay Louise L., *Your Can Heal Your Life* (Hay House, Inc. Carson, Ca. U.S.A. 1984)

Hoffman David Bsc., M.N.I.M.H. with Diana Deluca, *An Elders Herba: Natural Techniques for Health and Vitality* (Healing Arts Press, Rochester, Vermont, U.S.A. 1993)

Hozrat Inayat Khan, *The Mysticism of Sound* (Geneva: Barrie Books Ltd., 1960)

Hunt Valerie V. Infinite Mind, *Science of the Human Vibrations of Consciousness* (Malibu Publishing Co., Malibu, California, U.S.A. 1989, 1996)

Jackson Carole, *Colour Me Beautiful: Discover your natural beauty through the colours that make you look great and feel fabulous* (Ballatine Books, New York, N.Y. U.S.A. 1973)

BIBLIOGRAPHY

Jenson Bernard, *Nature Has A Remedy: A book of remedies for Body, Mind ans Spirit gathered from all corners of the world* (Dr. Bernard Jenson, Escondido, Ca, U.S.A. 1978)

Judith Anodea Ph.D, *Wheels of Life: A User's Guide to The Chakra System* (Llewellyn Publications St. Paul Minnesota, U.S.A. 2002)

Judith Anodea, *Eastern Body, Western Mind: Psychology and The Chakra System as a Path to Self* (Celestial Arts Publishing, Berkely California, U.S.A. 1996)

Johnson Steve, *The Essence of Healing: A Guide to the Alaskan Essences* (Alaskan Flower Essence Project, Homer, Alaska 1996,2000)

Kaminski Patricia and Katz Richard, *Flower Essence Repertory: A comprehensive Guide to North American and English Flower Essences for Emotional and Spiritual Well-Being* (The Flower Essence Society, Earth-Spirit, Inc. Nevada City, Ca, U.S.A. 1994)

Kaptchuk Ted J., O.M.D. *The Web That has No Weaver Understanding Chinese Medicine* (Congdon and Weed, Inc. Chicago, Illinois, U.S.A. 1983)

Ketherin Michaels and Corvus Night, *The Experiment: An Exploration of Perception and focus A Primer* (Greybear Publishing Co. Santa Fe, New Mexico U.S.A. 2002)

Keville Kathi, *Herbs – An Illustrated Encyclopedia: A Complete Culinary, Cosmetic, Medicinal and Ornamenta Guide* (Freidman/ Fairfax Publishers, New York, N.Y. U.S.A., 1994)

Keyes Laurel Elizabeth, *Toning – The Creating Power Of The Voice* (De Vorss and Company Santa Monica, Ca, U.S.A. 1973)

Krebs, Dr. Charles T., *The Energetic Structure of Man and the Universe* (Melbourne Applied Physiology, Melbourne, Australia, 2005)

Lavabre Marcel, *Aromatherapy Workbook* (Healing Arts Press, Rochester Vermont, U.S.A., 1990)

Lawlor Robert, *Sacred Geometry: Philosophy and Practice* (Thames and Hudson Inc. New York, N.Y. U.S.A. 1982, 1989, 2003)

Liberman Jacob, OD. Ph.D., *Light Medicine of the Future: How We Can Use It to Heal Ourselves NOW* (Bear and Company Publishing, Santa Fe, New Mexico, U.S.A. 1991)

Losier Michael, *Law of Attraction: The Science of Attracting More of What You Want and Less of What You Don't* (Michael Losier , Victoria, Canada, 2006)

Masaru Emoto, *The Hidden Messages in Water* (Beyond Words Publishing, Inc. Hillsboro, Oregon, U.S.A. 2004).

McIntyre Anne, *Flower Power: Flower Remedies for Healing Body and Soul Through Herbalism, Homeopathy, Aromatherapy, and Flower Essences* (Henry Holt and Company Inc., New York, N.Y., U.S.A. 1996)

Mein Carolyn L.D.C., *Releasing Emotional Patterns with Essential Oils* (Vision Ware Press, Sante Fe, CA, U.S.A., 1998)

Melchizedek Drunvalo, *The Ancient Secret Of The Flower Of Life volume 1 and 2* (Light Technology Publishing, Flagstaff, Arizona, U.S.A. 2000)

Melody, *Love is in the Earth: A Kaleidoscope of Crystals Updated* (Earth Love Publishing House Wheat Ridge CO. U.S.A. 1995)

Michaels Ketherin and Night Corvus, *The Experiment An Exploration of Perception and focus A Primer* (Greybear Publishing Co. Santa Fe, New Mexico U.S.A. 2002)

Mulders Evelyn, *Western Herbs for Eastern Meridians and Five Element Theory* (Evelyn Mulders, Winfield, B.C. Canada 2006)

Myss Caroline Phd., *Anatomy of the Spirit: The Seven Stages of Power and Healing* (Three Rivers Press, New York, N.Y., U.S.A. 1996)

Ozaniec Naomi, *The Elements of The Chakras* (Element Books Limited, Longmead, Shaftesbury, Dorset, Great Britain 1990)

Pettitt Sabina M.Ed., L.Ac., *Energy Medicine: Healing from the Kingdoms of Nature* (Victoria, B.C,, Canada: Pacific Essences,1993,1999)

Rados Ivan, *Create Yourself: Secrets of Self Discovery and Healing with Sacred Geometry* (Futura; d.o.o. Petrovaradin, Serbia, 2005)

Rafferty Phillip, *Kinergetics – Kinesiology and Healing Energy Unit 5* (Phillip Rafferty, Melbourne, Australia, 2002)

Reid Daniel, *The Shambhala Guide to Traditional Chinese Medicine* (Shambhala Publications, Inc. Boston Massachusetts, U.S.A. 1996)

Ryrie Charlie, *The Healing Energies of Water* (Journey Editions, Boston Massachusetts, U.S.A. 1999)

Scholes Michael, *Beyond Scents: Aromatherapy Home Study Course*

Scully Nicki, *Alchemical Healing: A guide to Spiritual, Physical, and Transformational Medicine* (Bear and Company, Rochester, Vermont, U.S.A. 2003)

Sellar Wanda, *The Directory of Essential Oils* (The C.W. Daniel Company Limited, Saffron Walden, Essex United Kingdom 2001)

Sharamon Shalila and Baginski Bodo J., *The Chakra Handbook: From a basic understanding to practical application* (Lotus Light Publications Wilmot, Wi U.S.A. 1988)

Smallwright Machelle, *Flower Essences: Reordering our understanding and Approach to Illness and Health* (Prelandra Press, Virginia, U.S.A 1988)

Smith Ed, *Therapeutic herbal Manual: A Guide to the Safe and Effective Use of the Liquid Herbal Extracts* (Williams, Oregon, U.S.A., 1999, 2003)

Sun Howard and Dorothy, *Colour Your Life: Discover your true personality through Colour Reflection Reading* (Judy Piatkus Ltd. London, England 1992)

Tenny Louise, *Today's Herbal Health* (Woodland Books, Provo, U.S.A., 1992)

Thie John, D.C., *Touch for Health: A Practical Guide to Natural Health with Acupressure Touch and Massage to Improve Postural Balance and Reduce Physical and Mental Pain and Tension* (De Vross and Company Publisher, Marina del Ray, Ca, U.S.A.1973)

Tierra Michael L.Ac., O.M.D., *The Way of Herbs* (Simon and Schuster Inc. New York, N.Y., U.S.A, 1980, 1983, 1990, 1998)

Wild Michael Bsc.Ed., *Meridian and Five Element Theory in Kinesiology* (Equilibrium, Ormond, Australia, 1996)

Wildwood Chrissie, *The Encyclopedia of Aromatherapy* (Healing Arts Press, Rochester, Vermont, U.S.A. 1996)

Willard Terry, *Edible and Medicinal Plants of the Rocky Mountains and Neighboring Territories* (Wildrose College of Natural Healing, Ltd., Calgary, Alberta, Canada 1992)

Willard Terry, *Herbs: Their Clinical Uses* (Wildrose College of Natural Healing, Ltd., Calgary, Alberta, Canada 1996)

Willard Terry Cl.H, Ph.D and Kelly Mary T. MA, *Mind – Body - Harmony: How to Resist and Recover from Auto-Immune Diseases* (Sarasotah Press Toronto Ontario, Canada 2003)

Wood Betty, *The Healing Power of Colour: How to use Colour to Improve Your Mental, Physical, and Spiritual Well Being* (Destiny books Rochester Vermont U.S.A. 1984, 1992)

Worwood Valerie Ann, *The Fragrant Mind, Aromatherapy for Personality, Mind, Mood and Emotion* (New World Library, Novoto, Ca. U.S.A. 1996)

White Ian, *Australian Bush Essences* (Bantam Books Moorebank, NSW, Australia, Auckland, NZ, London England, New York, N.Y. U.S.A., 1991,1992,1993,1994,1995,1996,1997,1998)

Young Gary, N.D. *Aromatherapy: The Essential Beginning – Essential Oils Refernce Guide – Science and Application Of Essential Oils* (Essential Press Publishing, Salt lake City, Utah, U.S.A. 1996)

BIBLIOGRAPHY

1. Keyes Laurel Elizabeth, *Toning – The Creating Power Of The Voice* (De Vorss and Company Santa Monica, Ca, U.S.A. 1973) p. 14.

Thank you for your purchase of the Essence of Sound, which is a reference guide to the Meridians, Chakras and Auric field band.

As a thank you for your service to yourself and others, I am gifting you with 35 reference charts. I created these additional resources for the busy practitioner. You will find these charts provide a quick access to various aspects of the energy field.

Please use this QR code to receive the gift of 35 charts You'll need to sign onto website to retrieve them.

This is a gift from my heart.
Go ahead, and sing a new tune! Shine in DeLight.

Enjoy!
Blessings, Evelyn Mulders